*The Intellectuals
on the Road to
Class Power*

Gyorgy

GEORGE KONRÁD

IVAN SZELÉNYI

The Intellectuals
on the Road to
Class Power

Translated by

Andrew Arato and Richard E. Allen

A Helen and Kurt Wolff Book

Harcourt Brace Jovanovich

New York and London

Library of Congress Cataloging in Publication Data

Konrád, György.
The intellectuals on the road to class power.

Translation of Az értelmiség útja az
osztályhatalomhoz.
"A Helen and Kurt Wolff book."
1. Intellectuals—Europe, Eastern.   2. Power (Social
sciences).   3. Social classes—Europe, Eastern.
4. Socialism in Eastern Europe.   I. Szelényi, Iván,
joint author.   II. Title.
HM213.K6813   301.44′5   77–92547
ISBN 0-15-177860-4

First edition

B C D E

CONTENTS

The debate in the Western working-class movement over intellectual and worker interests

The Bolshevik answer

IV

The Evolution of the Intelligentsia into a Class in the Socialist Societies of Eastern Europe

The technocracy and the ruling elite:
The ties that bind

The elite's counteroffensive

New opportunities for the intellectuals in the era of
compromise: Marginality freely chosen

The marginal intelligentsia and power

Two types of marginal intellectuals: Teleological
and empirical revisionists

Can the intellectuals acquire critical self-knowledge?
Some possibilities and impossibilities

PREFACE

My friend George Konrád and I wrote this essay between December 1973 and September 1974 in Csobánka, a small working-class commuter village in the Buda Hills, about an hour's drive from Budapest. In it we attempted to sum up the results of the studies we had carried on in Hungary since 1965 and to formulate our conclusions.

The Intellectuals on the Road to Class Power is not a conventional academic study. It is more an Eastern European *samizdat* and as such does not always meet the formal standards of Anglo-Saxon scholarship. We did not cite any literature and consistently avoided footnotes. We were writing an Eastern European sociological essay and not a research report in Kremlinology. Our aim was to clarify for ourselves the kind of society we were living in, without any internalized censorship and with due disrespect for all official ideological taboos, and we decided to publish the unaltered text of the book to document what kind of conclusions social scientists committed both to the cause of socialism and to critical social analysis could draw in 1973–74 in Eastern Europe.

In the course of our research we became convinced, little by little, that Eastern European socialism has produced a new system of oppression and exploitation of the working class, and that under the "dictatorship of the proletariat" it is actually the workers who make up the most underprivileged class. We came to realize that the dictatorship of the proletariat is a myth, an ideology which legitimizes the power of an oppressive new social force. We were not Communists, had never joined the party, and did not even think of ourselves as Marxists. But as professional sociologists we felt called upon to examine the functioning of the Eastern European social system from the point of view

of the oppressed. That meant that our critical analysis was bound
to have a socialist perspective. Since the existing critical socialist
or Marxist theories of Eastern European social structure did not
adequately explain the kinds of social conflicts we thought we
had uncovered, we decided to set down our own theoretical
explanation of the class structure of state socialism. This was
an overambitious task intellectually, and an impossible one politically. The best we could do was a rough sketch, more an
invitation to further study than a mature piece of research. In
the political climate of the mid-seventies any such work was
fated to become one more contribution to underground literature, and it is only by a stroke of luck that it has now become
possible for it to appear in print.

It is natural to ask how this book is related to other socialist
critiques of Eastern European society. Left-wing critics of Soviet-
type societies have been aware for some time that Eastern European state socialism has created a new system of oppression of
the working class. Theorists from Trotsky to Djilas and Kurón
have noted the emergence of new types of class conflict. In this
regard our book is very much in the line of traditional left-wing
criticism of state socialism. In the course of our endeavors, however, we found it necessary to reinterpret earlier "new-class"
theories. Previous left-wing critics identified the state and party
bureaucracy as the force opposing the working class, and drew
a crucial distinction between intellectuals and this new "bureaucratic elite," or to use the terminology of other writers, the new
"bureaucratic class" or "new bourgeoisie." But since the sixties,
it seems to us, this distinction between the bureaucracy and the
intellectuals has become more and more open to question. We
believe that the differences between intellectuals and bureaucrats
are gradually disappearing. We do not question that there are
conflicts, sometimes quite significant ones, between "free intellectuals" (scholars, artists, teachers) and technocrats (engineers,
physicians, and the like) on one hand, and the party bureaucracy
on the other. Nevertheless, we contend that these conflicts are
dying down and are, increasingly, secondary to conflicts between
the working class and a new class of intellectuals, of which the
bureaucracy forms a part. In other words, if there is a new dominant class in Eastern Europe it has been composed, since the

sixties at least, of the intelligentsia as a whole rather than just the bureaucracy narrowly defined. Djilas's theory of the "new class" served in its time to give many valuable insights into the social structure of Stalinism. We hope that our study will prove thought-provoking for those who are concerned with post-Stalinist Eastern Europe. Thus, without rejecting earlier theories, we have tried to place them in the historical context from which they sprang and to go on from there, building on them in the course of developing our own analysis.

In contrast to the Maoist viewpoint, we accept the socialist character of contemporary Eastern European societies. We define those countries as socialist because they have done away with private property in the means of production. The term "state capitalism" strikes us as misleading, since the concept of capitalism is meaningless without the existence of private ownership and of wage labor exchanged on a price-regulating market. Nor can we agree with the Maoist contention that the Stalinist period represented "real" socialism and the dictatorship of the proletariat, while the post-Stalinist period represents a restoration of capitalism. As we see it, the post-Stalinist era is an organic outgrowth of the Stalinist period. They are merely two phases of the same kind of socialism, and the present phase is certainly not a step backward. On the contrary, the changes which have occurred since the death of Stalin are basically progressive and point toward a more rational society, toward "socialism with a human face." They represent a step, even if not a radical one, toward the further emancipation of the working class.

The question of the socialist character of Soviet-type societies is crucial to our whole discussion. To brand the Soviet Union as state-capitalist is to evade the prime task facing contemporary socialist theory: the critical analysis of Soviet-type societies. Left-wing social theory must face up to the fact that socialist transformation—the nationalization of the means of production—has not brought about the results expected by nineteenth-century socialist thinkers. Not only has it failed to abolish alienation and inequality, or to produce a more democratic political system; it has in fact invented new methods of political oppression and economic exploitation. There is much to be learned from critiques

of state-socialist societies, yet their negative lessons should not
lead us to reject the idea of socialism. Our next task is to work
on the theory of an alternative socialism. Though the present
study refrains from making explicit the ideological implications
of our analysis, we hope that it too will ultimately contribute
to the theory of a new, self-managing socialism—a "free association of direct producers," rather than the class rule of intellectuals organized around the redistributive planning process.

Is our analysis Marxist? It is quite difficult to give an unam-
biguous answer to that question. Under Eastern European state
socialism Marxism, or to put it more precisely, "Soviet Marxism,"
has become a kind of state religion, and is unquestionably the
ideology of a new dominant class. To that degree Marxism is the
very subject of our critical examination. On the other hand
Marxism had a major impact on our methodology, and indeed
our book can be seen as a Marxist, historical-materialist critique
of Marxism. But it is important to point out that it does not bear
a Marxist stamp because it was written in Eastern Europe; we
did not clothe our message in Marxist jargon as part of an intellectual compromise, as is often the case with social science in
Eastern Europe. It is highly advisable to call yourself a Marxist
if you live in Eastern Europe, and it is not surprising that many
Eastern European Marxists, when they find themselves in the
West, suddenly turn out to be functionalists, Christians, or Zion-
ists. We followed a quite different and paradoxical course of
intellectual development. In our earlier sociological publications,
which appeared in Hungary and even won us some academic
recognition, we carefully avoided flirting with Marxism, consciously shunning the usual mandatory references to the "Marxist
classics." But when we started to work on the theoretical sum-
mary of our previous empirical work we suddenly realized the
analytic power of Marxist class analysis, and this book remains
basically within that paradigm of class analysis, as first formulated by Karl Marx and later somewhat modified by Max Weber.
We do not deserve the indulgence of our bourgeois colleagues,
for we used the tools of Marxism in this book not because our
academic establishment expected it of us, but on the contrary
because in the course of our work we came to discover the ex-
plosive critical potential of Marxist theory.

From the very beginning we were clearly aware that the task we had set ourselves was an impossible one politically. We consciously prepared ourselves for committing "scholarly suicide." We knew the political establishment would never accept the book we had in mind. In fact by 1973 both Konrád and I were under almost constant police surveillance, and that was one of the reasons why we moved our "workshop" out of Budapest and rented a peasant cottage in Csobánka, where we hoped to escape police harassment. In fact we soon began to suspect that the political police were keeping the house in Csobánka under observation too. We started taking precautionary measures, burying our unfinished manuscript in the garden every evening to make sure that the police could not seize it in an early-morning raid (we naïvely assumed that police raids take place only in the early-morning hours). Those were the strangest months of my life. We lived in a constant state of euphoria. We enjoyed writing the book, but in many ways we were unprepared to accept the consequences of our action. During the long, silent evenings in Csobánka we often talked about the possible sentences we might face, but I know that I at least was not ready to serve a long prison term. I was afraid, and it is difficult to explain why we went ahead with the whole project. The only explanation I can give is a bit pathetic: We wrote the book out of curiosity. We genuinely wanted to uncover the real nature of the new class oppression in Eastern Europe.

By late September 1974 we had finished the manuscript in its present form. We had three typewritten copies, but decided we also ought to have a microfilm copy, which would be easier to hide from the police. We asked a friend, the avant-garde poet and photographer, Thomas Szentjóbi, to make one for us. I suppose that by that time Konrád was being followed by police agents all the time, and they probably saw him hand the manuscript to Szentjóbi in a café. Two or three days later, anyway, the police raided Szentjóbi's flat with a search-warrant, claiming someone had reported him for turning out pornography, an absurd charge since Szentjóbi has always been the most modest of men and never showed the slightest interest in pornography. All the police found was the one thing they were obviously looking for—a manuscript of *The Intellectuals on the Road to Class*

Power. Szentjóbi was taken into custody and a few days later, just before the anniversary of the Hungarian uprising of 1956, we were also arrested, on a charge of "subversion."

The rest of the story is not very exciting and not very dramatic either. We spent altogether one week in jail; twenty years earlier we could have been executed for the same piece of work. But times had changed and in the mid-seventies the political police had to follow formal legal procedures, which we were also quite familiar with. Legally the prosecution was in more trouble than we were. In Hungarian law, you can be charged with subversion for writing something only if it can be proved that someone has read it. The police had only one copy of the manuscript at that time, and they could not find a single person who had read it. They interrogated a good many friends of ours, but since our friends knew the law too no one admitted having read the book (and in fact only a few of them had). There was also a mounting international protest against our arrest and a good deal of un-easiness among our fellow intellectuals in Hungary, who put pressure on the police either to bring a formal indictment against us, citing their evidence, or else to drop the case and release us. Since they did not have conclusive evidence, they finally decided to close our case with a so-called "prosecutor's warning." This is a curious legal procedure. When the prosecution does not want to bring someone to trial—mostly, I suppose, because they do not have a solid legal case—they warn him that in their judgment he has committed a crime, or was on the verge of committing one, and if it happens again he will be prosecuted. Our prose-cutor's warning was a serious one. We were accused of writing a book "which could serve as the program of a counterrevolu-tion." People were hanged after 1956 on such grounds. Still in jail, all three of us were told that we would have to mend our ways. We had to realize that our actions violated Hungarian law but, we were told, if we were unable to reform we would be allowed to emigrate. That came as a surprise; we could not re-call a similar offer in Hungary, at least not in the last fifteen years or so. After some hesitation we all accepted. Later Konrád changed his mind; Szentjóbi and I went into exile. In May 1975 I left Budapest for London with a one-way visa, three children, and four suitcases. In 1976 I accepted a post in sociology at a small Australian university, where the one copy of *The Intellectuals on the Road to Class Power* which we had managed to save from the police finally reached me, after many vicissitudes. From now on, I hope, it will live the normal life of a book and cease to be an exhibit in a criminal case.

Finally I would like to express my thanks to my former students at the University of Economics in Budapest for their encouragement, intellectual stimulus, and friendship during those most difficult years when I was working on the early versions and the final draft of this manuscript.

IVAN SZELÉNYI

Adelaide, March 1978

I

What Makes Us Intellectuals?

1

Theoretical Background to
the Self-Definition of
the Intelligentsia

In this essay we argue that under contemporary Eastern European state socialism, for the first time in the history of mankind, the intelligentsia is in the process of forming a class. Intellectuals there are a dominant class *in statu nascendi*. We, too, are intellectuals, members of the class that is the object of our investigation; consequently our task is self-critical. Marxist sociology of knowledge was the first major step toward the intelligentsia's critical examination of itself, for it made relative the "objectivity" of knowledge by discovering that all knowledge is existentially based, and that intellectuals, who create and preserve knowledge, act as spokesmen for different social groups and articulate particular social interests. This essay is an invitation to our fellow intellectuals to go on to a new stage of this critical self-examination.

In its search for the existential bases of knowledge the sociology of knowledge, whether Marxist or non-Marxist, has usually assumed that intellectuals have been neutral instruments in the hands of different social forces. The question of what effect the interests of intellectuals, as intellectuals, had on the knowledge they cultivated was never asked. It was assumed that they had no effect. We believe that the Eastern European intellectual vanguard abused our epistemological innocence and, while pretending to carry out the "historical mission of the proletariat," in fact gradually established its own class domination over the working class.

To put it in general terms: The first, Marxist stage of the intelligentsia's critical self-examination was epistemological; we propose that the second, in a sense post-Marxist, phase should be ontological.

Such an ontological critique of the role and social position of intellectuals requires an analysis of the social and historical circumstances in which a class position for the intellectuals could develop. We must also examine what structural positions intellectuals have occupied in other socioeconomic formations. Before we can document how and to what extent the Eastern European intelligentsia has succeeded in developing its class domination, we must attempt to work out a definition of the intellectual. Since our main task is to combine an epistemological critique with an ontological one, our definition cannot be a purely generic one, like most definitions of "true" intellectuals. In the analysis that follows we will attempt to define intellectuals in terms of both their generic and genetic existence, as well as in relation to their historical determination and transcendence.

ACCORDING TO THE MARXIST SOCIOLOGY OF KNOWLEDGE,
THE INTERESTS OF OTHER CLASSES SHAPE THE KNOWLEDGE
OF THE INTELLECTUALS

Ever since Marx it has been a commonplace of the sociology of knowledge that knowledge in general, and our knowledge of society in particular, is determined by the conditions in which it arises and expresses, directly or indirectly, a variety of interests in society. Yet Georg Lukács, in the critical and philosophical works of his Marxist period, was the first and up to now the only writer to attempt a full elaboration of Marx's rather sketchy theory of the intellectual superstructure of society. Lukács saw the culture of the past two centuries as a changing mixture of apology for the bourgeoisie, criticism of it, and bourgeois self-criticism. He applied, with considerable sophistication, a rather simple scheme of values according to which developing capitalism was progressive until 1848, but thereafter became retrograde, particularly after the Russian Revolution of 1917. Before 1848 a critical attitude, rationalism, coherence, wholeness, and humanism predominated in our culture; afterward apology, irrationalism, disintegration, decadence, and antihumanism. In this paradigm creative artists and scholars had no appreciable autonomy vis-à-vis the owners of capital and the social structure of capitalism, which were decisive. If they were honest, their response to the free-market economy—an economy regarded as being in perpetual crisis—could only be one of criticism or despair and, for the most radical if not always the most significant figures, identification with the standpoint and interests of the proletariat, specifically by joining the Communist movement. After that the only question was whether any given individual should choose to join it as a "common soldier," accepting the discipline of party membership, or link up with it indirectly as a "partisan fighter" enjoying more independence and freedom of movement.

It was Gramsci who quite properly drew from the work of Marx and Lukács the conclusion that every social class needs its own intelligentsia to shape its ideology, and that intellectuals must choose which social class they are going to become an organic part of. Since those tenets of Marxism which relate to the sociology of knowledge and the social position of the intelligentsia are based, like the fundamental principles of Marxism generally, on an analysis of capitalist society, it is understandable that for Marxist thinkers the notion of defining the intelligentsia as a class has never even arisen, for intellectuals are neither owners of capital nor proletarians. Kautsky and Lenin pointed out that on one hand the intellectual resembles the proletarian by reason of his social position, since he lives by selling his labor and so is often exploited by the power of capital; but on the other hand he differs substantially from the worker, for the intellectual performs mental work, often managerial work directing the efforts of other workers, and thanks to his higher income lives in a manner comparable to that of the bourgeois.

As a result Marxism regards the intelligentsia—like a number of other classes, for example the petty-bourgeoisie—as a *stratum* situated between the fundamental classes, and with that relieves itself of the trouble of offering a more precise definition. Thus the classics of Marxism did not even attempt to make the connection between social knowledge and the position of the intelligentsia into a subject of study. It was Gramsci who first made the attempt, dissatisfied as he was with a tautological description of intellectual activity which asserted that an intellectual is someone who does intellectual work, a banality tantamount to saying that a worker is someone who does physical work. His was a more sophisticated approach. Gramsci ascribed to intellectual activity an independent structural position in the ensemble of social relations. Its function was to formulate the interests and ideologies of the fundamental social classes. But even Gramsci did not ask whether the position of the intellectuals differs in different social systems and, if it does, how far their social position, and the changes it undergoes, determine the character of the culture they produce.

All these analyses created the impression that the intellectuals, the social bearers of culture, left on their works no trace of their own historically determined existence or of the interests which sprang from it, as if this peculiar agent were a mere transmitter which lent no modifications of its own to the ideologies it conceived. The intelligentsia, in this view, were mere technicians formulating ideologies determined by the interests of other classes; it would never have occurred to them to create a class culture corresponding to their own interests. And even if it had, the notion would have been an impossible one, for they could have learned from their own works that the intelligentsia itself, as a class, did not even exist.

ATTEMPTS TO RELATIVIZE THE DEFINITION OF CLASS
FROM DURKHEIM TO MANNHEIM AND THE NEW LEFT. THE
"TRUE INTELLECTUAL" AS THE AGENT OF TRANSCENDENCE

Critics of the Marxist sociology of knowledge started out by charging that its model oversimplified the relationship between knowledge and its existential foundations. Their criticism took two directions: On the one hand they questioned whether position in the social structure is the sole existential determinant of knowledge, while on the other they demanded a more precise description of the relationship between knowledge and its existential foundations, inquiring in particular whether there might

not be varying degrees of closeness or remoteness in that relationship.

Durkheim, in studying primitive forms of thought, pointed out
the decisive role of the modes, scenes, frequency, and organizational forms of social activity (festivals, rituals, ceremonies).
Max Scheler questioned whether all kinds of knowledge are determined in equal measure by their social roots. Different forms
of cognition, from vernacular language to technological knowledge, are not equally determined, as is apparent from the fact
that they change at different rates, suggesting that those forms
of knowledge which change more slowly are less determined by
their existential foundations. Karl Mannheim thought that class
position in itself was not enough to provide a comprehensive
definition of the existential roots of social knowledge. For that,
he thought, it was necessary to take into account such diverse
aggregations as generational, occupational, and status groups,
religious sects, and the like, and the mentality characteristic of
each. Mannheim's critique of the Marxist sociology of knowledge
was justified insofar as class position in itself is indeed an abstraction of a high order, especially when taken in conjunction
with the assumption that social knowledge reflects only sharply
polarized conflicts of class interest. Social interests do in fact
take on other dimensions as well, which in their turn evoke the
appropriate ideas and values. Mannheim demanded a more sophisticated and more historical description of the agents of culture, and sought to elucidate the rise of ideologies from a study
of their real environment. He did, however, believe there could
be a species of social knowledge which transcended the sphere
of ideology. In order to hold that belief he had to formulate a
concept of the intelligentsia which was in fact even more ideological than what had gone before. Marx was clear-sighted and
critical in his thinking when he asserted the determined nature
of all intellectual activity in capitalist society. His sociology of
knowledge reflects the essential functioning of its basic anatomy,
for indeed we cannot imagine any sociological or philosophical
activity which is not at one and the same time ideological.

In contrast to Marx, who avowed the ideological nature of
cognition, Mannheim—even while studying ideologies in specific
detail and setting them in their concrete historical context—

posited a higher, more real, more objective kind of knowledge, beyond ideology, which he gave the not altogether apt name of "utopian." In order to do that, however, he had to set up an agent which would stand above particular interests: This was none other than a free-floating *(freischwebende)* intelligentsia which would rise above the ideological conditions of its activity. In singling out the cream of the intelligentsia as the bearers of pure transcendence, Mannheim radically rejected Marx's thinking, even while concurring with Marx's intentions in his empirical descriptions; and in order to do so he had of course to posit a sphere of knowledge independent of particular interests in society.

It is worth noting that in recent years the radical left has likewise yielded to the temptation of drawing a line of demarcation between various kinds of intellectual activity. It has denied the name of "intellectual" to those brainworkers whose mental activity does not entail a radical transcendence of the interest-relationships of existing society. The rank of intellectual is reserved by many New-Left thinkers for those who formulate ideas which unconditionally and critically transcend the existing order. Such an ethical-normative definition of intellectual activity opens wide the gates to arbitrary distinctions between "true" and "false" intellectual activity, depending on the choice of values of the person who is making the distinctions. Thus here an intellectual is somebody who is hailed as one by another intellectual in sympathy with him. Moreover, certified intellectuals are such only in some of their actions, while at other times they remain technicians serving the capitalist order, like the atomic physicist who, according to Sartre, is a true intellectual only when he signs a petition against nuclear testing. Thus the concept of "intellectual," from being a real social category, becomes a badge of distinction which individual intellectuals confer on one another, and which they can just as easily take back—a kind of moralizing patent of nobility which, at the same time, cunningly removes the products of "true" intellectual effort *a priori* from the purview of any critical sociology of knowledge. The transcendent consciousness of "true intellectuals" cannot, by definition, be compared against the interest relationships which condition it.

In what follows we are at pains to subject to a critical self-analysis the immanence of this supremely transcendental manner of thinking on the part of intellectuals. In doing so we will rely on our experience of an Eastern European intelligentsia in the process of becoming a class, some of whose favorite mystifications we should like to expose in the course of this study. But we do not deceive ourselves for a moment that through such ironic self-revelation we can divest ourselves of our own character as Eastern European intellectuals.

THE KNOWLEDGE OF THE INTELLECTUALS ALSO REFLECTS THEIR OWN INTERESTS, AND WHEN THEY BECOME A CLASS THEIR KNOWLEDGE IS SUBORDINATED TO THOSE INTERESTS

There is nothing wrong with the proposition that under free-market conditions our social consciousness is determined by the major class interests in society, and that the intellectuals as a social stratum always form the intelligentsia of some class; thus each social class has its own intellectuals. In the social history of the twentieth century, however, decisive changes are evident: The consolidation of early forms of socialism in Eastern Europe, the emergence of state-monopoly capitalism in the developed industrial countries, and most recently the first signs of the technocratic global hegemony of multinational economic organizations. All of these changes critically influence the position of intellectuals in the social structure.

We were led to our present approach by way of sociological analysis of social planning, in particular of urban and regional planning. We saw the intelligentsia's new position of power unfold before us in many of its essential features. In the person of the planner the intellectual lays claim to a key role in the process of social reproduction. Examining this phenomenon more closely, we observed that in the early socialist planned economies of Eastern Europe and (though only partially and belatedly) in the world of state-monopoly capitalism as well, the conditions are emerging for the formation of the intelligentsia into a class.

We find it natural that a sociology of knowledge devoted to describing free-market capitalism should not even have raised the possibility that intellectuals could have their own interests, distinct from those of other social groups. Their subordination to other social classes was far more conspicuous, and for that reason their growing tendency to gain autonomy escaped attention. That tendency was manifest in two principal areas: the bureaucratization of the state, and the socialist labor movement. These phenomena did not go completely unnoticed; Max Weber called attention most clearly to the first, Mikhail Bakunin to the second. We cannot any longer avoid discussion of the separate and distinct interests of the intelligentsia in planned economies dedicated to rational economic growth, which redistribute the greater part of the national income through the state budget, restricting consumption and investment in agriculture and the infrastructure so that a large portion of the national income will be made available for rapid industrialization. These are the socialist economies of Eastern Europe. On the basis of the more detailed analysis which follows we place them in the category of rational-redistributive economies. In light of the emergence of the class position of this purposeful agent of redistribution we must reconsider the social role of the intellectuals, and the consequences it entails for their function of generating knowledge.

To anticipate one of the basic ideas of our study, we believe that the conditions under which society's knowledge is acquired are crucial when the social group which undertakes to create, preserve, and transmit both culture and social goals comes to function as a class, and so subordinates its cognitive activity to its own class interests. Indeed the question must arise: Is self-knowledge possible at all if the intelligentsia becomes a class? How far the intelligentsia under early socialism, or under the forms of post-industrial state-monopoly capitalism now appearing, is a *ruling* class in the traditional sense is, by comparison, almost of secondary importance. However that may be, according to our initial thesis the transformation of the intelligentsia into a class, principally in the rational-redistributive economies, has indeed meant that in the industrially backward agrarian societies of Eastern Europe the intelligentsia, organized into a government-bureaucratic ruling class, has taken the lead in modernization, replacing a weak bourgeoisie incapable of breaking with feudalism.

In our judgment the rational-redistributive system represents an autonomous form of economic organization closely bound up with the social and historical traditions of Eastern Europe and incorporating its own sovereign model of civilization and its own system of cultural goals. Thus it calls for analysis on its own terms, and is not to be explained according to bourgeois-liberal value-systems as the combination of a totalitarian political system with a wastefully disfunctional economy, no more than an accidental and temporary deviation from the legitimate and generally valid Western model of development. Early socialism can be regarded neither as the dénouement of a drama of social salvation nor as some sort of baleful mishap forced on the eastern half of Europe by devious political schemers. The system of rational redistribution, as a sovereign social and economic formation, is linked by a rich complex of structural and historical connections with those equally sovereign social and economic systems of traditional redistribution which economic history knows as the Asiatic mode of production. But essential structural factors relate it as well to the free-market economy which made possible the Western type of economic growth.

2

To What Extent Is Intellectual Knowledge Transcendent?

THE INTELLIGENTSIA DOES NOT JUST REPRESENT TRANSCENDENCE; IN REALITY IT REFLECTS A CONFLICT BETWEEN THE TRANSCENDENT AND THE HISTORICALLY DETERMINED

To this very day the sociology of knowledge has never inquired into the cultural meaning of intellectual activity. It has been content to treat the concept of the intelligentsia as a generic concept, and has seen in the intellectuals' tendency toward transcendence the essence of their function. It is their culture-creating activity which gives rise to this generic concept of the intelligentsia, a conception which defines intellectuals quite independently of historic ages and modes of production. Thence is derived their fundamentally teleological social mission, for culture is society's effort to give purpose and meaning to a world which in itself is purposeless. Our intention, however, in examining the actual position which the intellectuals occupy in a variety of concrete social structures, is to employ a genetic concept of the intelligentsia as well, which entails a description of the functions their cultural mission serves and the interests it articulates in specific social contexts. Indeed, the history of the intellectuals can be depicted as a series of conflicts between their generic and genetic roles.

In static preindustrial societies, where economic growth was practically nil, the teleological function of the intellectuals marked out for them their special sphere of activity. In the absence of any dynamic historical evolution and of the impetus which expanding production might have lent, these cultures displaced their goals to a realm outside society, a metaphysical dimension above and beyond man's historical existence. Following the rapid technical and economic growth which accompanied the birth of Western capitalism, life in this world was transformed, in the Protestant ethic, into a virtuous calling; the goal of human life was transferred to the realm of history, and society's goal became the cultivation of its own dynamism, which the Puritan discipline of capital accumulation furnished with a secularized rational theology. In preindustrial societies the intelligentsia was represented by the priestly caste, which in the interests of social stability synthesized the empirical, historical, and rational knowledge of the age within the context of a theological science oriented toward salvation. Modern Western civilization has called into question the teleology of religion, and with it the traditional role of the intellectual, which combined in the priestly function a variety of norms and types of knowledge. The intellectual has been transformed from a sacerdotal personage into a secular expert. In the state bureaucracy and in private economy alike well-paying jobs have multiplied; skilled professionals are able to capitalize upon their knowledge. Politics is divorced from theology, and the intellectuals, abandoning the sacral exploitation of their monopolistic knowledge, now offer it for sale on the open market. As petty producers and owners of a small stock of such knowledge they do not have any special class status on the labor market. Under modern Western capitalism the intellectuals make commodities of the ideologies they produce and offer themselves for hire to the real social classes whose ideologies they formulate, whose intelligence they will become. This new situation is in direct contrast to the earlier teleological and moral mission of their priestly estate; hence the term "professionals" is a more precise description of the new social situation of the intellectuals.

Though it was widely recognized in classical capitalist society that the intellectuals' subordination to other classes conflicted with their generic function and with the transcendent character of intellectual activity, those thinkers who reflected critically on this conflict took it as merely a historical episode, to be brought to an end by the intellectuals themselves either by vindicating their own universal, humanistic transcendence, above and beyond all particular interests, along the lines of Mannheim's free-floating intelligentsia, or else—according to the Marxian prescription—by embracing the cause of a working class assumed to be the agent of society's future collective interests, and enunciating its demands.

Both solutions have in common the assumption that the intellectual is capable of rising above his historical determinedness and absorbing his genetic being into his generic being. Indeed, it is precisely those who are able to do so who are regarded as true intellectuals. In line with this view sociological and philosophical thought has treated the concept of the intelligentsia as a moral concept; to our knowledge there has never been any serious attempt to arrive at a deeper understanding of the intelligentsia. The reason for this failure is to be sought primarily in the fact that intellectuals themselves have always been the bearers of transcendence in society; thus philosophy, searching for the essential nature of man in general, fixed upon the characteristics of the intellectual, until the intellectual began to appear —to himself—as the most universal, generic type of humanity. For our part we regard as unacceptable and useless for purposes of objective study the assumption that everything pertaining to

the genetic concept of the intellectuals—everything that is historically determined—ought to be treated as a denial of the
essence of intellectual life (its transcendence) or else as a nonintellectual element, and that the essence of intellectual life is
to be sought exclusively in its transcendence. We find it just as
unacceptable to disregard the degree of transcendence which is
evident in the activity of the intellectuals and to restrict our investigation solely to the genetic concept of the intelligentsia.
We see the task of empirical social research on the intellectuals
as precisely the investigation of the historical tensions between
their generic-transcendent and their genetic-historical character,
with a view to understanding how the relationship between these
two conflicting conceptions of the intellectuals has varied over
the course of time. We must label as ideological all philosophical
efforts to deny the historically determined character of the
intellectuals by identifying the empirical intelligentsia with its
own transcendence. The intellectuals of every age have described
themselves ideologically, in accordance with their particular interests, and if those interests have differed from age to age it has
still been the common aspiration of the intellectuals of every age
to represent their particular interests in each context as the general interests of mankind. The definition of universal, eternal,
supreme (and hence immutable) knowledge displays a remarkable variability over the ages, but in every age the intellectuals
define as such whatever knowledge best serves the particular interests connected with their social role—and that is whatever
portion of the knowledge of the age serves to maintain their
monopoly of their role.

HOW INTELLECTUALS ELEVATE THEIR OWN IMMANENT
INTERESTS TO THE STATUS OF TRANSCENDENT VALUES:
SOME HISTORICAL EXAMPLES

In the Trobriand Islands the shaman who watches over the
gardens possesses a knowledge that is partly agronomical and
partly magical. The former is quite modest in scope and hard
to keep secret; others can acquire it too. The shaman in a simple
tribal society could never ask that he be provided a living by

reason of this technical knowledge alone, or that it should entitle him to any special authority. And so he must put the emphasis on the magical elements of his knowledge, which in fact perform a great many functions: Through the magic of spell-casting or rainmaking, with its associated ceremonies, he reinforces the foundations of social solidarity, integration, and stability. It is a significant mark of this sort of knowledge that in it teleological and technical functions are only partly differentiated. In the consciousness of primitive peoples the relationship between ends and means is hazy; it is not clear that pregnancy is the result of sexual intercourse or that crops will yield a rich harvest if certain agricultural operations are carried out in the right order and at the right time. Hence it appears that the final harvest is the outcome of a whole series of magical acts, while the actual cultivation is only carried out parallel with them and almost under magical compulsion, perhaps largely to avoid the shaman's punishments. Thus simple agronomic knowledge is transformed into magical knowledge, even if we may suppose that the more intelligent shamans must eventually discover the causal connection between cultivation and harvest. But it is wise to keep this insight a secret. If their knowledge became common knowledge they would lose their magical authority and society would no longer maintain them for the sake of their monopolistic knowledge. At the same time it is in society's interests that agronomic knowledge should be rooted in magic, for if it were purely technical and did not enjoy the sanction of supernatural authority people might no longer fear the shaman or obey him and so, under primitive technical conditions, might not even produce enough to assure their continued survival. The shaman squeezes extra work out of the members of the tribe, which indeed goes to waste in good years for lack of techniques for preserving and storing the crop, but in bad years the tribe may owe its survival to the product of that extra labor. And so what we would today declare valueless and mere superstition in the shaman's science turns out to be this tribal intellectual's most transcendent knowledge, expressive of the comprehensive interests of the whole tribe while at the same time most effectively reinforcing his superiority in his social role. We may suppose that had there happened to be in Trobriand society a sociologist inclined to define intellectuals by their transcendent function alone, he would have acknowledged the shaman as a true intellectual precisely because of his magic rites, not because of any knowledge of agricultural techniques. Just as the concepts of end and means are not sharply distinguished in the primitive mind, so too the technical and teleological functions inherent in the intellectual's role in primitive society are not clearly separated, although the emphasis is always on the teleological aspect.

In early feudal societies—with the expansion of technical knowledge, the evolution of a separate state apparatus, and the appearance of central redistribution of the social surplus product —the focus of the intellectual's role shifts even more markedly in the direction of a teleological function based on mystic knowledge. The priest succeeds the shaman. The essence of this change lies in the fact that the intelligentsia, organized into a priestly order, is able to relinquish its technical functions either to artisans (still kept in a state of servitude) or to the newly emerged central military authority. The functions of benevolent magic are turned over to technicians, black magic to state organs of violence and coercion: soldiers, overseers, and clerks. The intellectual defines himself as the incarnation of pure teleology, because that affords him the best opportunity to maximize his social power and privileges (even if, with the differentiation of the intelligentsia into different social types—high priests versus prophets or even heretics—his success in this enterprise may prove rather uneven at times).

Thus the biblical Joseph, for example, was able to rise to a position in Egypt second only to Pharaoh's solely as an interpreter of dreams. Even though he was obliged to voice his ideas in oracular form rather than as rational hypotheses, we can still say that he was the ideologue of traditional redistribution; once he had acquired authority to redistribute as the interpreter of Pharaoh's dreams, his position came to be legitimized by the ruler's traditional authority. Joseph's knowledge was truly a mystic, teleological knowledge, freed of the technical burdens of magic, for separate specialists saw to the building of the storehouses and the preservation of the grain, while state organs of coercion assured that the cultivators would produce a surplus and supervised its collection and redistribution. Thus there appeared in feudal society a cleavage in the sphere of activity of the intellectuals: The concepts of ends and means, teleology and technique, were divorced from each other, with the priestly caste reserving to itself the function of setting goals while conferring the technical functions on society's pariahs. And so an ancient Egyptian sociologist would have accepted the creators of a teleological priestly ideology as genuine intellectuals, at the risk of disconcerting posterity's sociologists, who think true knowledge is rational, technical knowledge; for that has become an integral part of the science of the modern intelligentsia, and the teleology of the mystic seers is set down as a form of ignorance. From the vantage point of ancient Memphis the interpreter of dreams is the true intellectual; from that of modern Oxford, the pyramid-building forerunners of today's civil engineers.

In the millennial history of feudal societies the priesthood has been obliged, in order to safeguard its teleological function, to acquiesce in a certain division of roles. The more successful a sacerdotal intelligentsia in acquiring power, the less capable it is of fulfilling its transcendent teleological mission; it comes to bear an uncanny resemblance to the feudal overlords of traditional societies, abandoning what distinguishes it—its intellectual authority—and acquiring instead what is for all practical purposes a feudal authority. Prophetic and heretical movements serve the direct interests of the intelligentsia—albeit in opposition to a hierarchy attached to particular historic interests and a dogmatic theology bound to the age—because they appeal to universal values and strive to preserve a separate sphere of intellectual authority (or counterauthority), in an effort to prevent a feudal, patriarchal authority from taking the place of the intelligentsia's teleological monopoly of knowledge.

We would certainly not contend that the conflict between ascetic vanguard movements of an intelligentsia representing transcendence, and a conservative-clerical order in league with feudal authority (or occasionally usurping its role), can always be reduced to a simple antithesis of "progress" and "reaction." In the critical renovation of the Church, for example, the Jesuits were no less universal in outlook than the Protestants. But, after appropriating the ascetic ethic of the earlier mendicant-heretical movements, they sought alliance with the feudal orders against a Protestantism allied with the bourgeoisie. Their aim was to restore the hegemony of the Universal Church within the framework of the absolute monarchies, with a subordinate place marked out in a baroque-feudal society for a bourgeoisie deprived of its illegitimate power and subjected again to monarchical authority. Having said that much, we must not neglect to point out that the renewed Universal Church can be taken as a remarkable anticipation of the power of the universal intelligentsia. Both the Protestant and the Jesuit movements to reform the Church universalized particular interests of the intelligentsia, but they did so in different ways and in concert with different allies. Of course their choice of methods and allies affected the character of both movements. In seeking the alliance of the bourgeoisie the ideologues of Protestantism went beyond the alternative of reforming the Church from within. Although such religious-revolutionary dictatorships as Calvin's at Geneva or Savonarola's at Florence sought to construct an antifeudal clerical-intellectual regime, their attempts were in the nature of the case premature and short-lived, for at that time the intelligentsia was still not strong enough to exercise power on its own. The particular interests which the Protestant ideologues represented, on the other hand, were not the interests of a teleological, clerical intelligentsia, but rather those of a new practical-minded intelligentsia possessing special skills, whose interests were easily reconcilable with those of a bourgeoisie rising to power in the new market economy. The teleological thinkers of the Reformation and Enlightenment—the preachers and philosophers—mined the ground beneath their own feet in raising to the rank of genuine intellectuals the servile technical intelligentsia of earlier epochs, as most vividly illustrated by the intellectual coalition which produced the great French *Encyclopédie* with its summaries of the technical and scientific knowledge of the age. In return, however, the lawyers, engineers, economists, and physicians expressed their thanks by overturning the whole accepted value-hierarchy of knowledge, even going so far as to exclude theology altogether from the sphere of high and worthwhile knowledge.

The teleology of theology, or of the philosophy of history, was of no use to the bourgeoisie, for the goals of a free, self-regulating market cannot be posited *a priori*; they can only be observed *a posteriori* as the outcome of the latent logic of a competitive economy. Thus there was no longer any need for a privileged and prestigious order of intellectuals to give meaning and direction to social action. With Kant the spheres of rational and metaphysical thought, practical action and absolute value, were completely divorced. The former became the province of "professionals," intellectuals much sought after in the market economy and able to market their skills at a good price. The latter sphere was defined as the realm of pastors, academic moralists, and professional metaphysicians, themselves humble technicians of teleology who, with their modest corrective proposals (not much valued by market standards), have taken up their place too in liberal capitalism's division of intellectual labor. Outside the pragmatic, positivist mainstream of science these conservators of teleology go on practicing their metaphysical activity, verging now on charlatanry, now on the comic, and thoroughly deprecated by the guardians of the hierarchy of scientific values.

The intelligentsia's rejection of teleology was never complete and proved, moreover, to be only a brief historical episode. Soon after the emergence of a free-market economy attempts were made to reinterpret the concept of teleology. These took two different directions. One sought to reconcile the teleological outlook with the fact of dynamic social change. This synthesis found expression in an evolutionary positivism which spread outward from biology, sociology, and economics, and later in twentieth-century growth theories and the ideology of the scientific-technological revolution. In it the common intellectual outlook of post-liberal state-monopoly capitalism finds its theoretical framework. A paradoxical contemporary outgrowth of this evolutionism is the "growth theory" of zero-growth. With some slight ironic exaggeration one might say that teleology's third generation has now been born: First the teleology of nonrational zero-growth gave way to that of rational growth, which in turn is beginning to yield today to the teleology of rational zero-growth.

The other direction taken in the reinterpretation of teleology is represented by German classical philosophy in its Hegelian version. Kant drew a radical distinction between *Sein* and *Sollen*

—what is and what ought to be—relegating them theoretically to entirely different spheres of existence. Goal-setting activity was excluded from the sphere of rational cognition, and the concept of value, divorced from any notion of interest, was linked to a categorical imperative which could not be empirically derived. Hegel's metaphysical evolutionism, by comparison, signaled a decisive turning point: It promoted teleology from the realm of religion and theology to that of history. Hegel attempted to arrive at a synthesis of rational knowledge and teleology. But the attempt was a muddled and unsatisfactory one, for two reasons. In the first place it was not rational enough; it remained metaphysical insofar as Hegel's objective realism led him to explain mankind's empirical history in terms of the dialectical unfolding of the World-Spirit. Secondly, Hegel thought to see the purposefulness of history incarnated in the nation-state, a political organism separate and distinct (in his view) from the bourgeois economy.

Marx on the other hand recognized that it would become possible to set social goals scientifically only over the dead body of liberal capitalism, and only in an economy integrated into the state—only, in other words, if the bourgeois economy and the political state were merged in "civil society." With this insight Marx opened new vistas for the philosophy of history. On one hand he freed it from all traditional metaphysical elements and claimed to have placed it on a foundation of rational, positive knowledge. On the other, he offered a teleological framework for all kinds of intellectual activity. Marx radically reversed the Kantian dichotomy of *Sein* and *Sollen*, subject and object, and found in revolutionary practice the synthesizing medium which dissolved the contradictions between pure reason and practical reason, and between positive knowledge and values which cannot be empirically derived. The theory of scientific socialism is founded on the postulate of the unity of *telos* and *techné*.

Neo-Hegelianism could only become the ideology of the Prussian state bureaucracy; it was unable to resolve the antinomy of *telos* and *techné* (so axiomatic in the thinking of the age) because it was forced to come to terms with a market economy organized on principles alien to its own. The marginal intelligentsia, on the other hand—including some who deliberately made themselves marginal—were unable or unwilling on moral grounds to become integrated into either the bureaucracy or a labor market where they could capitalize on their expertise; they sought instead to transcend capitalist economy and political superstructure alike. Those intellectuals chose Marxist scientific socialism because it was not just one sociological and economic theory among many; it represented, rather, a practical step toward laying the foundations of a culture in which the antinomy of *telos* and *techné* would be eliminated not only in itself but for all kinds of intellectual activity as well. In the culture that would arise in this new political society the leading role would again fall to the ideologue who formulates social goals, who would place the total rational knowledge of the age at the service of teleology.

The society of rational redistribution which came into being in the aftermath of the Bolsheviks' triumph created a new value-system for intellectual activity and for knowledge in general. It encompassed the direction of society, social planning as an ideologically guided activity of technical experts. In this system of rational redistribution ideology was supreme. But in time those specialists who were constitutionally incapable of accepting this mandatory unity of *telos* and *techné*, or who rejected it on scientific grounds, began to question this state of affairs. And so we would not by any means assert that this unity was automatically assured. Indeed, the conflict of *telos* and *techné*, at first an internal division within an intelligentsia in the process of evolving into a class, gradually ripened into the major conflict in Soviet society. But before presenting that conflict in detail, in the course of our analysis of the social structure of rational redistribution, we must examine more closely the conflicts within the intellectual class—i.e., the conflict, under socialism, between the transcendent role of the intelligentsia and its historical role.

Our examples from the history of the intelligentsia in Western civilization illustrate the futility of seeking the essence of intellectual activity in a transcendence which, over the whole course of human history, finds expression in timeless, immutable values. What is to be viewed as transcendent in the knowledge of various ages depends on who is doing the viewing, and from what vantage point. Similarly, knowledge may have a different significance in different eras; at one time it may qualify as transcendent, at another as historically determined, and indeed with the passage of time it may lose its value altogether. In saying this we do not wish to deny the existence of transcendent elements in the activity of intellectuals, only to make them relative. We maintain, furthermore, that the question of which knowledge is to be regarded as transcendent can only be answered by examining how the interests existing in any age are structured, and in particular what position the intelligentsia occupies within the social structure.

And so we do not see the history of the intellectuals as a process of evolution in which intellectuals become increasingly independent of historical determination, and ever more free to realize their transcendence fully. It is not our purpose to demonstrate how or when the intelligentsia may become more of a bearer of transcendent values, or to what extent it may be transformed into a repository of absolute, universal interests in a world of particular and conditional interests. We are concerned rather to know what historical changes are traversed by the complex of conflicts between the generic and genetic concepts of the intelligentsia and between its transcendence and its historical determination.

It is one important characteristic of the intellectual life that in it this conflict emerges into consciousness, and recognition of it brings with it its own catharsis. The intellectual's schizoid character stems from the duality of his social existence; his history is a record of crises of conscience of various kinds, with a variety of origins. In their ideologies the intellectuals cultivate certain particular interests until they have universalized them, then turn about and expose the partiality of those ideologies. They defend the cult of achievement but angrily reject any suggestion that their own activity be judged by any sort of performance-principle. They articulate the rules of the social order and the theories which give them sanction, but at the same time it is intellectuals who criticize the existing scheme of things and demand its supersession.

Often the schizophrenia inherent in the intellectual's role is apparent in one and the same individual. The greatest of them incorporate the contradictions between their generic and genetic roles into the antinomies of their thought—which does not by any means prove that their thinking is inconsistent. More commonly this schizophrenia finds its protagonists in different individuals, and then we have such antithetical pairings as those of high priest and prophet, anarchist revolutionary and government official, apologist and social critic. If such an enterprise were not rendered futile precisely by the ambivalence of the most significant thinkers we might incline to see in the prophet, the revolutionary, and the critic the "true" intellectuals, excluding the high priest, the official, and the apologist from the intelligentsia in our sense of the word. But such a solution would be misguided if only because without Caiaphas there could have been no Jesus, without Pope Julius II no Luther, without Pobedonostsev no Tolstoy. Indeed, in the case of a few great creative intellects different periods in their own lives stand in an antithetical relationship to each other, without the works of either period losing any of their significance thereby; we need only think of Saul and Paul, the young and the old Hegel, Dostoyevsky the Petrashevist conspirator and Dostoyevsky the Slavophile, Malraux the revolutionary and Malraux the Minister of Culture as examples of a radically antithetical metamorphosis. It is a commonplace that the radical criticism of one age can become the apologetic conservatism of the next. Empirical social research cannot permit itself to select from the portrait gallery of the intelligentsia those visages which it finds attractive and call them the "true" intellectuals, while turning the less engaging portraits to the wall. Such a procedure may be useful for expressing one's own personal value-preferences, but it is of little help in understanding the social character of the intelligentsia, and it is particularly inappropriate for purposes of uncovering the relationship between the intellectuals and power.

3

The Historical Determination of the Intelligentsia

A FALLACIOUS QUESTION: HOW MUCH KNOWLEDGE DOES
SOMEONE NEED TO BE AN INTELLECTUAL? DIFFICULTIES
OF A STATISTICAL DEFINITION

In the course of our earlier analysis we questioned the validity
of philosophical definitions of the intelligentsia arrived at on
the basis of values. But that does not at all mean that we automatically accept the descriptive, statistical concept of the intelligentsia, which treats as an intellectual anyone having a defined
store of knowledge and engaged in one of a number of defined
occupations. We are not even convinced that a descriptive, statistical concept would generally serve, without further modifications, as a genetic definition of the intelligentsia, by comparison
with the notion which we have advanced above and tried to
elaborate on to some extent. Our doubts are based primarily on
the fact that a statistical definition (as contrasted with a transcendent one) is only apparently value-free: It substitutes a
quantitative criterion for a qualitative one, replacing the dichotomy between "real" knowledge and knowledge that is "not real"
with a different one between high and low, or complex and
simple knowledge—a new distinction which in the last analysis
has to be weighed in a no less transcendent manner. Thus a descriptive statistical definition contains, behind its semblance of
abstract and ahistorical neutrality, decided evaluative tendencies
of its own.

Although we do not consider a statistical definition really adequate for understanding the genetic aspect of the intelligentsia,
we do still believe that in modern rational economies it has some
value as an approach to the problem. The rational economy and

the rational state recognize intellectuals as specialists working in defined specialties. Market economy forces them to choose between professions. A modern social statistician would be in difficulty if he tried to classify the versatile polymaths of traditional society as intellectuals or not on the basis of their occupations, for in those societies each of them partook of the overall knowledge of the day to the limit of his ability and to that extent became an intellectual. That was true not only for exceptional personalities like Aristotle or Leonardo but for the average cleric as well, who above and beyond his religious functions might also be simultaneously a teacher, architect, physician, or agronomist. In market economies, however, it is not at all inappropriate to define the *professional* intelligentsia as comprising all those engaged in the professions and possessed of a common, socially standardized training usually associated, in our time, with the holding of a university degree. The diploma is an outward sign, trivial in itself, attesting that a person in a given occupation probably does really know what he is supposed to know.

In rational-redistributive economies it is even more useful, perhaps, to employ occupational categories in defining the intelligentsia. There the professionalization of functions has gone even further: Society has converted into professional pursuits certain activities which were taken up in the past on some other basis than education (on the basis of property-ownership, for example). Thus those who carry out these activities are now defined as intellectuals. In market economies, since the expense involved in becoming an intellectual is fairly uniform, the social rewards accorded the professionals have also been leveled out to some extent. That in turn makes each occupational group into a relatively homogeneous intellectual stratum. This homogeneity leads to the development of a manifold identity of interests: It is in the interest of every degree-holder that a defined level of income and social prestige should be associated almost automatically with the possession of a degree. It is also in their interests that the acquisition of a university degree should be an almost automatic prerequisite for the attainment of that level of income and prestige. (We must add by way of qualification that in market economies university graduates cannot achieve this latter goal unqualifiedly, for there the possession of private

wealth in itself offers a royal road to status advantages.) Behind
the expansion of universities under modern capitalism the interests of an ever more homogeneous intellectual stratum can
be clearly discerned. The university is the Trojan horse through
which the intellectuals seek to bring ever wider sections of the
economy and society under their control.

In rational-redistributive societies there are more immediate
reasons why the intelligentsia is becoming more and more homogeneous. In those societies performance is not measured by the
profit motive. Instead, the complexity of the knowledge used in
one's work serves as the criterion of compensation, and it can
be directly measured; it is in fact equivalent to the level of one's
prior qualifications. The skilled craftsman has to be paid more
than the laborer, the technician more than the craftsman, the
engineer more than the technician. Thus the prestige and, more
materially, the pay accorded to university preparation is automatically assured. And so in rational-redistributive societies it is
felt to be an anomaly if a greengrocer or auto mechanic earns
as much as a university teacher. Parallelism of educational attainment and pay scale has become such a mandatory principle
in the ethos of redistributive society that the mechanic, instead
of priding himself on making as much as a professor, feels
ashamed of it, and considers it a natural vengeance of fate when
the tax authorities put an end to this momentary anomaly.

The interests of the socialist intelligentsia, which has already
been rendered relatively homogeneous in this way on the basis
of educational level, are quite different from those of the intellectuals in market economies. They are bound up with a defense
of the value of the university diploma, which leads to restrictions
on the number of degrees that can be obtained. Thus the number
of university admissions is limited by administrative means, and
the competition on the entrance examinations for the limited
number of places remaining is so intensified that ten applicants
may appear for each place; for the only legitimate way to rise
in society leads by way of the university. And so a constant
struggle goes on between those intellectuals who have arrived
and for that very reason wish to restrict the number of qualified
competitors for intellectual status, and young people striving to
move up through the relatively narrow channels of social mobil-

ity. A momentary compromise in this struggle was signaled by the development of a number of inferior, intermediate-level institutions of higher learning which afford some scope to the desire to get ahead, without however conferring complete intellectual credentials. Aside from competition's being discouraged in this way, the security of the intelligentsia's positions is further assured by the fact that if someone with a degree accepts a lower-ranking job he is made the object of general social disapproval, and such deviants can expect punishment from a number of quarters, ranging from the press to the public prosecutor's office.

If until now we have attempted some defense of the statistical definition of the intelligentsia, we are now at a point where it begins to appear that it will not take us very far. For, in fact, the given level of division of labor and the complexity of the knowledge required for certain work do not by any means determine directly which kinds of work society will label as intellectual. That determination is itself made in a context of interest-relationships, and the issue in the struggles of the intelligentsia is precisely *which* kinds of work society will define as exclusively intellectual work, compensated with all the influence and material reward that go with intellectual status. And so we must also apply to the statistical definition of the intelligentsia reservations of an epistemological nature, since we do not possess any absolute cultural yardstick for measuring what is high knowledge and what low. Nor can we accept as anything but an oversimplification the functionalist argument that society needs to have performed certain kinds of work requiring more complex knowledge, so that, since only a few people have such knowledge, they are assigned disproportionate rewards. This reasoning assumes the existence of functional connections between occupation, knowledge, and power. We consider this way of ranging those three factors into a causal sequence to be itself one of the ideologies of the intelligentsia. It is in the interests of the intellectuals that occupations guaranteeing superior social rewards and influence should be designated as intellectual occupations, and the way to achieve that is to make sure that the knowledge needed for them attains the degree of complexity which society regards as characteristic of intellectual knowledge. The saying

"Knowledge is power" implies a dual process: Knowledge creates its own kind of power, but at the same time power also brings into being its own knowledge. Thus, for example, when economic enterprises come to be bureaucratically structured and managerial positions appear, each with its sphere of power, those positions are quite creditably filled at first by people who have not the foggiest notion of what "managerial science" is. But soon management becomes an activity demanding complex knowledge, among other reasons because then it can be designated an intellectual activity, and the rapid expansion of management studies is the means to this end. The process is not one whereby managerial science evolves first and then works out the principles of scientific management which make it possible to administer giant industrial enterprises; quite to the contrary, the giant enterprises with their managerial posts come first, and only afterward does management science appear, as a device for selecting people to fill the positions. Acquisition of a knowledge of scientific management is more important for purposes of regulating the competition for leading positions than it is in actual management. In saying this we do not mean to deny that a part of the knowledge acquired at university by the practitioners of various intellectual skills does indeed find functional use in the world of concrete work; nevertheless, the other and perhaps greater part of that knowledge serves another and as it were secondary purpose—it entitles one to enter the industrial bureaucracy where the really relevant skills of management can be acquired in the course of actual work.

The essence of the intelligentsia's social function does not lie in the fact that knowledge of a certain complexity guarantees power and reward in certain positions; rather, the intelligentsia seeks to obtain power and reward for itself by exploiting its relative monopoly of complex knowledge as a means of achieving those goals. The heart of the matter, then, is not to be found in a knowledge that is functionally necessary, but rather in the desire to legitimize aspirations to power.

Thus a king, for example, probably needs to know a great deal in order to occupy his throne, but that still does not make him an intellectual. He is not a king because he knows a great deal but because his father was a king before him and doubtless taught him to be a king too. Although his functions demand considerable knowledge, it is not his knowledge but tradition which legitimizes them. It is the firstborn of a king's sons who succeeds him, not the most intelligent. Similarly, a capitalist may need advanced economic, legal, and technical knowledge to run his enterprise, yet his Oxford degree does not make him an intellectual because it is not his formal knowledge but his ownership of capital that gives him a right to appropriate and reinvest the profits of his enterprise. Signor Agnelli no doubt has more knowledge, and more complicated knowledge, than many highly qualified Italian intellectuals, but he is still a capitalist, not an intellectual. But should some future Italian government nationalize the Fiat works, while keeping Agnelli on in his executive position because of his managerial abilities, he would then become an intellectual. The elected politician too is an intellectual only in a doubtful sense even when he has considerable educational background. His authority is legitimized not by the technical abilities at his command, but by the fact that a majority of the voters have expressed confidence in him, and if he loses his electoral majority he loses his right to exercise power, even though his knowledge has not diminished a whit. When an American Senator has to vote on a bill, he finds it wiser to study the letters his constituents write him about it than to consult the scholarly literature on the subject. Obviously tradition, ownership of capital, and political representation carry with them sufficient legitimation for positions of authority which, for the rest, do require considerable knowledge in order to be filled well. Thus it is not merely knowledge which makes someone an intellectual, but the fact that he has no other title to his status except for his knowledge. And the range of positions which can be held on the basis of knowledge alone varies from society to society and from age to age.

WHAT KIND OF KNOWLEDGE DOES SOCIETY REWARD WITH INTELLECTUAL STATUS AND AUTHORITY?

What sort of knowledge in itself confers a title to social reward and authority and, *in itself*, relieves the possessor of any necessity of directly, physically producing use-values or performing any physical, mental, or even supervisory services of a routine na-

ture? The question is all the more apt since there are industrial
and agricultural skills which often demand a great deal of complex technical knowledge, yet no one thinks of calling their
practitioners intellectuals on that score, much less of exempting
them from the obligation of performing physical labor. On the
other hand there must be many activities defined as intellectual
which do not require more, or more complicated knowledge,
than a trained electrician or gardener possesses; yet no one questions the intellectual character of those activities for that reason.
Students of personnel management would be hard put to measure
empirically the amount and composition of the information
needed in various lines of work. Intellectual knowledge does
not then differ from the knowledge used in other skilled activities in its quantity or complexity so much as in its character
or quality (by which we do not mean to imply any superior
valuation).

Thus intellectual knowledge is not knowledge of a higher order; its qualitative distinctiveness consists only in the fact that
it is concerned with the values which a society accepts as part
of its culture. That in turn means that society deems those values
pertinent for orienting and regulating the behavior of its members. Orientation: The intellectual works with alternative values
while only referring to them in passing, thus working out the
techniques for choosing among different values. Regulation: In
working with nonalternative values the intellectual *prescribes*
them, thus laying down a given technique for a given value.
Thus the element of *telos* is still present in the activity of intellectuals even if we still regard *techné* as the most valuable
element in intellectual knowledge. Max Weber recognized this
fact when he introduced the concept of value-relatedness *(Wert-
bezogenheit)*. In essence, Weber asserted, even the most positive
knowledge must have at least some reference to values. Society—
or at least the common consensus of intellectuals—declares only
those forms of knowledge to be valuable which bear some relevance to the concepts that regulate the spontaneous teleology of
society. Such forms of knowledge must at the very least be
capable of being brought into relationship with such questions
as: What is good? What is bad? How are we to act?

In this sense the physicist who examines the structure of the atom and the policeman who examines the contents of writers' manuscript drawers are both intellectuals, even though the former's connection with values is remote while the latter represents them very immediately indeed. But even this latter, supremely direct representative of values is an intellectual if his work has cross-contextual validity—if the police investigator not only confiscates a given manuscript but also sorts out the others in the drawer according to how dangerous they are and informs the author on what pages he overstepped the bounds of legality, thus functioning as an intellectual censor, even an ideologue. By cross-contextual significance we mean that intellectual knowledge offers models which are applicable in different contexts; their validity transcends the individual situation. Suppose A tells B that his (A's) wife has been unfaithful. So far this is merely information of individual validity about a melancholy turn of events in A's life. But if A unfolds his tale on such a level of symbolic generality that others feel themselves drawn emotionally into his feelings in this little drama of adultery, if by sympathizing with A's story they come to understand their own marriages better and draw from it lessons on how to treat their own wives, then A's communication acquires cross-contextual significance; it rises to the level of intellectual knowledge. A chair made by a craftsman differs from a factory-made chair in that it is not just for sitting on. It is a work of art, not just something made to be used; one can contemplate it and in so doing understand what the craftsman was telling society about beauty in furniture and how we should furnish our surroundings, for his chair is at the same time a judgment on other chairs.

Knowledge which is not objectified in material goods and services but is meant solely to influence others is still not, in itself, intellectual knowledge; it becomes so only when it acquires cross-contextual significance. A prison guard, for example, must know the penal regulations and must see that the convicts obey them, but he is still not an intellectual, for the norms he represents apply only to the prison situation. From him the prisoners can only learn how they are supposed to act in the normal circumstances of prison life. It is the director of rehabilitation who conveys to them the rules and values which operate both in prison and outside, in normal and unforeseen situations alike.

He is the spokesman of the official ethos. His tools include the private counseling session and the prison newspaper, written in a thoroughly edifying style, in which the most confirmed recidivists hail their punishment and vow to begin life afresh as new men on the completion of their sentences. The guard, who is not an intellectual, dispenses *rules*; the rehabilitation director, who is one, provides *models*.

Intellectuals, then, are the monopolistic proprietors of knowledge which society accepts as having cross-contextual validity and which it uses to orient its members. For that reason, and only for that reason, it is willing to provide for the support of those who possess that knowledge and to relieve them of other kinds of work, always provided of course that they use their knowledge in a way society deems proper. To be sure there are in everyday life many elements of cross-contextual, orientational knowledge which anyone may employ. All parents, for example, convey such knowledge to their children, but they do not become intellectuals by that reason alone, for that knowledge is not their monopolistic property; and so they cannot demand that society provide them with a living in exchange for it. If then we want to know what intellectual status is in a given society we must look for that point in its structure at which society accords material rewards and authority over others solely on the grounds that those having such status are monopolistic proprietors of the kind of knowledge described above.

We remarked before that any social order will reward its intellectuals with material benefits and power only so long as they use their knowledge in a way that society deems proper. An individual does not lose his intellectual status, however, if he employs intellectual knowledge in a manner that deviates from, or even directly flouts the values of his society. In that case his intellectual status is indicated not by the rewards accorded him but by the severity of the sanctions brought against him. The figure of Giordano Bruno would probably not loom so large in the historical pantheon of the intellectuals if he had never been burned to death for writing the *Three Dialogues*. There are some who become writers thanks to a favorable critical reception, and others who are made into writers by forced-labor camps. Of course there is no question of a society's official arbiters of culture deciding who is an intellectual and, more particularly, who is not. But neither is it a matter of the members of society casting a species of majority vote on the subject, perhaps by responding to some sort of public-opinion poll. Intellectuals are defined as such by the social structure. By that we mean that whether the powers that be in society like it or not there objectively exist in the social structure functions whose executants are objectively intellectuals, and if they cannot be rewarded for their activities then they have to be punished for them. A court which sentenced a writer to prison because of the contents of his manuscript would seek in vain to deprive him of the name of writer as well, for the sentence itself defines him as a writer. If his work had not been an intellectual product—cross-contextual, having general reference, possessing an orientational value—he would not have been convicted for it in the first place. How different societies decide which uses of intellectual knowledge to reward and which to punish is another matter. The more tolerant ones are less stringent, but for that very reason they specify concretely and exhaustively what uses of intellectual knowledge are punishable. Societies which legitimize conflicts of interest can tolerate sociological treatises which submit their class structures to sharp critical analysis, may indeed even reward their authors with academic chairs. Criminal prosecutions are leveled only against writings which incite to violence against definite persons or institutions—sabotage, seizure of hostages, and the like. (Of course one may question whether such works, lacking cross-contextual validity, can be regarded as intellectual products at all.) It is true, of course, that such societies employ other sanctions besides criminal prosecution against nonconformist intellectuals; among other things they may exclude them from the mass market of cultural production and consumption, and in such cases repressive tolerance is replaced by a kind of lofty indifference.

Other societies are less tolerant. They indicate only very generally and elastically what sorts of intellectual knowledge they consider deserving of punishment, abandoning even repressive tolerance in favor of a repressive intolerance. In those societies not only appeals to action but also nonconformist theoretical analyses can incur prosecution, and it is left to the tactical judgment of the criminal authorities to decide in which cases measures against deviant theorists are warranted. Poor Galileo had no wish to be subversive, nor would the Holy Office have put him on the rack solely over such an abstract and theoretical matter as his refutation of the Ptolemaic cosmogony. Nevertheless his doctrine was branded as an "incitement against the fundamental institutions" of the Roman Catholic Church, an indication that that organization was ideological to the point of endowing all intellectual knowledge with canonical significance.

To avoid any misunderstanding, let us reiterate that it has not been our intention, in analyzing the genetic concept of the intelligentsia, to cast doubt on the legitimacy of defining the intelligentsia statistically, through the enumeration of occupational groupings. Much less was it any part of our purpose to devise a new nomenclature of occupations for socio-statistical use. We were in search of an answer to the question: By what criteria do various societies recognize someone as an intellectual? An elucidation of this question may of course supply, as a by-product, a background of social theory helpful in deciding which occupations should be regarded as intellectual in statistical studies undertaken in societies where the intelligentsia does appear as an aggregate of certain defined occupational groups. The structural concepts which we have mentioned as criteria for intellectual status are also useful for determining to what extent a concrete individual, activity, or occupation should be considered intellectual in character. We have deliberately avoided such traditional sociological quibbles as, for example, whether an engineer or a schoolteacher is an intellectual; instead, we have tried to determine whether intellectual knowledge is present in such extreme cases as those of the prison guard and the rehabilitation director. In our judgment there is no insurmountable theoretical barrier between intellectual and nonintellectual activity, and we have only been concerned to ask: What is the likelihood that society will recognize certain occupations as being intellectual in character? It is up to later empirical research to draw the exact dividing line, ranging the most diverse occupations on a scale from zero to one hundred and deciding at what point along the scale occupations deemed intellectual begin. Like all drawing of distinctions this will reflect a considerable element of arbitrariness, of course, and will give rise to stirring debate in various quarters.

We have asked which people are recognized by various societies as intellectuals so that, from there, we could go on to the next question: What structural position is marked out in various societies for the intellectuals? Or, putting it more concretely: Is it ever permissible to use the category of *class* to describe the social position of the intellectuals, and if so under what historical circumstances? In the second chapter of this essay we will give an affirmative answer to that question, in analyzing the integrated economic systems of rational-redistributive societies. And this answer brings with it a new question: In an age when the intellectuals are being formed into a class, what conflicts arise between the intelligentsia's transcendent mission and its historical determinedness, and how are those conflicts reflected in the image which the intelligentsia creates of itself?

II

The Intelligentsia
in the Social Structure

4

When Is the Concept of Class Applicable?

Every more or less complex society has its intellectuals—people whose knowledge is accepted by society as intellectual knowledge in terms of the criteria outlined above, and who regard that as a sufficient warrant for receiving social authority and reward. Their position varies however from one society to the next, just as power itself is legitimized in different ways in different societies. The relationship of the type of power legitimized by intellectual knowledge to other kinds of power also varies. The study of social structures demands that we look into the following questions: What factors legitimize authority in different societies? And what relationship do these variously legitimized forms of authority bear to one another?

Every society can be characterized by the dominant principle of legitimation which prevails in it. It is this basic legitimating principle which defines the social structure and marks out the places in it of those who justify their power on other principles. We accept the fundamental premise of Marxian sociology that the basic structure of society is determined by the way that society reproduces itself, and more particularly by the disposition made of the social surplus product, who controls it, and on what principles. On this thesis we must conclude that in every society a legitimated right to dispose over the surplus product is elevated to the general and dominant principle of legitimacy, subsuming within itself other principles of legitimation.

This fundamental structure ranges the members of society into subordinate and superordinate positions, along a hierarchical scale—the producers of the social product and its expropriators, hence oppressed and oppressors. It also indicates the conditions on which members of society come to occupy these positions or exchange them for others. Finally, it is this basic structure which creates the coherence of the groups that form around identical positions, enabling them to recognize their identity and through that recognition to construct their own culture and ethos. Thus it is that we can characterize aggregates of individuals in identical situations in different ways, and so we think it likely that the intelligentsia, for example, can be described differently in different periods of its social history when it occupied different places in the social structure, sometimes as a social order or estate, sometimes as a stratum, and sometimes as a class.

SOME NOTES ON THE MARXIST CONCEPT OF CLASS

In attempting to define the basic structure of capitalist society Marx set out from the relations of property-ownership. He described the structure of capitalist society as a class structure in which the basic classes are, on the one hand, the owners of the means of production (or capital) and, on the other, those who do not own their own means of production and who merely supply the property-owners with their labor-power. Bourgeoisie and proletariat occupy the two fundamental positions in this dichotomous structure. On the basis of what has already been said we can assume Marx recognized that in capitalist society it is property-ownership which legitimizes control over the surplus product. Thus he was correct in declaring the ownership of capital to be the fundamental factor determining the structure of this type of society.

Difficulties involved in the historical and sociological use of Marx's concept of class. The problem of the Asiatic mode of production

Marx believed that in the relations of production he had found the key to a description of all societies past, present, and future as class structures (or, as the case might be, classless). Nevertheless it was only capitalist society that Marx subjected to concrete and detailed analysis and, even though he emphasized that from his standpoint the entire history of mankind was a history of class struggles, he used the category of class very cautiously in analyzing precapitalist societies (which he nonetheless still generally termed class societies). During the 1920s Marxist and especially Soviet scholars found themselves in great difficulty when they were obliged to apply a concept of class derived from property-relations to the great mass of historical and economic data which had accumulated on Asiatic societies. The mode of ownership characteristic of Asiatic societies was prebendal property—a nonheritable estate conferred upon an official in exchange for service to the state, whose revenue the holder could enjoy but which he could not sell or otherwise transfer; nor could he even make changes in the mode of cultivation practiced on it. The Asiatic mode of production seemed to suggest unmistakably that the feudal lord partook of social authority and a disproportionate share of the surplus product not in the capacity of a property-owner but in that of an official. Thus it became a matter of debate whether the social position of such landlord-officials as, for example, the mandarins of China, could be described using a concept derived from ownership of the means of production.

This question arose not only in connection with the Asiatic mode of production but also in the study of Eastern European history, particularly Russian history of the sixteenth and seventeenth century, for there too the landholding service nobility were really officials and soldiers who were given the use of various lands by the Tsar in exchange for services rendered him, but provisionally and subject to revocation at any time. And so those historians who were prepared to be more flexible in the face of the empirical data proposed that these "Asiatic" social formations should not be treated as feudal and recommended the term "Asiatic mode of production" to indicate their distinctiveness. Behind this suggestion, however, more orthodox scholars saw a theoretical abyss yawning—if only because its acceptance might supply a precedent for removing other types of societies from the scope of the universally valid blueprint which the Marxist philosophy of history offered. It would, moreover, have given others the right to deal with various kinds of feudal or slave societies not on the basis of property-relations, but in terms of concrete relations of power and authority. Even in the case of the Western European societies which Marx knew so well it became doubtful whether precapitalist social structures could be analyzed at all on the basis of property-relations (even though those societies appeared most susceptible to a Marxist analysis, for private property in one form or another can be found over the whole length of Western history). Perhaps the more acute of the orthodox theorists also sensed that such a relativization of the role of property-relations might also come to influence the way Soviet society viewed itself. In that event the fundamental tenet that the basic classes of Soviet society evolve in conjunction with its two forms of property (collective and state property) would have been called into question. In other words, it would no longer have been possible to derive the structure of Soviet society with any assurance simply from the negative observation that in the Soviet Union there were no means of production in private hands. In the light of these considerations it is perhaps easier to understand why the study of medieval Chinese economic history became a political crime in the Russia of the early 1930s, to such a degree that many of the practitioners of that discipline were obliged to bid farewell not only to their scholarly research but often to their very lives as well.

Difficulties in applying the Marxist concept of class to the analysis of the social structures of socialist Eastern Europe

Even the sharpest of the orthodox theoreticians could not, for all the grisliness of their methods of disputation, bury the problem itself; they merely succeeded in putting it off for three decades. It was hardly a coincidence that just at that point—when the Asiatic mode of production had come to be tolerated again as a seemingly harmless notion and was being used by historians and philosophers in some of the Eastern European countries as an accepted analytical category—sociologists should have begun to justify the old suspicions by calling into question the relevance of property-relations to any analysis of the structure of socialist societies. Having arrived at a recognition of the irrelevance of property-ownership as an analytical category, the sociologists went on to attempt a positive, substantive analysis of socialist society. Their work took three different directions.

Those whose approach was more empirical soon found themselves obliged by their concrete researches to discard the traditional type of class analysis based on property-relations, for the classification of the population into a working class based on state property and a peasantry based on cooperative property soon proved incapable of explaining a whole range of empirical phenomena, from the distribution of income to the diversity of life-styles. In its place they substituted a statistical method of analyzing social stratification. But in doing so they neglected to ask: What criteria do define the structure of socialist societies, if not property-relations? The possibility that the concept of class might be applicable was simply left aside, even though it was obviously accepted as an ideological premise, for Soviet Marxism holds that only fully communist societies are classless, while socialist society is described as composed of a working class, a class of peasants, and a stratum of intellectuals. But in so doing it does not even look for the real dimensions which define classes. This circumstance forced Eastern European empirical sociology into a theoretic eclecticism recognized by its critics of East and West alike. The latter rightly demanded a structural theory of Eastern European society more coherent than this set of empirical stratification-categories, something that would pull together such discrete indicators as type of work performed, level of qualification for it, degree of complexity of the knowledge needed for it, possibility of managing one's own work, number of subordinates, and the like.

This criticism has given rise to a neo-Marxist attempt to modify the notion of property, which, applied to socialist society, would yield a concept of class having real content. We refer to the theory of the "new class" or "collective ownership class." Yet these notions, however radical they may be politically, are marked by an unchanging theoretical conservatism. Their proponents go on clinging firmly to the idea that property-relationships determine the content of class-relationships, but in order to maintain this thesis they are obliged to empty the concept of property of all meaning. We would argue as follows: If under the Asiatic mode of production property-rights are so tenuous that the real social authority and position of a holder of such a right cannot be explained on the basis of property—for the right attaches only to him personally and is only for his personal use, while the income is shared with the real owner, the ruler—then does not the category of property seem even more devoid of meaning in socialist economies, where a plant manager may perform certain ownership functions but where his share in the income of the enterprise is legitimized in exactly the same way as the simplest laborer's wage (even if the manager's share is larger)? Even if we were to call the plant manager an owner that would still not be sufficient grounds for determining his social situation. Moreover, this argument narrows property-ownership down to an impersonal, functional right of disposing over the surplus product, banishing every element which might suggest that "ownership" and "right of disposition" are not identical concepts. If we need the notion of property to tell us who disposes of the social surplus in certain circumstances, and under what conditions, then formal logic alone demands that property-owning be a richer and more specific concept than the mere exercise of a right of disposition. Simplifying the circular logic inherent in the notion of the new class, we find ourselves confronted with the following series of questions and answers: Who disposes over the surplus product in socialist society? Answer: the collective owners, the new owners. And who are these new, collective owners? Answer: those who dispose over the surplus product.

There was only one way out of this tautology, and it began to be taken in Eastern Europe in the latter half of the 1960s, in the form of research into the mechanics and legitimation of the right to dispose over the social surplus. By examining the nature of bureaucratic rule these theorists sought to arrive at a structural analysis that would be new in content. As soon as we turn to the analysis of bureaucratic rule, however, we overstep the limits of the concept of property-relationships and find ourselves dealing with a more general notion that lies behind it: the relations of authority and rule in society, and the question of how rule is legitimized. We feel obliged to assume in advance that property is only one possible way of legitimizing rule, and that other bases of legitimation are conceivable as well.

SOME REMARKS ON MAX WEBER'S CONCEPT OF CLASS

In his analysis of social structures Marx committed the same error with which Karl Polanyi reproached those economists who in analyzing nonmarket economies thought in terms of market categories and market rationality. Marx projected the notion of class, which was relevant in societies where ownership of capital really did give a legitimate right to dispose over the surplus, back onto societies in which the principles of legitimation were different and where for that reason property-relations in themselves were not decisive in defining the social structure. For that reason Weber's attempt to pin down the range of legitimate validity of Marx's concept of class appears all the more justified. It was no accident that Max Weber, who had devoted a great deal of study to the economic history of Asia and the special conditions in which European capitalism developed, was the first writer who thought it necessary to render more precise Marx's categories for analyzing social structure. Weber employed the concept of class to describe social structures based on a free-market economy. In his analysis class relations always emerge from a market situation. Under free-market capitalism the labor market gives rise to the most fundamental class relations. There the owners of capital and the owners of labor-power meet and enter into transactions with one another, and that is what delineates the two basic classes of capitalist society, capitalists and workers. Up to that point Weber really did no more than apply his own terminology to the interpretation of Marx's theory of classes. But Weber went further than that, for in holding that the notion of class was applicable only in market economies and under market conditions he also asserted that it was not valid for precapitalist societies. Indeed, a considerable part of Weber's work was devoted precisely to discovering what other means of legitimizing authority exist in precapitalist societies, and what structures of social domination are built upon them. But if we accept Weber's proposition that it is proper to speak of classes only where market conditions exist, then we must abandon the use of the concept of class in dealing with socialist societies, which are fundamentally redistributive in character.

Nevertheless, we will continue to use the notion of class in discussing modern societies with redistributive economies, to that extent lending the concept a more general meaning. Like market economies, modern redistributive economies may be regarded as rational economies, in which the power to dispose over the social product is legitimized on rational principles. In capitalist societies the power of disposition over the surplus product is legitimized through a rational criterion, ownership of capital; in order for someone to have a portion of the surplus product at his disposal he must be a capitalist. In modern redistributive systems it is the teleological redistributors who dispose over the surplus product; in order to become one of them an individual must possess specialized knowledge, or in other words must be an intellectual. It is our contention, then, that in modern redistributive economies the teleological redistributors occupy a structural position around which a social class may form.

It is not the purpose of this study to provide a description of the class structure of socialist societies in general. For the time being we do not even wish to take a position on the question of whether the social structure of early socialism can best be described as a dichotomous class structure, or whether it is more useful to work out for it a multidimensional class structure like Weber's. The aim of this essay is simply to examine whether it is appropriate to describe the new social position which the intelligentsia occupies in modern redistributive economies as a class position. Indeed, neither Weber's nor Marx's concept of class is apt for that purpose, for it was not the purpose of their conceptualizations to present a complete descriptive cross-section of society, and when they attempted it they generally overstepped the bounds of their own class-concepts strictly defined to characterize society as a complex system of classes, strata, and status groups.

5

Models of Economic Integration and the Social Structure

MODEL OF ECONOMIC INTEGRATION OR MODE OF PRODUCTION?

We propose to analyze the position of the intellectuals in various societies in terms of the models of economic integration which those societies display. We understand by model of integration a concept analogous to mode of production, but substantively superior in that it also takes in the systems of authority and rule in various societies and not just their relations of production. In analyzing various models of integration emphasis will be placed on the legitimization of social authority. Of course these models of economic integration can also be taken as models of reproduction, but coupling together the institutions of social reproduction and social authority anchors economic concepts in a sociological framework and does away with the rather sterile problem which appears in formal sociology as a dualism crying out for concretization: What deterministic relations exist between the technical aspects of production, and authority or culture (described as a superstructure in Marxist sociology)? Something of this sort is all the more necessary because every concrete social analysis is bound to come to the conclusion that base and superstructure stand in an interdependent, mutually determining relationship, and singling out the criteria of primacy within this mutual dependence has importance only for the history of philosophical thought since Hegel.

Earlier we asserted that property-relations play a decisive role only in certain historical contexts, which gives them only a relative importance. Although we consider justified the exceptional significance which Marx attached to property-relations in capitalist society, we believe that the elevation of this contextual category into a suprahistorical absolute is a very dubious procedure. To the category of mode of production we attribute a purely formal economic value, since we do not regard property-relations, independent of their conditioning circumstances, as affording any universal principles for explaining the process of social reproduction. Indeed, their too-frequent use only leads, in our judgment, to bypassing precisely those problems which belong at the center of sociological research: What is the meaning of property, or any other social institution, in the concrete system of institutions of any society? A great mass of research in sociology, economic history, and anthropology, from Weber to Malinowski and Polanyi, proves that there is hardly a single precapitalist society in which property-relations can offer an adequate explanation of social authority. Those societies can best be analyzed in terms of traditional, political, legal, and cultural factors acting as principles of legitimation, even though in them property has a greater or lesser importance as one institution among many.

That is why, in seeking the place of intellectuals in the social structure, we set out not from the category of mode of production but from Polanyi's models of economic integration. We said before that, with the emergence of the teleological redistributors, there appears in the social structure a point around which a class may coalesce. That assertion implies another—namely that, extending Weber's interpretation, we will speak of class not only amid free-market conditions but will assume the existence of a historically new model of economic integration in which we consider the formation of the intelligentsia into a class to be a possibility: the redistributive economy of early socialism.

ECONOMIC INTEGRATION AND SOCIAL AUTHORITY

Growth or stagnation?

The type of economic integration which offers a basis for the formation of the intelligentsia into a class—rational redistribution—differs from the sort of redistribution ideally typified in the Asiatic mode of production (which we will henceforth call traditional redistribution), and also from the self-regulating market ideally typified by nineteenth-century Western European capitalism. We see the distinction between these three integrational models in the way each interprets the overall challenge to which it must respond in its own way. Systems of traditional redistribution are not called upon to respond to the demands of growth; a dynamic economy is not one of their goals or values. Such a system works satisfactorily even when it assures no more than the simple reproduction of society. Typically, traditional redistributive systems are powerfully conditioned by their ecology; the simple reproduction of society depends heavily on chance environmental and topographical factors, and therefore social survival demands that these natural conditions be brought under control (in particular through irrigation works, justifying their designation as hydraulic societies).

Under the Asiatic mode of production the members of society accept as legitimate the authority of the central redistributive apparatus to appropriate a part of their production as social surplus because the central authorities, by maintaining the system of dams and irrigation canals, guarantee the society's continued survival. The common feature of free-market and rational-redistributive economies, on the other hand, is that both assure an expansion of production, orienting the members and institutions of society toward economic growth. The difference between the last two appears in the way the challenge of growth is met: The free market builds the imperative to expand into the market mechanism itself, and the goal of growth, internalized in this way, is then controlled through an impersonal profit mechanism. Rational-redistributive societies treat economic growth as an external challenge, a politically defined goal dictated by the desire to catch up with the developed Western economies. In this externality of the goal of growth rational redistribution resembles the more traditional variety, for whom the challenge of nature appears as an external menace, and it is for this reason that institutions of authority which are similar in many ways arise in both.

Independent economy or coordinated economy?

All redistributive systems are characterized by the coordination of economic and political power, by contrast with free-market

economies, where for the first time in history political and economic institutions are separated. It is this coordination of political
and economic institutions which lends a certain limited sense to
the superficial comparison of rational-redistributive with precapitalist systems in such phrases as "feudal socialism." For purposes
of analyzing the concept of class, however, the most important
difference between those two models of integration is to be
found in the way the organs of combined political and economic
authority are legitimized. In older redistributive societies tradition legitimizes the appropriation of the surplus product, and so
the rule of traditional authority is the prime structural feature
of this type of economy.

Legitimizing control over the surplus product

Under the Asiatic mode of production the power to redistribute
is founded upon traditional status; its legitimacy cannot be called
into question on the grounds that it is not exercised rationally
enough or efficiently enough. Modern redistributive economies,
on the other hand, like free-market economies, are rational and
geared to dynamic growth. They are based on the performance
principle and accept the criterion of maximum return at minimum
cost; they strive for the most efficient use of capital, create comparable institutions to assure the organization of technical and
industrial labor, and make achievement, not ascribed status, the
criterion of class membership. The Asiatic mode of production is
also characterized by a centralized state bureaucracy, a pyramidal conduit serving the whole redistributive system. In a
somewhat similar way modern redistribution substitutes governmental administrative decisions for the decisions of the market,
creating through the sum of those decisions a bureaucratic network which tends to become centralized and to encompass the
whole society. Since no one owns any appreciable amount of
property everyone in rational-redistributive society, from top to
bottom of the pyramid, is an office-holder. Nevertheless, the features which Weber discerned in analyzing the workings of the
rational bureaucracy of modern capitalism are also to be found,
in many respects, in this organization of office-holders, and they
distinguish it from traditional bureaucracy with its nonrational

recruitment procedures and operational principles. This modern bureaucracy, in which interest-relationships are impersonal, has to show effective results, and accordingly its various rungs are occupied by people possessing various degrees of bureaucratic knowledge.

Historically and technologically, market economy and rational-redistributive economy are contemporaries. Thus their common feature is the rationality of power. In the latter system authority to redistribute the surplus product from a central point is not granted according to inherited status, much less by tradition or charisma, but by a purposive rationality—an ideology which has grown into a common consensus that the organs of central planning and redistribution are capable of redistributing the surplus product in the most rational manner. In market economies, too, the right to dispose over the social surplus is legitimized according to a rational criterion, except that there it is ownership of capital which bestows legitimacy.

Differences in the way the surplus product is determined

Our three models of economic integration not only legitimize the right of disposition over the surplus product differently; they also determine the surplus product itself in different ways. In market economies it is determined by economic criteria alone. The surplus product is equivalent to the difference between production costs and market prices; its size is regulated by the market mechanism itself. All redistributive systems, on the other hand, have in common the fact that the surplus product is not determined by economic means alone; its magnitude is the result of political decisions. In these societies the surplus product is as much as the central authorities can extract without provoking uprisings against themselves. In traditional redistributive economies, however, the size of the surplus is relatively limited. Rational-redistributive systems, on the other hand, are the most effective of all at maximizing the amount of surplus product withheld from the personal consumption of society's members and mobilized for purposes of expanding production. From that it does not follow, of course, that in the rational-redistributive systems the social capital retained is allocated more efficiently than it would be if a market mechanism were making the decisions about its use. On the contrary, every economist knows that while the proportion of national income devoted to investment in the socialist countries is substantially larger than in market societies on a comparable level of development, the efficiency of the capital invested is lower. It is no less a commonplace that market economies display their efficiency above all in the way they satisfy consumer needs and the infrastructural requirements of consumption, while at the same time they generally devote a smaller share of their resources to such ultimately extraeconomic purposes as armaments. That is the reason relatively developed socialist societies can create military establishments on a par with, or even larger than, those of market societies more developed than they.

Expansion of the size of the surplus product is not an essential feature of traditional redistribution. If it happens nonetheless the increase goes not to expanding production but toward swelling the mandarin bureaucracy. We might add that in such systems only a few goods become salable commodities, for in the redistributive process most goods circulate in kind, which further limits the amount of goods that can go to make up the surplus product. Thus for the most part traditional redistribution goes together with a subsistence economy. The necessities of life are consumed in their immediate natural form within the communal organizations of production, so that often it is only luxuries which enter the redistributive stream. Then there is the fact that societies characterized by traditional redistribution are not great centralized empires, and even when they are forcibly organized into empires they frequently fall apart again into regional satrapies constantly at war with one another. If any one region succeeds in imposing its rule on the others, it is still incapable of integrating them economically, and attempts only to hold the various regions together as long as possible by means of ideology and sheer military power. Sooner or later, however, anarchy and corruption dissolve the imperial structure, a process whose ultimate economic cause is to be found in the fact that the redistributive mechanism itself limits the kind and amount of surplus product available for redistribution.

Commodity relations under rational redistribution

Rational redistribution, in contrast, by rationalizing the tools of power, is able to increase the size of the surplus product considerably. In this process an important part is played by the fact that although the price-regulating function of the market is eliminated commodity relations are not; in fact they are made universal. We know of no other model of economic integration which converts so large a proportion of all products into commodities. The entire labor supply becomes a commodity, for the political machinery of rational redistribution destroys all traditional productive units, replacing them with a vast bureaucratic apparatus. This universalization of commodity relations does not take place according to the logic of the market, however. It is the rationality of the planning process, not the decisions of owners of capital, which redistributes the retained surplus product, whose size cannot be effectively regulated by the market. The extension of commodity relations does not weaken the redistributive system. On the contrary, it strengthens it, for the prices of the increased quantity of goods brought into circulation by minimizing how much of his own production the peasant consumes—and by minimizing, in a particularly thorough and inflexible fashion, the price of labor—are basically determined not by the market but by the decisions of the authorities. This key structural feature is motivated primarily by the desire to put a relatively large percentage of the national income to use through the channels of the state budget, and to make even consumption dependent, in large measure, on allocations from a central source rather than on wages arrived at through transactions on a labor market.

Although the first great spurt of economic growth in the rational-redistributive societies coincided everywhere with the transfer (by means of collectivization) of a large quantity of peasant labor from small-scale agriculture to industry, and thus with the rapid conversion of the independent small producers who made up the bulk of the population into wage workers, the "sale" of labor in the redistributive economy still cannot be regarded as "market commerce" in Polanyi's sense. A worker who is forced to sell his labor, sometimes by police measures, cannot enter into transactive relations in any kind of "labor commerce" with the organizations that offer employment; he is more or less at their disposition. In these circumstances there is no connection between the worker's wage and the size of the surplus product he turns out, nor theoretically can there be any. Just as prices are not economic but political prices, so too wages are not economic but political. Consequently, only the patience of the population determines their lower limit. In the light of all this it can be understood why wage differentials are governed not by the actual demand for various kinds of labor, but by an abstract hierarchy of qualifications.

The universalization of commodity relations: Stalin's revolution

Today both Chinese ideologists and the Western New Left brand Eastern European economic policy since Stalin's death as revisionist because a few pieces of market machinery have been fitted into the overall redistributive mechanism, and an ever-growing number of consumer goods have been defined as commodities, removing them from the sphere of direct allocation. But in fact it would be more correct to say that the great turning point in the history of the Eastern European economy was the introduction of Stalinist economic policy, which found a country where three-quarters of the population were small peasant producers and in a few years' time transferred nearly all available labor to the "socialist labor market." Stalin and his entourage realized that neither extorting capital from individual peasant holdings through a system of forced deliveries of crops, nor giving free rein to the open marketing of peasant production, as recommended by Bukharin, could greatly increase the surplus product available for rational redistribution. That objective would be served only by curtailing the peasant's self-sufficiency, treating all labor as a commodity, and extending the range of consumer articles that could only be obtained with money as rapidly as possible.

Thus, far from abolishing commodity relations, Stalin universalized them. Henceforward the size of the surplus product which the central authorities could skim off the economy was limited only by political factors. That enabled the planners to take into account only political and power considerations (rather than economic ones) in deciding what would be a requisite or sometimes just barely tolerable standard of living. Over the years experience yielded the elementary political insight that living standards had to be raised in some modest degree (but enough for the population to notice it) if the state apparatus wanted to avoid such outbreaks of discontent as occurred in Hungary in 1956 or Poland in 1970.

The recent economic reforms do not limit redistribution; they only make it more rational

By comparison with the Stalinist revolution the economic reforms adopted in some of the Eastern European countries during the 1960s, which introduced monetary indicators in place of administrative directives in the management of the enterprise, were only of secondary significance. Since these reforms never disturbed the redistributive interpretation of labor as a commodity and did not attempt to replace the worker's dispositive situation with new, transactive relations, they did not bring the rational-redistributive system a single step closer to a market economy.

Western leftist critics of early socialism almost without exception misunderstood this extension of commodity relations in the Eastern European societies. The gradual disappearance there of utopian-socialist illusions about the possibility of direct, moneyless redistribution leads them to think that Eastern Europe must be headed, as a result, toward a market model of economic integration, and that the institutional conditions for a restoration of capitalism have been created inside the socialist system. They should bear in mind, however, that the universalization of commodity relations takes place strictly according to the logic of redistribution, not just in the sense that the price of every key commodity (including labor) is regulated by central decision, but also in that the apparent market elements in fact only increase the proportion of the surplus product which can be diverted into the stream of central redistribution. The alternatives of plan versus market, natural indicators versus monetary indicators, represent in fact only structural options within the framework of redistribution. Even the most radical proponents of market devices in Eastern Europe have only designed measures to increase, by monetary means, the size of the surplus product available for central redistribution, to a degree that was not possible for the socialist system in its first period, when some limitations on commodity relations still survived.

In sum, all these reformers recommend is that products on whose redistribution only formal administrative decisions can be made should not be introduced into the central redistributive process. They deem illusory the appropriation of such components of the surplus product as are destined to be reallocated to the producers anyway; subsidizing the price of milk or meat, for example, and balancing that section of the state budget by taxing other articles in trade, has in this view only the appearance of being a redistributive decision. What all these reforms strive for is precisely to make rational redistribution more rational, by purging it of traditional elements.

An economy by no means approaches the free-market model merely because it expands the range of products which are treated as commodities. The decisive question is still how the surplus product is determined, and here rational redistribution is still unalterably characterized by the integration of political and economic power and, as a result, by administrative decision-making uncontrolled by economic processes. And so we must defend the Eastern European economic reformers of the 1960s against the charge of revisionism; indeed we see in them the direct heirs of the rationalizing tendencies of Stalinist economic policy. Their reforms have not in the least questioned redistribution's basic principle of legitimacy—the principle that it is the teleological redistributors who should decide over the social surplus product, not owners of capital or self-managing owners of labor-power. They only want to be rid of bungling, untutored party bureaucrats who run the economy with arbitrary, haphazard directives, and put in their places "computerized" planners with a high level of econometric knowledge, who can govern economy and society more effectively.

Special characteristics of the Chinese social and economic structure

Western European New Left writers customarily cite as an alternative to the Eastern European model of development the economy of China, in which market relations and distribution of product other than in kind play a rather modest part. Because of that they tend to see the Chinese model as a more likely point of departure for a genuinely socialist economy. In our opinion Chinese socialism differs from the Soviet model primarily in resembling traditional redistribution more closely than it does the typical rational-redistributive system. Central redistribution of the Chinese type draws only a relatively small fraction of the social product into the state budget. In China the Stalinist revolution has never taken place; the central government has converted into commodities neither labor nor consumer articles, nor even the bulk of the agricultural means of production. The Chinese state has not become the kind of regime required for modern rational redistribution, in that the individual members of society—particularly the villagers who make up eighty-five percent of the population—are not brought constantly and immediately face to face with the central authorities.

China may still be termed a "segmented" state in the sense that redistribution does not take place through a rational bureaucratic apparatus working from the top down, nor does it encompass the whole of social and economic activity. But that does not at all mean that the Chinese organizational model is any less bureaucratic than the Soviet one, or that it really affords greater scope for self-management. The lowliest official in the technical bureaucracy stands high above the locally organized communal units, ostensibly autonomous and basically self-sufficient economically. The technical bureaucracy is in fact smaller than in the Soviet Union, but on the other hand the range of products regulated by it is larger, for in China officials must supervise the actual physical distribution of goods in kind, which in the Soviet system is merely regulated in broad outline by the bureaucracy.

The surplus product which flows from the Chinese communes

into the hands of the central distributive apparatus is relatively smaller, but that does not at all mean that the producers have any greater a voice in determining the size of the surplus product taken from them than do the producers under the Soviet model. In fact the Soviet citizen still has greater autonomy in his choice of consumer products, for he can spend his wages as he likes on the (admittedly narrow) consumer-goods market. The fact that his labor has been made a commodity subjects him all the more to the professional bureaucracy, of course, but it also makes him freer of them to the degree that the control exercised over him is more impersonal and does not extend to every moment of his life, his leisure time as well as his working hours. In China, on the other hand, an enormous unpaid bureaucracy is ranged alongside the paid professional bureaucracy, and extends its watchfulness over the individual into every aspect of life.

Since Chinese society is not integrated through a central rational-redistributive system, ideological and political controls even stricter than those found in the Soviet model are required in order to assure the integration of state and society. The latter can only be achieved if everything that happens in society is imbued with ideological significance and the most banal acts are given symbolic meaning, so that every manifestation of the individual's life can be weighed in the scales of loyalty or treason. That is what makes the life of the Communist movement seem more spirited in contemporary China, even if the parades and slogans of the organizationally mobilized masses never represent the articulation of a particular interest in society. The purpose of these rituals is to compel the masses to express their dedication to the organization of Chinese society, in which the people under one leader advance toward a single goal, and usually the masses need to be mobilized whenever the leader identifies his next rival in the Politburo and undertakes to oust him and his supporters from the upper levels of power.

For all that the organizational forms of traditional redistribution survive relatively intact in China, Chinese society itself is no less bureaucratic than Soviet society; it is only so in a different way. Since a relatively smaller fraction of the social product is made available for central redistribution, fewer redistributors are needed, hence fewer intellectuals. But since contemporary Chinese redistribution, in contrast to the traditional form, is already rational in its essential structural components, class positions for the intelligentsia already exist in theory under Chinese socialism, and the formation of the intellectuals into a class is now possible within the foreseeable future. Today, however, the appropriated surplus product still goes primarily to meet military needs; only a small fraction of it is returned to the civilian economy in the form of production subsidies. Thus it is that in contemporary China the teleological redistributors are themselves, first and foremost, soldiers. So too the power struggles in the Chinese leadership are restricted to groups within the elite; they reflect the rivalries between the party bureaucracy, the state bureaucracy, and the military, and do not involve intellectual groups outside their ranks.

Thus when Liu Shao-chi advocated an extension of rational redistribution on the Stalinist model, which would have resulted in a rapid growth of the Chinese working class and urban population, he was in fact advancing a class program for the intelligentsia, even though on the ideological plane he and his supporters had to come forward as spokesmen for industrialization and the working class. It was no accident that after the collapse of his reform efforts reprisals were directed in the main against intellectual groups outside the inner circles of the central bureaucracy. In banishing university professors, scientists, and artists to village reeducation camps the authorities settled accounts with those elements of the intellectual class which sought, under the guise of rationalizing the redistributive system, to expand the class power of the intellectuals at the expense of the central bureaucracy.

In that respect the Cultural Revolution was no more than a struggle of intellectuals belonging to the ruling elite against the coalescence of the intellectuals outside it into a class. It was accompanied by a struggle against the state bureaucracy, which, although it has a stake in the prevailing order, is more interested by reason of its technocratic tendencies in broadening the intelligentsia's power base. Maoist ideology's *bête noire* was the technical expert whose social status made him relatively independent of the political hierarchy. Therein lies a certain resemblance between the principles of Maoism and Stalinism, however much the basic differences in their social and economic policies may seem to go against it. Stalin made a worker out of the peasant, kept agriculture as a separate branch of the economy while appropriating its entire surplus product, subordinated its development ruthlessly to that of industry, and in the pursuit of all these policies crowded the villagers pell-mell into the cities. Mao did the exact opposite of all these things. Yet they had in common the power monopoly of the party, and they defended it by the most brutal means in order to prevent the evolution of the intelligentsia into a class. The purges of the 1930s in the Soviet Union were bloodier than the Cultural Revolution in China because (among other things) the danger of the intelligentsia's coming to form a class was more immediate there. With regard to the economic structure it was Stalin himself who, in forcing the pace of social development in the direction of a rational-redistributive system, created at the same time the conditions for the formation of the intelligentsia into a class. To the degree that the rulers of China will have to abandon the structural principles of traditional redistribution in favor of further elements of rational redistribution, struggles within the intellectual class will come to replace political conflicts within the governmental elite in China as well.

III

---

*The Intelligentsia's Evolution into
a Class: The Historical Background*

6

The Intelligentsia: Social Estate, Social Stratum, or Class?

Earlier in our discussion we pointed out that different societies define intellectual knowledge in different ways, and assign different structural positions to its possessors at different times, depending on what significance the kind of power legitimated by intellectual knowledge has in the process of social reproduction. We said that it is permissible to speak of a class position of the intelligentsia only in societies where, in keeping with the principles of rational redistribution as a mode of economic integration, intellectual knowledge by itself confers the right of disposition over the surplus product. Socialism then is the first social system in which expert knowledge emerges from society's subconscious and becomes, by the end of the era of early socialism, more and more openly the dominant legitimating principle.

We also pointed out that although every complex society accepts intellectual knowledge as legitimating various kinds of authority, until the appearance of the rational-redistributive system this legitimation was everywhere subordinated to the society's dominant principle of legitimacy. In complex precapitalist societies, in Western European feudalism, and under the Asiatic mode of production intellectual knowledge secured for its exponents the authority of a social order or estate. Under free-market conditions it won them the position of a social stratum, an intermediate structural position which put intellectuals partly in the situation of owners of capital, partly in that of owners of labor, thus making it possible for them to decide

autonomously whether to become the organic intellectual stratum
of one or the other class.

In precapitalist societies the situation of the priesthood represents the structural position to which intellectual knowledge entitles its possessors. Even if every intellectual is not a priest and
every priest is not an intellectual, still every kind of intellectual
knowledge is hierarchically ranked by the priestly order, the
bearer of the teleology of religious transcendence. Doctors of
theology and canon-law jurists, the direct personifications of the
telos, are elevated to key intellectual positions, while surgeons,
architects, and even painters are reduced to the level of handicraftsmen (although the last of these may be allotted an intermediate position when they depict the spirituality of theology in
works of church art pleasing to the hierarchy). Since traditional
societies award power and privilege only to transcendental theological knowledge every other form of knowledge brings its
owner power, or else just a bare living, to the degree that it is
related to theology. In the classical conditions of traditional
society a man who openly questions any basic teaching of the
Church cannot on principle be an intellectual, no matter how
learned he may be.

The intelligentsia sought by professionalizing themselves to
escape from just this feudal situation, appearing on the free
market as a stratum emancipated from the constraints of feudal
subordination. Soon they went on from this stratum-position to
take the first step toward forming themselves into a class, by
formulating the ideological program of a society in which intellectual knowledge itself would be the dominant legitimating
principle for the exercise of power. On our hypothesis the history
of the changes of structural position undergone by the intelligentsia can be described as a process of transformation from an estate
to a stratum and from there into a class, these three structural
positions corresponding to the conditions of traditional redistribution (Western European feudalism), free-market capitalism,
and rational redistribution.

For us, however, estate, stratum, and class offer more than just a historical typology of the intellectuals' structural position. For we assume that in every age the intelligentsia is differentiated relative to these three structural positions, even though the character of the differentiation is determined by the intelligentsia's basic situation in each age. Thus while under traditional redistribution intellectuals occupy a primarily feudal situation, the outlines of their future role as a stratum begin to appear even there: Intellectuals who feel little compulsion to defend their feudal status—who, indeed, thanks to some unusual skill, feel it as a curb on their activity—manage somehow to escape it and look for takers outside the clerical estate for their skills or productions. They find them in the princes, great feudal lords, and urban patricians, in all those power centers which even while accepting the Church's hegemony still seek to limit it, even at times defending their particular interests against the Church's supreme authority by force of arms. Intellectuals who seek this kind of interstitial status—be they painters or physicians, mercenary captains or astrologers, chroniclers or musicians—are forerunners of the intellectuals of market societies, and the marginality which frees them from their feudal situation more or less forges them into a unitary stratum.

For all that the intelligentsia may win for itself a stratum or even class position, its feudal characteristics still do not disappear completely. Even under classical free-market conditions medical and legal associations still defend their members against competition in a strikingly corporative or "feudal" manner. Military and naval academies and foreign-service institutes use corporative status-requirements in choosing among applicants for admission. Those admitted are inculcated with the rules of group conduct, while at the same time they become entitled to special privileges which endow them with the character of a closed corporate elite within the intelligentsia as a whole. Under rational redistribution, as we shall see, the governing elite also acquired a privileged role which has enabled it, during the early socialist period, to place its corporate interests above the class interests of the intelligentsia and—so long as the era of early socialism lasts—to prevent the emerging intellectual class from acquiring and exercising real class power.

Different intellectual groups in rational-redistributive society may be bound together by their stratum-interests, too. It is in their interest, for example, that professional knowledge be accepted as valuable in itself, even apart from its teleological component, i.e., independent of the intellectuals' redistributive authority. Within any age we can understand the internal articulation of the intelligentsia, the conflicts among various intellectual groups, and the ideological alternatives of intellectual culture only if we examine the conflicting ways in which its dominant structural position interacts with elements of the two other possible positions.

THE SCHIZOID CHARACTER OF INTELLECTUAL CULTURE AS
A MOTIVE FORCE OF CHANGES IN THE INTELLIGENTSIA'S
POSITION

In order to coalesce into a class the intelligentsia had first to outgrow its traditional corporative situation, become secularized, and create a new type of specialized knowledge, the knowledge of the intellectual professional. But the ambition that would drive the intelligentsia to fight for a class position of its own could only be born in the drama of the individual intellectual. Thus the intellectual class finds its immediate historical forerunners in that intellectual stratum which found itself unable to reconcile its historical situation and its transcendent mission with the conditions of market economy, and in response to that dilemma developed the ideology of rational redistribution or socialism.

For that reason we must take a cursory look at the situation of the intellectual under capitalist free-market conditions, in order to trace how the intelligentsia in capitalist society develops that schizophrenia for which it comes to seek a remedy in the idea of socialism. We must also look for an answer to the question of why that idea was never able to become the dominant ideology of the intellectuals in the classical market societies, and why the path leading toward the coalescence of the intelligentsia into a class was blazed precisely in Eastern Europe—in countries where the free market was limited in scope and where, as a result, the intellectuals were never able to carve out for themselves a solid position as a social stratum. Although the class ideology of the intelligentsia was formulated by Western intellectuals, its aims were achieved by the Eastern European intelligentsia, only a fraction of whom had succeeded in freeing themselves from the constraints of feudal society. The bourgeois market economy did not afford enough employment opportunities to the Eastern European intellectuals, and so if they were not to slip back into a feudal situation they had to struggle for a society in which the intelligentsia itself, taking over the historic role of the bourgeoisie, would not only cast off the lingering shackles of feudalism but would rise above the laws of the market and subordinate the economy (and within it, of course, the labor market) to the class interests of the intellectuals.

7

The Intellectual Stratum in Market Economies

THE INTELLECTUAL BETWEEN CAPITALIST AND PROLETARIAN

The basic class structure of capitalist free-market societies is shaped by the dichotomy between owners of capital and owners of labor-power, who are deprived of the means of production. In this dichotomous structure intellectuals, like owners of any other type of product or labor, are obliged to sell their intellectual products or their labor in accordance with the laws of the market. Since intellectuals, as proprietors of specialized intellectual knowledge, do not possess capital or means of production, they most closely resemble workers in their basic structural situation.

But the special character of intellectual knowledge lifts them out of the ranks of the proletariat. The intelligentsia stands closer to the proletariat in respect of the position it occupies in the market, but closer to the bourgeoisie in terms of its income and style of living. While the worker, particularly the unskilled worker, is at the mercy of the market, the intelligentsia is able to assure itself to some degree of a monopoly situation by making the filling of intellectual positions dependent on the completion of a university education, which is expensive to acquire. Thus specialized intellectual knowledge, acquired and defended through the universities, has a relative scarcity-value on the labor market, which is to say that the intellectuals have succeeded in assuring that the market for intellectual labor is and remains a sellers' market.

Intellectuals appear on the labor market not only as owners of labor-power, however, but also in a sense as owners of capital too. They can use their specialized skills as a means of production as well, and thus many of them do not offer for sale their labor so much as the intellectual products of their knowledge. An architect does not absolutely need to go to work for a capitalist enterprise; he can have an independent practice, just as doctors and lawyers may, and in like fashion the practitioners of most intellectual professions can decide for themselves whether to work for a salary or to offer their services or products for sale on the open market. Thus a significant percentage of the intellectuals have the opportunity to be intellectual entrepreneurs rather than wageworkers whose labor, sold on the market, goes to produce profits for others. They themselves can share in profits (the classic example is the lawyer who sometimes receives as his fee a percentage of the profits of the financial operations he has been involved in). In capitalist society, then, the intelligentsia is bourgeois as much as it is proletarian, and Marxist analysis is correct in describing it as a stratum.

THE PRICE OF LIBERATION FROM FEUDAL DEPENDENCE:
DEPENDENCE ON THE MARKET

Having become a social stratum, the intellectuals need no longer render the kinds of personal services which, in an earlier era, they were obliged to perform for their feudal masters through the institution of patronage, the material foundation for much of their activity under feudalism. The musician was compensated for entertaining his lord, the historian for exalting his personal or family merits, the architect for building a castle according to his detailed instructions, the astrologer for reading his destiny in the stars; the patron took these intellectual activities as services due to his person and compensated them accordingly.

The intellectuals have more freedom on the open market, for now they work not for patrons but for buyers who are generally anonymous or with whom, at least, they stand on a footing of equality in the market. On the other hand, the whims of the market are just as difficult to fathom as the whims of patrons. The patron framed his demands according to a fixed and familiar system of values, but the intellectual producing for the market is confronted with a constantly shifting value-system which he has to interpret. In creating his intellectual products he runs the risk of not finding buyers for them.

This changeover can favor his creative efforts, for it offers the possibility of influencing the public's value-system, bringing it closer to his own; but on the other hand it can be harmful too, for it is quite possible that in his own day the market will reject what he finds valuable (even though posterity may eagerly embrace it). Whereas earlier the artist or scholar stood lower in the social scale than the patron, the bourgeois intellectual feels himself at least the equal of the bourgeois, if not indeed his superior. This pride is reinforced by the cult of creative individuality which goes with the spirit of capitalism and which surrounds the creative artist or scholar, not only in intellectual circles but also among a wider public influenced by intellectual culture, with a prestige at least equal to that accorded ministers of state or captains of industry.

Thence arose the demand of the intellectuals that their works (more affectingly, their creations) be judged not by the standards of their consumers, who in the last analysis know less about their art than they do, but by the aristocracy of the inner circles of their craft, which actively oppose their own avant-garde norms to the accepted mass standards. Thus intellectuals who were unable to market their labor or their intellectual products forged a moral weapon out of their rejection while at the same time laying the foundations for the early intellectual counterculture of the great urban artist-ghettos, a fertile seedbed for political as well as artistic rebellion.

THE INTELLECTUALS' HOSTILITY TOWARD THE MARKET

Thus the validity of the free market came to be questioned first in the market for intellectual products, for the creative intelligentsia found it unworthy that an impersonal market should determine the value of their works. Soon afterward appeared those ideologies which called into question the validity of the market in general, seeing in it the fundamental evil and in commodity relations and money the antithesis of culture; and so they advanced a program of humanization with the elimination of competition and of market relations in general at its core.

The romantic age in art and the age of utopian socialism in political ideology were characterized by the demands of the intelligentsia for a new teleological mission for itself. The intellectuals would no longer accept the notion that market demand expresses society's real needs, and saw in themselves the avant-garde whose task it was to formulate real needs and a progressive system of values. Thus they attempted, at least in utopian fashion, to describe the social conditions under which the avant-garde's norms could spread until they became the norms of society as a whole, through the efforts of intellectuals to teach, to enlighten, and to lead the way toward the abolition of the regulatory principles of the market.

In casting doubt upon the rationality of the market's operating principles the intelligentsia rendered its own place in the social structure problematical. The role of an organic intelligentsia was no longer enough, the intellectuals were not satisfied with enunciating various particular interests in society; they had to represent more, the interests of society as a whole. This mission of the intelligentsia acquired at the same time a moral impress, and so those intellectuals who served the market, surrendering to the vagaries of demand, were branded as immoral; they worked as spokesmen for partial, hence lower-ranking, interests rather than for those of all society.

The demand for a new teleological mission for the intelligentsia was also articulated in the ideologies of the utopian socialists. But since they offered only a moral condemnation of the conflictual class-relations of capitalism they were unable to endow the notion of an overall social interest with scientific, much less political, content. Historically, Marxism's great ideological innovation lay in combining an analysis of the real class relations of capitalist society with a concrete version of the mission of the radical intelligentsia, i.e., with the task of articulating the interests of the working class. In the Marxist prognosis the proletariat would rise to become the ruling class by identifying its interests with the interests of all humanity; therein Marx saw the abolition of all partial interests, through their merger into a single common interest. Thus the socialist critique posited an identity of interest between an intelligentsia striving to realize its transcendence and a working class struggling to acquire a consciousness of its class situation.

In the Marxist system of thought the intellectuals' own aspirations to power are sublimated, and the intelligentsia comes forward as the spokesman for proletarian power. Marxism gave intellectuals a justification for working to promote the development of the working class, for given the dichotomous structure of bourgeois society in the age of classical capitalism no alternative was imaginable to capitalist interests except the interests of the workers. The left intellectuals of the day were not aware that in the idea of a socialist society they were enunciating the ideology of class power for the intelligentsia. At that time, indeed, an intellectual class was only a possibility, while the working class was an empirical reality. Consequently they could not know that a century later the intelligentsia would begin to take form as a class; indeed a century ago the intellectuals could not even have had a coherent awareness of themselves as a social stratum.

The intellectuals, in other words, did not think of themselves as an intelligentsia; they identified with the social class or group from which they sprang or whose interests they expressed. They fell into the same ironic trap of historical self-projection as did those bourgeois revolutionaries, the Jacobins, who thought themselves the spokesmen of the whole people against feudal interests rather than the representatives of that very bourgeoisie which they viewed with such suspicion. A whole historical era had to pass before Marx could mock the bourgeois politicians of the revolution of 1848, with their Jacobin phraseology, as epigones and parodies of the real thing, pointing to the fact which the June days in Paris had made painfully clear. Jacobin phrases now only concealed the narrow special interests of a bourgeoisie which could respond to the barricades of the workers who made up the bulk of the city's population only with the *ultima ratio* of cannon. And so, just as the Jacobins could not see that their ideology expressed the interests of a capitalist class which was only just coming into existence at the time of the French Revolution, so too the socialist thinkers of the nineteenth century could not see that their ideology expressed the interests of a distinct intellectual class which did not exist before the socialist revolution, but was destined to emerge in its wake.

THE DEBATE IN THE WESTERN WORKING-CLASS MOVEMENT
OVER INTELLECTUAL AND WORKER INTERESTS

Here we should enter a modest qualification, however. The First International—the earliest broad international organization of the revolutionary labor movement to draw no distinction between the defense of the workers' immediate interests and the long-range strategy of socialist revolution—broke up precisely because the leaders of its two most important factions, Marx and Bakunin, each suspected the other of trying to acquire power for a narrow intellectual elite rather than for the workers. Bakunin saw the danger in terms of statism, Marx in the elitism of the shadowy conspiratorial *Alliance* which lurked behind the anarchist movement. In the following decades, however, as social-democratic mass parties came to be organized around the most pressing immediate interests of a now greatly enlarged working class, socialist ideology was combined with bourgeois-democratic parliamentarianism, and trade-union struggles in defense of economic interests were supplemented consistently only by such political demands as could be achieved through parliamentary legislation serving workers' interests on a national level, rather than just in one plant or one branch of industry. But that also meant that the social-democratic parties no longer considered timely the question of taking power politically or of constructing a new socialist order, or of proletarian revolution generally. To that extent they accepted, at least on the level of tactics, the class rule of capitalism, projecting the aim of achieving the dictatorship of the proletariat into an indefinite future. Looking at it in another way, they gave up precisely those objectives of the workers' movement which later, following their attainment in Eastern Europe, turned out to be the conditions for creating the class rule of the intelligentsia.

THE BOLSHEVIK ANSWER

In order to restore to the socialist movement an integral politics, concerned with both the workers' immediate economic interests and the prospects of socialist revolution—in order, that is, to subordinate the workers' struggle for their immediate interests to the struggle for political power—a party of a radically new type was in fact required. By Lenin's definition those who joined the Bolshevik faction had not only to accept its political program but also to submit to the discipline of the leadership's decisions, and to work actively in the party's organizations as professional revolutionaries, at times under conditions of illegality demanding great personal sacrifice.

This program necessarily carried within itself the possibility, recognized by every social-democratic theorist from Plekhanov and Martov to Kautsky and Rosa Luxemburg, that the party would develop into an elite vanguard in whose activities the broad masses of the working class would be unable or unwilling to participate. Instead, the most prominent positions in its ranks would be filled by intellectuals willing to embrace the transcendent value-system of socialism as their life's work, men and women who thanks to their families or their intellectual activity would be able to survive under marginal conditions, emancipat-

ing themselves from the empirical interests of the working class
as well as from their own.

Such a change could come about only if socialist thought
struck root in social conditions where the intelligentsia had not
been seriously corrupted by the lure of the market into espousing
various particular interests, and where the actual working class,
because of its relatively small size, could be replaced by a
philosophical abstraction which would not contradict the axiom
that the intellectuals, organized into a party, were the true
representatives of the workers' interests. For the idea of scientific
socialism to be transformed into a program of class power for
the intelligentsia, the socialist movement had to ripen into
Bolshevism amid the social conditions of Tsarist Russia—in an
atmosphere of sham parliamentarianism and of a police power
exceptionally repressive by the standards of the day, which drove
all proletarian political activity underground.

The Western socialist movement of the first two decades of
the century lagged behind Russian developments; only during
the revolutionary crisis at the end of World War I and after the
triumph of the Bolsheviks did it come to understand the historic
originality of Lenin's once-scorned strategic innovations. At that
point the Western movement split into Communists and Socialists.
The schism in Western socialism also heralded something else,
however: the "great transformation," the age of the disintegration of the free, self-regulating market, an age in which the
Western intelligentsia had to seek a new place for itself amid
the conditions of state-monopoly capitalism.

8

The Intellectuals under
State-Monopoly Capitalism

Under the impact of the Great Depression capitalist societies
incorporated a number of redistributive mechanisms into their
economies, partly from reasons of social policy, partly in order

to bring the business cycle under some kind of regulative control. The traditional free-market economy of the nineteenth century disintegrated as state-monopoly capitalism withdrew ever-larger sectors of the economy from the workings of the market mechanism, replacing it with redistributive mechanisms. How did this "great transformation" affect the structural situation of the intellectuals in those societies which, while retaining the principle of private property in the means of production, accorded the intelligentsia an ever-larger role in the management of economy and society? Does the patent fact of the rapidly growing power of the intellectuals permit us to speak of the intelligentsia's evolution into a class under state-monopoly capitalism?

STATE-MONOPOLY CAPITALISM AND SOCIALIST
RATIONAL REDISTRIBUTION

For all that it adopted certain redistributive mechanisms, capitalist economy was no more transformed into rational redistribution than socialist economy became capitalistic by giving market-type commodity and money relations a place in the regulation of its economic processes. There is a qualitative difference between the two systems; they run on fundamentally different principles. There is no gradual transition between monopoly-capitalist market economy and rational redistribution; it would be pointless to ask what proportion of economic activity is regulated by the market, or by redistribution. It would be equally pointless to set up a graduated scale beginning with the United States, where redistribution is at a minimum, and ranging through Sweden and Yugoslavia, where the role of redistribution is roughly identical, all the way to the Soviet Union or even to China, where the role of the market is as slight as is that of redistribution in the United States.

The fundamental question in comparing economic systems is: What criteria legitimate the right to dispose over the surplus product in one or another economy, and what factors determine the relative size of the surplus product itself? However much the state may tax the surplus product, a society still remains capitalist so long as the market determines the surplus product, in terms of the difference between production cost and selling price, and so long as capital ownership confers a sufficient title to dispose over the surplus product. Capitalist economies utilize redistribution precisely in order to improve the workings of the market, but subordinate it to the logic of the market, while socialist economies utilize market relations to improve the efficiency of redistribution, subjecting them however to the logic of redistribution.

Thus the introduction of redistributive mechanisms has made state-monopoly capitalism more efficient, but has not brought with it a class position for the teleological redistributors. Consequently the economic conditions for the formation of the intellectuals into a class are absent in the Western societies. It is true, of course, that redistribution itself has greatly enlarged the economic power of trained professionals, and that process has been accompanied by efforts on the part of an ever-growing technocratic intelligentsia to acquire something like class power. But if state-monopoly capitalism accords an ever-larger role to the redistributors, their status still does not become the focal point for a merging of the economic and political spheres, or for a monopolistic ideology which universalizes redistributive relations in every area of economy and society.

It is one of our fundamental theses, in analyzing the structure of socialist society, that the status of teleological redistributor is only the key structural position of the emerging intellectual class; that class in its entirety takes in not only those who are directly authorized by reason of their office to dispose over the surplus product, but also all those who create and maintain the rational-redistributive ethos, and make out of it an ideology which pervades the society's entire culture.

Though professional redistributors do make their appearance under state-monopoly capitalism, they form at the most an intellectual stratum, as it were the organic intelligentsia of the ruling class, even though as a technocracy they do possess some independent economic and political power. But that alone is not enough for an intellectual class to form around the technocracy, if only because the hegemony of intellectual knowledge as a principle of legitimation is limited (or prevented from appearing altogether) by the operation of two other principles of legitimation: the sovereignty of a political mechanism based on representation in the area of governmental budgetary allocations, and the immediate right of disposition of capital-owners in the sphere of capitalist industrial policy.

These two other principles of legitimation force the technocracy to seek its own security in a purely executive function, for that is the sphere which its principle of legitimation entitles it to, and it can rise above it only by influencing political decisions by giving expert advice which reflects its own goals, or by reducing political questions to technical ones. But since in a pluralistic economic and political arena every technically formulated political question comes into conflict with other formulations and recommendations, embodying other interests, eventually every competing interest acquires its own technocratic apparatus. And so there ensues the open, public struggle of various technocratic groups—a struggle which makes it inaccurate to use the singular in speaking of the concept of technocracy. In reality we can speak only of competing technocracies serving a variety of interests organized along different lines in society.

THE POLARIZATION OF THE INTELLIGENTSIA UNDER STATE-MONOPOLY CAPITALISM

Under state-monopoly capitalism, then, the intellectual stratum, which typically occupies an intermediate position between capitalists and workers, undergoes a noticeable differentiation. One occupational group of intellectuals emerges with its power substantially enhanced, in many respects coming to share economic power with the owners of capital and political power with politicians chosen on the representative principle. At the same time, however, other groups of intellectuals are distinctly proletarianized, becoming simple owners of labor-power. In order to put intellectual knowledge to work it no longer suffices to have information stored up in one's brain; the material and technical tools of intellectual labor are increasingly required—ever-costlier laboratory equipment, computers, and the like—all the new and complex means of production of the scientific-technical revolution, which only large capitalist or technocratic organizations can afford and without which intellectual knowledge cannot realize its potential.

With the development of a high level of instrumentation, co-operation, and teamwork, scientific work becomes an increasingly capital-intensive activity, and researchers have to find a place for themselves in large productive organizations. An ever-smaller percentage of research costs goes to researchers' salaries, an ever-larger share to pay for equipment and for servicing it. This circumstance makes those who finance research very cautious; they have to be certain that their investment in research will yield a satisfactory return. To that end they must if possible choose from among the intellectuals competing to engage in research those whose solid and specialized training, disciplined working habits, and ability to subordinate themselves to cooperative work, promise dependable results, even if brilliant individual discoveries can perhaps no longer be expected of them. And so the role of individual ingenuity and of the individual researcher's personality is constantly on the decline in these factories of science, while that of routine, impersonal work keeps on growing.

Thus the lucky groups of intellectuals whom the administrators of research work select to harness to their expensive equipment come increasingly to feel their alienation from research which is imposed on them from above and which, by reason of its high degree of specialization, can no longer be comprehended in its entirety. To carry on their work these intellectuals need the tools provided by capital just as much as workers do, and so with respect to both the character of the work-process and their situation on the labor market they have come to occupy, in the last analysis, the same position as highly skilled workers.

The interests of the capital committed to scientific research demand that the universities turn out a labor force which meets the requirements outlined above. Through a policy of subsidies capital has attempted to influence the universities to become specialized factories for the production of specialized workers, operating with the same dependable mass-production methods as a great modern factory.

The central motif of the student movements of the 1960s was the rejection of this process of proletarianization. The students would not acquiesce in the conversion of the universities into high-level institutes for training skilled workers, which would have made the proletarianization of the intellectuals an accomplished fact. The young intelligentsia instinctively resisted the attempt to take away their monopoly of "cross-contextual, orientative" knowledge. And so they protested against a university in which they could acquire knowledge usable only in one context and under direction from above. The students reacted especially sharply against the efforts of the great capitalist corporations to create institutions of higher learning patterned after their own operations, which would have provided a thorough practical education but one so specialized that its graduates would have been virtually bound to a single context, in their case that of the sponsoring corporation's personnel pool. The rebellious students insisted on their own value-system and demanded an education that could be used in a variety of contexts. We might say that they wished to preserve the intellectual character of their labor-power, rather than see themselves reduced to mere owners of labor-power. To put it more ironically, they wished to preserve their character of owners of a special kind of capital.

It is a peculiar paradox of state-monopoly capitalism that while it reduces competition in the major branches of industry, augmenting the security of the producers and guaranteeing the successful marketing of the product in every field from auto manufacturing and the oil industry to agriculture, it makes use of redistributive subsidies to a much lesser extent in the market for intellectual labor and intellectual products. The monopoly position of the intelligentsia on the labor market is declining, and for that reason the latter is becoming less and less of a sellers' market. Now that the boom of the 1960s is over efforts are underway again to restrict the number of students admitted to university, and the universities' funding has been cut back as well. Meanwhile the market for cultural products—publishing, the film industry, the graphic arts—is still governed almost exclusively by the laws of the classical nineteenth-century competitive market. If an economist wanted to reconstruct a model of the free market from today's capitalist economy, he would choose the market for books or films as his paradigm rather than that for steel, petroleum, or automobiles.

Thence arises yet another dichotomy in the ranks of the intelligentsia in the age of state-monopoly capitalism. Those intellectuals who bring only their trained labor to the market are obliged to put on a spiritual uniform; they present the public appearance of faceless apparatchiks. Those, on the other hand, who live from the sale of their works—artists above all—must engage in strident self-advertisement in order to create individualized images for themselves. This last example graphically illustrates the difference between the situations of the intellectuals under state-monopoly capitalism and rational redistribution. The technocracy of the capitalist countries is unable to give other intellectual strata a major share in the benefits of the redistributive mechanism by extending subsidies to both the universities and the artistic world. And so the technocracy cannot come forward as the agent of the homogeneous interests of the whole intelligentsia, so that other intellectual strata do not coalesce around it into a unitary class.

It is precisely in the sphere of art and ideology that the ruling intelligentsia of the rational-redistributive societies has most thoroughly abolished the laws of the market mechanism, as expressed in the declared principle that in socialist society culture is not a commodity. Hence the practice of determining how many copies of a book will be printed quite independently of any estimate of its readership, and often independently of its inherent value as well, so that the size of the printing (and hence the author's honorarium as well) is most closely correlated with the dispositive status of the author. Thus a profound identity of interest is created between the technocracy which manages redistribution and creative intellectuals who are forced to live from state subsidies, and who are considered successful or unsuccessful quite independently of the judgment of the public, because in the first instance their fortunes depend on the approval of the cultural bureaucracy. That identity is also apparent in the fact that by contrast with their Western counterparts, who try to set themselves off, even in personal appearance, from managers and government officials, Eastern European creative intellectuals do their best to look the part of *comme-il-faut* artist bureaucrats, from their haircuts to their neckties.

If, however, state-monopoly capitalism fails to use the methods of government interventionism to protect important groups of intellectuals from classical free-market competition, it does offer them by way of compensation considerable freedom in choosing the content of their works, just as liberal capitalism did, while the technocracy of rational redistribution allows no such liberty. Thus while rational redistribution, following its own logic, denies that culture is a commodity in socialist society, it also demands of the artist that he reproduce in his works the class culture of the intelligentsia, the ethos of rational redistribution. State-monopoly capitalism, on the other hand, in leaving a small preserve to individual freedom in a culture industry subordinated to the laws of the market, provides an existential basis for the counterculture of the artists and other intellectuals, the ideological home of the New Left's rebellion against technocracy.

A variety of ghettos beckons to the intellectual who is unable or unwilling to fit into the private or public techno-bureaucracy, from the artists' ghetto to the ingrown culture of the radical political grouplets to the prestigious ghetto of academic life. However much they may differ in externals, in income level and customs of internal social intercourse, all these ghettos are alike in isolating their denizens in a closed universe, set apart not only from other social classes but even from other groups of intellectuals. Thus these marginal intellectuals are deprived of the consciousness-raising experience which their Eastern European counterparts undergo, of attracting everyone's attention, from the political police and technocracy to the academic and artistic intelligentsia. Like other members of his class, moreover, the marginal intellectual in Eastern Europe has the opportunity to come into contact socially with any other intellectual. Nothing is more surprising to the Western visitor who is introduced into intellectual circles there than the absence of ghettoizing tendencies and the extent to which personal connections cut across official hierarchies and occupational boundaries: in one company he may find an academic economist, a physicist, the managing director of a bank, a poet, and a film-maker, and he will be surprised to learn that they are "stars" for their whole class, not just for their peers in their own narrower professions. The Western visitor may even have his envy aroused by the paradoxical distinction which the highest party, state, and police organs bestow by their close attention to every intellectual product of any consequence whatever and of course to its author as well, irrespective of whether his amorous or his political vagaries are the object.

If the sharp-eyed Western visitor is also a sociologist he will soon recognize on the basis of his personal experience alone that his Eastern European friends are all members of one and the same class, that a common class culture unites them, and that even when they criticize their politicians they are not criticizing them as representatives of another class. Thus even its marginal members are imbued with the consciousness of the leading class. For all these reasons the Western visitor is bound to see that the Eastern European intellectuals he meets, though less affluent and less free than he is, are moving directly and inexorably toward acquiring class power. And that is more than he can say of a Western intelligentsia fragmented by conflicting interests, whose power-legitimating principle is anything but dominant under state-monopoly capitalism.

THE INTELLIGENTSIA'S NEW ASPIRATIONS TO POWER

Our last remarks require some qualification, particularly with respect to the directions and prospects of the intelligentsia's aspirations to power. The New Deal, state-monopoly capitalism's first broad-scale political construction, already represented a compromise between national capital and the national state: In the interests of its own survival capital relinquished some of its power to the national state, and indirectly to the techno-bureaucratic intelligentsia. Thus the New Deal was an important way-station in the intellectuals' struggle for power, but it was still insufficient to permit an intellectual class to form around it, for it raised only one occupational group of intellectuals to positions of power and privilege. The technocratic intelligentsia came to share in power with capital, and thus a conflict between technocracy and capital was added to that existing between capital and labor as one of the prime contradictions of state-monopoly capitalism.

More recently, however, a new and even more serious contradiction has been added to those existing within the national economy, as a result of the trend toward worldwide economic integration: It is the conflict between national capital, the national state, and a third factor, the technocracy of the great multinational corporations, which has made itself increasingly independent of private capital and now aims at economic power on a world scale. In attempting to explain the inflation of the 1970s observers have generally pointed, among other things, to the fact that organizations like the multinational corporation increasingly elude the control of the national state, thus withdrawing from the commitment made under the New Deal to harmonize their corporate interests with those of the government bureaucracy. The multinational corporation is all the less willing to subordinate its goal of profit maximization to the national interest because it can easily transfer its capital and even its headquarters across national boundaries. It creates a supranational bureaucracy which identifies with the corporation rather than the mother country, and rewards them not only with high salaries and great social mobility but also with similar working and living conditions anywhere in the world, so that we can justly speak of the birth of a new kind of organization man. We may be seeing in the multinational corporations' executives the forerunners of a new "world-intellectual," and to that extent the multinational corporation can be regarded as a new strategy on the part of the intellectuals to increase their own power. The multinational technocrats have rebelled against what they consider a petty compromise between national capital and the national government's bureaucracy, and have removed themselves from the control of both. And so we can hardly avoid the conclusion that at some point a new agreement will be required between the multinationals' world-intelligentsia, national capital, and the national bureaucracy, for only such a compromise can assure the economic and indeed the political stability of the Western world.

At the present time, then, the Western intelligentsia is following two contradictory strategies in its effort to enhance its power position. One is the extension of redistributive mechanisms within the framework of the national state; that is the traditional Left's program of nationalization, which has itself displayed two new tendencies recently. One of these is the rapprochement of the Communist parties of Western Europe with conservative-nationalist political bureaucracies representing national capital, on a platform of opposition to the multinationals. The other is the rapprochement between the Communist parties and the techno-bureaucracy of the national state, which has carried along with it many radicals of the New Left as well, reinforcing existing technocratic tendencies in the Communist and Socialist parties toward participation in a politics of technocratic reform. Such policies, they believe, would bring about a more modern and efficient state apparatus and a general extension of redistribution, with more attention to social-welfare measures. In abandoning the goal of proletarian revolution and seeking an understanding with the intelligentsia, particularly (and this is the really new element in the situation) the technocracy, the Communist parties have created the possibility of infiltrating the apparatus of the national state and the great national enterprises; thus long before the day of any eventual parliamentary victory they might be able to bring under their control more and more centers of decision-making (regional governments, university senates, government bureaus, and the like). They hope, in other words, to take the fortress of state-monopoly capitalism from within by introducing into it the Trojan horse of technocracy. This way of looking at the matter brings out even more clearly the sociological content of the compromise which we foresee between the national and international technocracies; the contending parties on both sides are all intellectuals, and so any compromise they reach cannot be merely an agreement between different sorts of capitalist interests; it will also be, in at least equal measure, a bargain struck between intellectual groups aspiring to power in national and international organizations, respectively.

In the years to come, then, we can look for a continued struggle between the intelligentsia's power-legitimating principle and the alternative principles of capital-ownership and political representation, not just on a national but on an international plane. Although the intelligentsia is almost certain to emerge from this contest in a stronger position, it is equally probable that it will not be able to make its principle of legitimation prevail totally. And so the Western intelligentsia will continue on its long odyssey toward the goal of organizing itself into a class. Its road is the road of Western civilization, which has turned out to be a byway from the standpoint of the aspirations of the intellectuals to class power. Meanwhile their progress is followed, sometimes enviously, sometimes maliciously, by an Eastern European intelligentsia which has arrived at the threshold of class power by a shorter route, however high a price they and all the other classes had to pay for it along the way.

9

The Eastern European Intelligentsia's Road to Power

THE SHORTCUT

Only in the West do we observe the phenomenon of intellectuals who sell their knowledge or their cultural wares on the open market being formed into a social stratum. In Eastern Europe the intelligentsia relatively early on conceived the intention to strive for something like class power. It avoided the detour on the road to class power which the position of a stratum would have entailed for it under liberal capitalism, and within a very short period of time transformed itself from an estate into a class.

The Eastern European intellectuals of the nineteenth century were unable for the most part to find employment on the private labor market, for the stunted bourgeois economy of the region was incapable of supporting a large professional intelligentsia. They could either find a place in the state bureaucracy, accepting a form of modernization directed from above, or else they could turn radically against the centralized absolutist regime. Professional competence was irrelevant; the state paid primarily for loyalty, and anyone who did not wish to turn into a cringing state secretary could find a rather obvious alternative in the radical intelligentsia, even perhaps in the role of professional revolutionary.

However antithetical the two roles of bureaucrat and revolutionary might be, however, they had in common the element of a social teleology oriented toward growth, whose ultimate form is the idea of socialism. In preindustrial societies the teleology of the priestly intelligentsia pointed to a world beyond ours. In bourgeois civilization growth is an end in itself, built into the automatism of the market; for the last hundred years asking what purpose it serves has been labeled "metaphysical speculation." That is why positivism has been the most appropriate philosophy for a Western professional intelligentsia which looks askance at any ideology with wider historical and philosophical goals, and which reverts to teleology only in the age of the bureaucratization of capital, when as technocrats they can convert the problems of society into technical problems and formulate their own goals as scientifically the most rational goals for society as a whole. In Eastern Europe modernization was not so much an internal imperative as a political and military necessity, a response to an external challenge: If Eastern Europe was not to become a colony, it had to close ranks to overtake a more rapidly developing Western Europe. From the outset the Eastern European intelligentsia embraced either a dynamic nationalist teleology, as state officials, or, as revolutionaries, the teleology of a dynamic socialism. It made of them a powerful weapon in its struggle to win class power, and in the aftermath of victory combined the two into the ethos of socialist state redistribution.

The evolution of the intelligentsia into a class was a possibility inherent in the social conditions of Eastern Europe. It was Lenin's greatest insight that socialist revolution was possible precisely in Eastern Europe, and only there. The intellectuals, not the proletariat, were the ones prepared to make a successful revolution possible. Neither a Western feudalism affording some scope to commodity-producing private property nor a market economy firmly founded on private ownership of capital offered the only possible model of integration for economies entering upon the road of growth. The economic system characteristic of Eastern Europe in the modern era not only lagged behind the Western model; it also differed from it qualitatively. We may term it early rational redistribution, bearing in mind that socialist rational redistribution with its universalizing of the state's role in economic development is by no means modeled upon it. The Eastern European intellectuals did not develop the ethos of the teleological redistributor as a result of accepting the teachings of Marxism-Leninism; they worked it out themselves over the course of centuries as a consequence of the position they occupied in the social structure of early rational redistribution, only to realize that that ethos was identical with the spirit of socialism.

At the turn of the century the Eastern European and especially the Russian intellectuals were not a class; they were only preparing to become one. They overtook and went on ahead of the Western intelligentsia by not trying to catch up with it, by organizing themselves into a radical marginal intelligentsia to struggle for a new type of society in which they could make their own principle of legitimation the dominant one and acquire a commanding structural position in society, transforming their quasi-feudal situation directly into a class position. To understand in some measure how the Eastern European intellectuals could set foot upon this shorter, though bloodier, road to class power, we must outline briefly the singularities of their situation and their ideologies in the age of early rational redistribution.

THE CHARACTERISTIC EASTERN EUROPEAN MODEL OF
ECONOMIC GROWTH: EARLY RATIONAL REDISTRIBUTION

The influence of the Asiatic mode of production

In the twelfth century the society and culture of the principality of Kiev or Novgorod, or of the Polish or Hungarian kingdom, was simply poorer than that of contemporary Western Europe. Only in the course of the following centuries did this simple quantitative backwardness give way to qualitative differences which attest to the existence of a new and different kind of organizational principle. These differences clearly reflect Turkish and Tartar influence and the impress of Asiatic redistribution. The unrelenting pressure of the seminomadic military

empires had the same significance for the peoples of Eastern
Europe as did the danger of floods for the societies of China and
Mesopotamia. Turkish and Tartar expansion represented a constant challenge, to which the autocratic rulers who had emerged
from feudal anarchy responded by strengthening their centralized
military and administrative organizations even more. But the
Mongol and Turkish conqueror did more than just set back and
rigidify the social and economic development of the peoples
whom they subjected and put to tribute: They also left a permanent stamp upon their civilization. In this way a special
model of traditional Asiatic redistribution spread westward, one
in which central redistribution did not serve a hydraulic economy but went rather to support standing armies. In these
militarized societies private property, commodity production,
feudal differentiation, and legal separation of powers could not
develop. But a military nobility (functioning primarily as a tax-
collecting bureaucracy) could evolve all the more easily. Nor
did the Russian church represent a countervailing power; on the
contrary, it was compelled to assure the readiness of an enserfed
peasantry to render taxes to the Tartar Caesars. The Russian
princes, for their part, held their authority from the Khans, and
the more reliable they were in remitting their taxes the more
unlimited was the power they could exercise over their own
society. Centralized military power, centralized bureaucracy, enserfed peasantry, and the destruction of every municipal or
feudal rival for power—that was the way the rulers of Eastern
Europe assured their survival, whether they became vassals of
the Tartar and Turkish empires or went on fighting against them.

The service nobility

Although the rulers of Eastern Europe learned from the Asiatic
model of social organization, they did not take it over whole
cloth; rather, they adapted it to European conditions. Their bor-
rowings were made to serve the purpose of economic growth,
and eventually to enable them to throw off the yoke of their
Asiatic conquerors. It was above all in Russia, in the expanding
principality of Moscow, that the organizational forms of the
Tartar military empire were taken over. In order to construct
a new type of centralized state, however, the grand dukes of

Moscow had first to alter the nobility's situation in society and with it the system of landholding. It was essential to the survival of the state that the ruler refuse to share power with the feudal nobles of his entourage, converting them instead into a military-official service nobility. And so the Muscovite rulers broke the power of a nobility founded on patrimonial landed property, with its roots in feudal autonomy; in its place they set the institution of limited, prebendal land tenure, dependent on the state, in which the nobility was in theory only the usufructuary of state lands assigned to it in exchange for service. Ivan the Great, Ivan the Terrible, and Peter the Great all strove alike to make all surplus produce available to the court and army, to curtail the influence of the hereditary nobility, and to augment the importance of the nonhereditary service nobility as a counterweight to them. They sought to make the service nobles even more dependent by making the demands of civil and military service more stringent, and by frequent reshuffling of landed estates and their occupants. The service nobility were in the first instance military commanders, obliged in exchange for their privileges to raise on demand a certain number of soldiers from the villages entrusted to them and to supply and arm them, without protest and on pain of execution. This military obligation in turn took the service nobility away from their estates and so made it impossible for them to administer their lands, thus reducing them to the status of tax collectors over the villages assigned to them. As a result they sought to extort as much as they could from the soil as quickly as possible, and made no attempt to introduce more intensive methods of cultivation; they practiced a predatory economy. In the absence of any intensive agriculture the Russian nobility had no use for a more skilled labor force or for cultivators who were more conscientious because they had a stake in the land; its chief concern was to secure an adequate supply of servile labor. To achieve that the peasants had to be bound to the soil, in a condition of servitude little removed from slavery.

The "second serfdom"

A further consequence of prebendal landholding was to deprive the peasantry of ownership of the land. In Western Europe the influence of the Roman church and of the surviving traditions of Roman law enabled the institution of private property in land and the system of plots divided among the villagers to prevail over the Celto-Germanic village commune; there dues in kind soon replaced labor service as the predominant form of feudal obligation due the lord, which in turn gave the peasant an incentive to practice a more intensive agriculture and expand his production, since a growing share of his increased output remained in his own hands. Western feudalism thus rested on a firm foundation of noble and peasant private property in land. In Eastern Europe during the early Middle Ages the institution of peasant landholding was also on the rise, affording the peasantry increasing opportunities for expanded commodity production. But this Western type of development was reversed there by the advent of the "second serfdom," which bound the peasantry to the soil and severely restricted peasant landholding, and which in Russia found organizational form in the institution of the village commune.

The peasants organized in the village commune, with its system of collective responsibility, merely held the land; they were not its owners, nor was the lord; the sole owner was the state, personified in the ruler. Under this system the peasant gained nothing by producing more; the individual had no incentive to increase his output because the surplus product was not his to keep. The village commune was content with simple reproduction; commodity production did not develop. The peasantry, thrown back upon simple consumption of its own produce, developed domestic industry; hence there was no ready demand in the villages for industrial products made in the towns and available only in exchange for money. As a result the urban population did not become specialized for handicraft work and was itself compelled to go on living primarily from agriculture. And so no strong, self-conscious artisan bourgeoisie could arise, of the sort which, reinforced by the influx from the neighboring villages, might eventually have won autonomy for themselves within a feudal system, and municipal autonomy for their cities.

The destruction of the rights of the free peasantry and their incorporation into a prebendal system of landholding organized and administered by the state represented a historic turning point in the history of Eastern European feudalism. Forced to perform labor services, reduced to near-slave status, the peasantry of Eastern Europe came to differ considerably from that of the West. While in the West the peasantry at the dawn of the modern era won the right to produce and market commodities themselves, so that a propertied class of peasant small producers increasingly took the place of the peasantry of feudal times, in Eastern Europe a new period of economic history began, that of the "second feudalism," with the peasantry reduced to serfdom once again. The economic geographies of Western Europe and Eastern Europe diverge profoundly along the frontier between these two divergent processes—a line roughly paralleling the western borders of Prussia and Hungary—with capitalist tendencies triumphant on one side and the second feudalism in the ascendant on the other. This "second feudalism" was not in fact so much a restoration of earlier feudal conditions as the beginning of the evolution of a new and specifically Eastern European set of conditions. In this new system there were no inherent economic incentives to develop more productive agricultural techniques, and so neither the enserfed peasant nor the nobleman enrolled in state service could enter upon the road of bourgeois development. Nor, in the absence of expanding commodity production, could there appear a bourgeois intelligentsia able to live by offering its intellectual labor and its cultural products in the open market.

The two Eastern Europes

For the sake of precision we should point out that modern Eastern Europe falls into two distinct areas. One is Orthodox Eastern Europe, encompassing (besides Russia) Romania, Bulgaria, and Serbia. The other is the westernmost portion of Eastern Europe, a band extending from the Baltic through Poland and Hungary to Croatia and reflecting the influence of Latin Christianity; this area displays, within the framework of an essential similarity, certain substantial divergences from the Russian model of development. In this region the peasant could never be bought and sold apart from the land, hence he did not live in virtual slavery; and eventually the monarchs regulated the upper limits of labor obligations and gradually put an end to the peasants' attachment to the soil. Collective landholding vested in the village commune did not extend to all the land; separate peasant plots, legally distinct from the lord's private demesne, made their appearance. The market towns played a significant role in commodity production, and their legal status was superior to that of the peasant villages; the towns in general were relatively independent of the feudal lords. The Catholic and Protestant churches brought the region into the sphere of influence of Western European culture, and in general there were no closed frontiers toward the West. Personal, cultural, and market contacts alike connected the western perimeter of Eastern Europe with the West. But fundamental features common to Eastern Europe were clearly apparent in the organization of the state and the system of land tenure.

The military challenge to growth: Ivan the Terrible, father of early rational redistribution

So closely were the military and economic systems interwoven in Eastern Europe, so powerfully did the former batten upon the latter, that in the end it was the military challenge that determined the organization of society. In this it differed structurally from Western Europe, which was able to absorb its challenges, converting them into an internal impetus to growth. There the major areas of social activity were separate and distinct from one another; legitimate and illegitimate powers could coexist side by side within a less centralized society, and the state itself was not forced by a critical military situation to range into a single military hierarchy, at the service of an absolute ruler, a variety of social groups imbued with the pluralistic spirit of feudal autonomy, mutually checking one another's power, and obliged to relate to one another through contractual agreements. Western principles of social organization were present in the patrician democracy of the city-state of Novgorod in the twelfth and thirteenth centuries, and in the noble democracies of Poland and Hungary; but the seeds of Western-type feudalism were not hardy enough there to withstand a Turkish-Tartar expansionism which put Asiatic redistribution at the service of military aggression, and so Eastern European society, by the time it managed to free itself of its Oriental conquerors, had already learned from them how to organize society from the top down and had taken from them the model of the autocratically centralized state. More than types of weapons and foods and the names of plants were exchanged between these two civilizations; patterns of social organization were borrowed as well. Ivan the Terrible, for example, who finally broke the power of the Tartar khans and had himself crowned Tsar of All Russia, decimated and plundered the hereditary aristocracy and organized a part of the service nobility into a modern political police; with the surplus product collected by the state he established foundries, arsenals, and shipyards, and manned them not with wage workers but with serfs at forced labor. His merchants were compelled, through government subsidies or without them, to set up workshops producing to meet military orders, and when his treasury ran dry he plundered his own cities. Thus in his methods of rule Ivan took at least as much from the Tartar khans whom he defeated as from the Western princes with whom the Russian state, under his rule, began its centuries of warfare. Nor are we confronted here with an eclectic mixture of influences, but with the emergence of a new form of economic integration and political rule, an autonomous model of growth which we have called early rational redistribution.

Eastern Europe, however, was a target not only of expanding Asiatic military empires but of aggressive Western monarchies as well. In Ivan's own time Polish, Swedish, and Lithuanian expansion already presented a greater danger than did the fading power of the Mongols. It was not enough to adopt the all-embracing despotism of the Asiatic mode of production; a response also had to be found to the Western challenge, which appeared primarily in the form of heavier and more effective artillery, impervious to arrows and swords. At the dawn of the modern era the West, thanks to a more advanced weapons technology, acquired military superiority over the East, and in recognition of that fact the Eastern European states had to import arms. If under prevailing social conditions development was slow, if the whole social superstructure nourished by the village communes was part of a centralized state apparatus, if the monarch would not tolerate any kind of autonomous initiative, leaving his subjects only the freedom to serve him with their goods and their labor, if the Church too was ruthlessly subjected to the state, then there was no internal social force which could overcome the prevailing economic stagnation, and the economy could be modernized only from above, through the commands of an autocratic ruler.

The transition to seigneurial economy: Autocracy's compromise with the great landlords

The Eastern Europe of the early modern period was the scene of empire building on a grand scale. The realms of the Romanovs, Habsburgs, and Hohenzollerns, with their relatively modern administrative apparatuses, their loyal court nobilities, and their merchants who acted almost like state officials, required well-equipped standing armies skilled in the art of modern warfare in order to meet the threat of foreign aggression or rebelliousness among the many nationalities under their rule. For want of any other means arms imports had to be paid for by exporting agricultural products and raw materials, and that required an agrarian system that could produce more commodities. In Eastern Europe great noble landed estates worked by an enserfed peasantry produced the surplus needed for export. Modern agricultural technique was not required, only cheap labor, and serf labor cost next to nothing. Since its productivity was very low, a great deal of it was needed; for that reason labor was constantly in short supply in Eastern Europe. Neither willing nor able to pay their serfs money wages, while at the same time they constantly brought new lands under their direct cultivation, the great landed proprietors looked to the state to guarantee a minimum of labor discipline, to keep their exploited peasants in place and to keep them bound to the soil.

The state was glad enough to do so, in the knowledge that the great landholders could keep and bequeath their estates only so long as they served the monarch unconditionally. In essence, then, these estates had a prebendal character, as attested by a constant succession of confiscations of property and trials for treason. The landed proprietors had to pay a price for the support of the state; they had to become first loyalists and finally courtiers. The repeated decimation of the boyars and their forced absorption into the Tsarist state machine, the futile conspiracies and rebellions of the Hungarian magnates, the forcible recruitment of the Junkers into the Prussian bureaucracy, the successive and useless risings of the Polish nobility (in the course of which the Russian and Austrian governments even incited the peasants against them)—all demonstrate conclusively that for two centuries the great landed nobility had no choice but to serve an imperial power bent on expansion in the capacity of a commodity-producing aristocracy.

In a paradoxical reversal of the normal sequence, the nation-state emerged in Eastern Europe before the nation did, and a modern, centralizing bureaucracy appeared ahead of a bourgeois market economy. In the absence of a bourgeoisie, a landed aristocracy integrated into the central administration assumed the task of building a modern economy and a hierarchically stratified society from the top down. Thus arose the Eastern European pattern of modernization—what Lenin called the Prussian way—which differed fundamentally not only from Western European capitalist development but also, because of its capacity for growth, from the Turkish and Tartar varieties of Asiatic distribution, geared only to military expansion; a difference underscored by the eventual triumph of the Eastern European monarchies over the decaying Turkish and Tartar empires.

In order, however, to consolidate a system of seigneurial cultivation based on serf labor and capable of producing for export, a greater degree of security had to be accorded the great landed proprietors. In particular, the system of direct prebendal tenure, which occasioned great personal insecurity and impeded the development of agricultural technique, had to be eliminated. Patrimonial, hereditary landed property had to be reestablished, with the proviso that the restored hereditary nobles would continue to serve the state. Only firstborn sons were allowed to remain at home; the others still had to enter state service as officials, or in the army, or at court, and if in time they managed to whittle down their mandatory terms of service as a reward for changing from muttering boyars into compliant courtiers, they still had to abandon all hope of acquiring corporate autonomy vis-à-vis their rulers. The Russian, Austrian, and Prussian monarchies of the eighteenth century owed their stability to an alliance of mutual interest between a landed aristocracy converting to commodity production on their own account (the "Prussian way") and an absolutist government which guaranteed that the labor force would be at their disposal. It was in the mutual interest of the partners to this alliance to limit the right to own land to noblemen and to keep inviolate the nobles' privilege of drawing upon unpaid serf labor. And in fact a military-bureaucratic-police absolutism was able to keep these privileges intact in the face of all those interests in society which believed that economic growth could be achieved more effectively through peasant production, commercial and industrial freedom for the bourgeoisie, and consequently the abolition of noble privilege and the introduction of a liberal, constitutional form of government in which a parliament elected by the people, not a monarch by the grace of God, would exercise sovereignty.

The role of the state in industrialization

The centralized state could not hope to build up a modern army if it only imported arms; it had to manufacture them as well. The economic organization of the new industry was determined in advance by the alliance of monarch and great landed nobility. From the very beginning this alliance inhibited the growth of small and medium-sized landed property and the transformation of the serfs into industrial wageworkers or independently producing small farmers; as a result no broad internal consumer market could arise for industrial products. Industry had to be created through state intervention; in the case of the arms industry it could rely on government orders for a secure market. It is a commonplace of Eastern European economic history that in that part of the world industry was not the offspring of agricultural and commercial capital but of state subsidy primarily, and the industry thus created was not a textile or other light industry producing for the internal consumption of the population; it was an arms industry, or heavy industry producing to meet the needs of the army. The state guaranteed it not only a market but also a supply of cheap serf labor, for the state was the biggest landowner too and owned many serfs. State serfs worked both in government-owned workshops and in those run by merchants who themselves had been virtually conscripted by the government to manufacture arms, in exchange for assistance in the form of subsidies. The situation was comparable in the manufactories established by the landed aristocracy, whose labor needs were likewise met by serfs legally obliged to perform labor services.

The economic policy of early rational redistribution was characterized, then, by agrarian development on the Prussian model. The great estate predominated, worked by cheap labor, first by serfs, then after emancipation by farm laborers paid in kind and still burdened by a variety of quasi-feudal obligations. All of this entitles us to call the peasants' situation in Eastern Europe in the second half of the nineteenth century a third serfdom, especially in view of the high labor obligations they accepted as the price of emancipation. This economic policy could not stimulate the transfer of excess labor from the agrarian sector to the capitalist labor market, in the form of free wageworkers; it kept the peasantry, who made up over four-fifths of the population, at a very low standard of living and freed the serfs without land or with very little, thus discouraging peasant production of a surplus for market sale, over and above immediate consumption needs. In all these ways it narrowed domestic demand for industrial products. It placed the industrial bourgeoisie, whose chief customer was the state, in a position of dependence. What the state could not buy went sooner for export than to the domestic market. In these circumstances an independent bourgeoisie, able to formulate its class interests vis-à-vis absolutism or the nobility, could hardly develop. State subsidies and contracts, and the assurance of a supply of cheap labor, guaranteed the loyalty of the factory owners to the alliance of nobility and autocracy. The most that changed in this situation was that by the turn of the century a highly concentrated heavy industry, grown strong on foreign bank credits and on new markets opened by state development of the economic infrastructure (especially railway-building), had taken its place (jointly with bank capital,. together forming a new force, finance capital) as a third independent partner in the coalition of interests which characterized early rational redistribution. Even so, however, the state bureaucracy still held on to its key position in the alliance, even at that date.

It was a constant goal of government economic policy, throughout the whole era of early rational redistribution and indeed on into the age of socialist rational redistribution, to maintain state control over the labor market. Control over the peasantry was achieved through the village commune, which was collectively responsible for each of its members meeting his service obligations, while the system of internal passports made it possible to regulate peasant migration to the cities. The nobility were not their own masters either. Service nobility and hereditary aristocracy alike were obligated to perform state service; they could not devote their full time to the cultivation of their estates, and they were bound to absorb the mentality of the army and bureaucracy. For centuries the Russian nobility were largely forbidden to travel abroad, and a passport was a mark of exceptional imperial grace, even accompanied as it was by a ban against Russian noblemen entering the service of any foreign power, even a friendly one; emigration carried the stigma of *lèse majesté*.

Early rational redistribution between the Asiatic mode of production and the Western European model

The modernization of the Asiatic mode of production and its adaptation to the conditions of Eastern European feudalism never permanently produced a completely unchecked despotic state with all power concentrated in the hands of the ruler. In the first stage of early rational redistribution, which lasted roughly until the emancipation of the peasantry in the middle of the nineteenth century, the centralized state was obliged to compromise with the great landed nobility. However bloody the autocrats' methods in settling with their boyars at the beginning of this first phase, however thoroughly they tried to establish a prebendal system of land tenure, sooner or later they had to accept (though not unreservedly) a form of patrimonial landownership along the lines of European feudalism. They had to accept the heirs of the boyars, the court nobility *(dvorianstvo)* as part of the scheme of things, even if they never let the institution of private property in land develop as far as it did in Western Europe; until the twentieth century restrictions were placed on the sale of land owned by the great nobility and the Church. We would argue, then, that early rational redistribution began in the late seventeenth and early eighteenth centuries, when the autocracy came to understand that it could not manage the economy and govern the state without the aristocracy, while the aristocracy realized that it had no alternative but unconditional loyalty to the monarch, and not the slightest chance of mounting any effective opposition to him.

Thus the requirements of military security forced the economically backward Eastern European monarchies to treat the economic accomplishments of the Western countries as an external challenge, to set themselves the task of emulating and overtaking the West, and to concentrate their resources on that objective. Traditional redistribution bred anarchy and corruption, and drew only a small range of products into the redistributive process. Its very organization limited the size of the surplus product and therefore the power of the state as well, and so a structural reform of the Asiatic model was needed if the redistributive mechanism was to bring Eastern European civilization closer to the Western standard. The reigns of Peter the Great, Frederick the Great, and Joseph II mark the beginning of a century-long reform movement which led to the transformation of rational redistribution. But efforts at social and economic reform during the presocialist stage of rational redistribution were confused and ambiguous. On one hand the absolutist rulers were unable or unwilling to part once and for all with those elements of political authority which were legitimized by such nonrational factors as ties of family and blood; on the other hand new tendencies kept appearing, right up to the socialist revolution, which brought their social systems closer to the market model.

Count Witte, with his program of railway-building and industrialization, took a giant step in the direction of rational redistribution in turn-of-the-century Russia, forcing agriculture to contribute heavily to the accumulation of industrial capital. Stolypin's reform, which by abolishing the village commune stimulated the better-equipped peasant proprietors to produce for the market, was another turn in the direction of market economy, even if one of its immediate purposes was to broaden the social basis of support for the Tsarist regime. The German and Austro-Hungarian empires in the latter part of the nineteenth century leaned heavily on private capital in their industrialization programs and allowed it considerable independence. Though the bourgeoisie were still not admitted to the ruling political elite, a liberal, constitutional system did emerge toward the end of the century. True, it left few important decisions to parliament, reserving those for the central administration—which was on a par with any in Europe, so much so that around half of all professionals found employment in its ranks—but still it opened the way to social and political organization and the handling of conflicts along Western European lines. Thus the efforts of the liberal bourgeoisie and of a rapidly advancing Social Democracy to introduce political democracy of the Anglo-Saxon type were not at all ungrounded. Such hopes were encouraged by the emergence in the second phase of early rational redistribution, which lasted from the emancipation of the peasantry to the Russian Revolution, of a third major political factor sprung from the alliance of centralized bureaucratic state and capitalizing Junker landowners: Finance capital, based on a modern, highly concentrated heavy industry. These three social and economic forces, relatively autonomous vis-à-vis one another, had an interest in a moderate liberalization which would reflect the equilibrium existing among themselves, and which for that reason enjoyed a degree of stability that made possible the limited articulation of other social interests as well.

The evolution of modern bureaucratic structures in Eastern Europe

It was a centralized monarchy intent on catching up with the West which created a bureaucratic apparatus directed from above, one which proved its military effectiveness during the First World War, when the German army owed its successes to a then-novel system of war economy administered by the state; nevertheless the bureaucracy always tended to become more than a mere instrument and soon began to regard its own aggrandizement as its highest aim. It discovered a social force whose interests linked it to the hegemony of modern bureaucracy, the hegemony of the state over society. That force was the bureaucratic intelligentsia, an army of professionals in the service of the civil and military administration, men for whose services an inadequate demand existed in the bourgeois private economy and who could never have found there such privileged and almost hegemonic power.

The prospect of subordinating itself to the bourgeoisie and functioning as its organic intelligentsia had little allure for a state intelligentsia which had grown secure and powerful in office, and had acquired some of the arrogant outlook of the bureaucratic milieu; even before the revolution it had in some ways acquired superiority over a bourgeoisie which in Eastern Europe was relatively subservient and, in addition, was made up to a considerable extent of members of ethnic minorities. Still, this largely gentry-descended state bureaucracy could not have swept its allies from the arena and transformed its partial bureaucratic power into a monopolistic class power if its apparent enemy and uninvited secret ally, the marginal intelligentsia, had not blazed the way. It is true that many of the official intelligentsia were swallowed up in the cataclysm of the revolution; but those who survived found themselves in the comical situation of Monsieur Jourdain, who discovered to his astonishment that he had been speaking prose all his life. However much they loathed the Reds, the bureaucrats who had run the war economy could not help realizing, once the storm had passed, that they had been thinking all along in terms of the red logic of an expanded rational redistribution. To understand this meeting of minds, however, we must go back and trace the other process which led up to it: the evolution of the intelligentsia's position within the structure of early rational redistribution.

THE INTELLIGENTSIA IN THE FIRST PHASE OF EARLY
RATIONAL REDISTRIBUTION

The secularization of the intellectuals in Western and Eastern Europe. Prolongation of their feudal status in the East

Prior to the eighteenth century intellectual movements appeared only within the Church, or else against it, in the form of the schismatic and Protestant churches. In Catholic Europe the ideas and social groupings which led to the gradual emancipation of the intellectuals took form amid the clash of Reformation and Counter-Reformation, in Orthodox Europe in the conflict between the state church and the conservative Old Believers. Within Europe's two great churches it was the intelligentsia which was most conspicuous at the point of collision between orthodoxy and heresy, struggling to win independence from feudal authority and even from the absolute monarchies, and furnishing the ideologies for the great social struggles of the day. The spiritual leaders of the peasant wars of the fifteenth and sixteenth centuries—the Czech Jan Hus, the Hungarian Lőrinc Mészáros, the German Thomas Münzer—were clerics or former clerics. On the other side the flowering of the mendicant orders during these two centuries bore witness to the growing spiritual and secular authority and independence of the intelligentsia, regardless of whether they inspired radical movements, like the Franciscans of the Strict Observance in Hungary, or produced the officials of the Dominican and Jesuit Inquisitions, who identified themselves with the spirit of a new feudalism. It was at this time that the Thomist ideal of a theocratic state ripened, inside the Counter-Reformation, into a social experiment, while in the absolute monarchies clerical politicians and counselors were in the front rank of the decisive figures of the day. In all of them, priests or ex-priests, friars or preachers, the aspiration of a spiritual authority to extend its sway over society was clearly formulated, albeit in categories drawn from Christian theology.

In the seventeenth and eighteenth centuries, following the defeat of Eastern European peasant rebellions led by heretical clerics, the feudal intelligentsia's power aspirations found expression in the absolutist bureaucratic state, and in an official state church which had recovered some of its strength, though now linked closely to the state if not actually subordinated to it.

In northwestern Europe the revolutionary movements of the Reformation triumphed, and clerics came to express the interests of the rising bourgeoisie. There heresy gave way to a lay spirit, bourgeois and presbyterian, outside the framework of the old Universal Church. Calvin's intellectual dictatorship yielded to the bourgeois self-discipline of the Protestant ethic, and an expanding market offered roles to intellectuals who were becoming professionals, and ever more secular in outlook. At the beginning of the seventeenth century the typical English intellectual was still a preacher, and a playwright was at best a hanger-on at court, at worst a good-for-nothing on a par socially with jugglers and bearbaiters; the typical eighteenth-century English intellectual was a lawyer, and the writer who lived by his pen, like Defoe or Dr. Johnson, had acquired a new respectability. The Dutch painter could sell his pictures, the learned man could open a school and charge tuition, a flourishing press could make a treatise or a novel into an object of widespread demand, and the Royal Society, while cultivating philanthropy, could also provide a living for the inventive scientist. The intelligentsia did not need to utilize the political apparatus to assure itself of a function. Instead it became the organic intelligentsia of the bourgeoisie and articulated the ethos of a secular, liberal, rational market economy based on the principle of achievement. The economic theory of Smith and Ricardo was the symbolic manifestation of the spirit of that intelligentsia, which, merging into the bourgeoisie, found a place for itself in the market, leaving theology and teleology far behind.

In Eastern Europe there was no room for this kind of secular accommodation. Under the aegis of the second serfdom a baroque, monarchic society emerged whose twin pillars were the centralized imperial bureaucracy and a rigidified but still resurgent Church. They offered continuity, power, and jobs to an intelligentsia unable to slip its feudal ties and forced, in the end, to abandon the struggle for emancipation. The hierarchical structure of the baroque social edifice was sanctioned by the ideology of the Counter-Reformation religious orders, and intellectuals from those orders played a key role in organizing the new society. In devastated Hungary, for example, following the expulsion of the Turks, the Jesuits took the lead in building a new civilization; from their ranks came the architects and surveyors, the natural scientists and poets, the physicians and teachers; they directed the work of reconstruction and the redivision of the land. The townsmen, subservient and few in number, also came under ecclesiastical authority, and lived out lives closely regulated by the demands of religion. From social intercourse to family life, from public health to stage performances, from social welfare to the ceremonial sequence of holy-day and every-day, the life of village and town passed under the flexible but unrelenting tutelage of the Jesuits. The dominant ideas of the age were fidelity, subordination, and an ecstatic but controlled devotion to the higher powers who, in the cupola paintings of the churches with their sophisticated use of *trompe-l'oeil*, spiraled upward into a hierarchically graded heaven. Such ideas necessitated a transcendent, paternalistic intellectual authority, a strict and vigilant intellectual police which did not allow the interests of a separate stratum of bourgeois intellectuals to take shape in opposition to the stability of a unified imperial-ecclesiastical order. Here the careers of the intellectual rebels of the time are characteristic. The leader of the Hungarian Jacobin movement, for example, Ignác Martinovics—an accomplished natural scientist and ingenious philosopher, for the rest—exemplified in one lifetime all the possibilities that were open to the Eastern European intellectual in the eighteenth century. A Jesuit and seminary professor, Martinovics became first an informer and secret agent in the police-intelligence-propaganda apparatus of Joseph II's enlightened absolutism and then, having seen that neither the Church nor the imperial bureaucracy really served his teleological ideals, went on to try and emancipate himself from both by setting up a sophisticated conspiratorial organization. He became the leader of the antifeudal and antiabsolutist movement of the Jacobin intellectuals, and eventually one of their executed martyrs.

The organized governmental and police intelligentsia

If the underdeveloped market economy of Eastern Europe could not provide the conditions for the secularization and emancipation of the intelligentsia, still there were always places for educated men in the imperial administration. The army and the state-subsidized industries needed technical experts, recolonization projects demanded geographers and geologists, the nobility wanted to convert its fortified castles into châteaux set in parks in the French manner; the rulers established academies and universities, official and semiofficial gazettes started up, and censors' posts waited to be filled. An organized administrative and judicial machinery was developed on formal legal principles; the economic departments and the taxation system cried out for professional personnel. In every administrative or ecclesiastical center from Vienna to Petersburg rose splendid baroque public buildings which had to be filled with qualified officials. Talented men found not only a role for themselves; in the state they found an employer as well. Consider the versatile Lomonosov, eighteenth-century Russia's first great secular intellectual: His voracious plebeian spirit spanned the whole range of intellectual knowledge of the day, from experimental physics and chemistry to geography, history, economics, and even the composition of heroic odes. His staunch respect for authority was not the result of naïveté or timidity, for he was a passionate partisan of the reforms of Peter the Great. If industry, mining, or agriculture needed developing, it would never have occurred to him to do anything but organize a ministerial department with comprehensive powers to direct it. He consciously placed all his scholarly activity at the service of the absolutist state. In his odes he celebrated Russia's campaigns of conquest and colonization. If from time to time he had his differences with other administrators he never attacked absolutist centralization as such, only its more irrational manifestations, which conflicted with the spirit of Peter's reforms and with the ethos of early rational redistribution; he could not have imagined anything more sensible or more beneficial for Russia than the Petrine outlook. If we compare his profound moral conformism with the sardonic attitude of his contemporary Voltaire (or with the attitude of that other partisan of Catherine the Great, Diderot), then the difference between the social structures and the intellectual strategies of the two Europes is readily apparent. In the West a third force had already arrayed itself against the coalition of centralized state and landed nobility, and was to succeed in overthrowing it at the end of the century. In Eastern Europe, on the other hand, no alternative existed to this coalition, and anyone who wished to put his knowledge to some use in society had to enter the service of the absolutist state, or else abandon intellectual activity altogether.

A large and well-organized police apparatus also grew up,

which supplemented the military by anticipating trouble through
its network of informers; in it large numbers of intellectuals filled
civil positions. These were the forerunners of the twentieth century's police states. Even in the early nineteenth century their
information storage and retrieval techniques were a model, far
ahead of their time; thanks to them there was no place in Eastern
European society where the eyes of the police did not penetrate.
In those multinational empires their growth was spurred by the
rise of nationalism, which threatened the success of colonialism,
and by the difficulties of keeping a subjugated peasant population in line. The Tsars were preoccupied with the pacification
of Transcaucasia, the Ukraine, and the Cossack regions, and with
the rebellions of the Polish nobility; the Habsburgs with Italian,
Hungarian, Czech, and South Slav separatism; the Prussian
monarchy with the possibility that the other German states might
unite under democratic auspices. To add to it all there appeared,
in the early nineteenth century, the liberalism of the lower
nobility, directed against the coalition of absolutism and aristocracy and demanding the abolition of serfdom. All these stir-
rings made it the first duty of the police to nip in the bud every
effort of the nationalist or democratic intelligentsia to emancipate itself, and to persecute freedom of thought in any form. In
all three states of the Holy Alliance absolutism, with its bureaucracy and police, fought the liberalism of the young gentry
intelligentsia. Thence arose the characteristic attitude of the
Eastern European intellectuals, who, unable to express their
ideas freely and work for reform openly, turned to conspiratorial
underground organization. Police persecution forged the revolutionary Eastern European intelligentsia at an early date. Eastern
European absolutism forced every progressive movement into
the mysterious yet complementary world of police agents and
conspirators. Thus appeared that fateful pairing of roles: On one
side the police official, himself an intellectual because duty-
bound to weigh what danger thoughts might hold; on the other
the rebellious intellectual, forced to regard the most innocuous
new idea as a challenge to the whole system and driven to learn
conspiratorial techniques. And these intellectuals, feeling themselves threatened in their very character of intellectuals irrespective of what class interests they voiced, naturally felt a solidarity

with those of their peers imprisoned for their words or writings, and so rather early on found their own identity in the role of a critical intelligentsia. With some slight, ironic exaggeration we might say that the Eastern European intelligentsia's aspirations to class power owed their early maturation in no small measure to the early development of police repression in Eastern Europe.

The appearance of a liberal noble intelligentsia

At the beginning of the nineteenth century the forerunners of the later professional intelligentsia were to be found not only in the ecclesiastical and state bureaucracies, but also among the educated noble landowners of modest means, the gentry. Under the influence of French culture the lesser nobility came to feel that their station in life, and a proper use of their leisure, required a familiarity with classical and modern authors, knowledge of foreign languages, a passion for botanizing perhaps, the preparation of elaborate plans for developing their estates, music-making and poetry-writing. The nobleman who went on working in the civil administration, or who had completed his term of military service, also began to learn how to relax and enjoy life's pleasures, perhaps in a château he had designed himself. Thus around the turn of the century the aristocracy, with its broad international culture, was joined by a new cultivated class of middling landowners. From now on a knowledge of Montesquieu had its place in the manor houses of the gentry as well as in the châteaux of the great landowners; everyone ordered the new journals, at once fashion magazines and literary periodicals, and soon a reading public formed for whom culture quickly became not just a means of occupying one's leisure but also a medium for expressing opinions on public life. There developed a fairly broad stratum of gentry intellectuals, many with university educations, often active in nationalist movements; individual members of it might devote the bulk of their time to literature, history-writing, or natural science, even when those were not their main source of livelihood. Eastern European noblemen learned a great deal from their stay in Paris as officers during the post-Napoleonic occupation; many who went there then or later as gentlemen returned home intellectuals. Taking advantage of their new-won

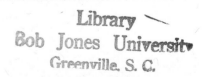

right to travel they set out on grand tours on the fashionable English model, visiting the great cities of Western Europe, taking a few philosophy courses at Jena or Berlin, studying agriculture in Holland, the textile industry in England, the educational and legal systems in France; and if they had been known to gamble away several villages in a single tipsy evening, it might also happen that on returning home they would devote themselves, out of guilt at their provincial boorishness, to improving the condition of their neglected people—reforming their barbaric language, introducing the achievements of modern civilization, founding academies and libraries, writing romantic epics and plays, working to uplift a peasantry still living in huts of mud and wattles, regulating rivers, establishing credit banks, model farms, and progressive societies of noble intellectuals. They tried to take part in public life in order to urge fargoing reforms of the feudal structure; wherever they looked, they saw things to be done all around them. But at the same time, and despite their occasional successes, they constantly ran up against the relentless opposition of an increasingly rigid and ever less enlightened absolutist bureaucracy, and of an aristocracy most of whose members had grown narrow and short-sighted, and clung stubbornly and fearfully to their privileges. This then was the situation in which they defined themselves, in opposition to the social structure of the day, as intellectuals. Even if they still lived mostly from the income of their estates they were no longer primarily landowners but the pioneers of the Eastern European gentry intelligentsia, and as such they articulated the most important structural conflict of the first phase of early rational redistribution.

The gentry intellectuals: Their interest as landowners in Western-style capitalism and peasant emancipation

That system in fact carried within itself the seeds of its own dissolution. The lesser nobility had little stake in the social and economic policies of early rational redistribution. It drew little benefit from serf labor. A small estate could be made to produce a large income only if intensive cultivation were introduced, and that required capital and a supply of reliable, free wageworkers who could be entrusted with more complex tasks. The aristocracy on their broad domains might content themselves with extensive methods of cultivation, using serfs obligated to perform labor service; the small estate worked with serf labor could not compete with large extensively cultivated holdings. It could not go over to commodity-production or join in the export of grain to the West. For that reason the lesser landed nobility were not altogether mistaken in thinking that the advance of capitalism would make them more competitive. But in order to foster the development of capitalism they had first to achieve the emancipation of the serfs. In the absence of a bourgeoisie, then, the program of the bourgeois transformation—and, indeed, even that of the democratic revolution—was systematically worked out by a new type of independent intelligentsia drawn from the lesser nobility. This intelligentsia had an interest in rationalization and secularization, in extending the scope of the market, and in the expansion of credit; its very existence demanded the modernization of noble landed property and the introduction of Western conditions generally into the social and economic system of early rational redistribution.

The early transcendence of the amateur gentry intelligentsia. Intellectual consciousness courtesy of the police. Career or conscience?

Nevertheless, material interests alone do not suffice to explain why it was precisely the nobility that produced Eastern Europe's first great movement of the intelligentsia and its first critical, Western-oriented reform generation, the equivalent of the Enlightenment on the Eastern European scene and of no small intellectual weight in its own right. In the Eastern Europe of the early nineteenth century the intelligentsia could only have been a noble one, for no bourgeois market economy had developed capable of providing a sufficient demand for trained intellectual labor and its products. The Western road to the emergence of a secular intelligentsia free of feudal obligations— the assumption of the functions of a stratum of free professionals —was not open in Eastern Europe. And so the economic basis for the exponential growth of the intelligentsia was noble landed property. It was possible and to some extent inevitable that their activity should retain a certain amateur character, for it was worthwhile to become an intellectual only if one could support oneself from landed property, or from an official post acquired through social position rather than specialized knowledge. Even those burgher and peasant sons who after finishing their schooling obtained government posts became nobles sooner or later; in Russia, for example, the upper seven of the fourteen grades in the civil-service hierarchy automatically conferred nobility on those who attained them. Thus nobility was generally a prerequisite for obtaining a government post, and even where the requirement was disregarded noble status was often acquired as a result of state service. And so if a small bourgeois intelligentsia did appear it was quickly co-opted into the ranks of the nobility.

This noble intelligentsia was part of a fundamentally feudal society which sheltered intellectual activity from dependence on market competition, throwing a kind of feudal shield over it. Such an intelligentsia, which owed its livelihood and its elite style of life primarily to its estates and derived only a supplementary income from writing poetry, history, or economics (or from official, military, or teaching posts in the state service), could not develop to any great extent the characteristics of an intellectual stratum. Their social position made them relatively independent of the whole social structure and reinforced the transcendent character of their intellectual role, elevating many of them above the genetic interests of the nobility. For they owed their intellectual status not so much to the nobility's need for an organic intelligentsia to articulate its interests as to the fact that their social and economic independence allowed them to devote themselves—both for amusement and from a sense of duty, but in any case freely and voluntarily—to intellectual activities which in the West had come to command considerable prestige. It was this pronounced transcendence of the gentry intelligentsia which made it possible for them to become the spokesmen of a bourgeois transformation which, if it did not necessarily stand in opposition to noble interests, was not necessarily in complete harmony with them either. One reason the Western intellectual was willing to enunciate bourgeois interests was that he hoped thereby to escape from personal subordination to a feudal lord, exchanging it for dependence on an impersonal, pluralistic market where no principle of deference operated. The Eastern European gentry intellectuals of the Enlightenment were free even of this personal motive, for as intellectuals they generally were not in the service of any lord. And if they were still not completely free in their intellectual avocations, it was neither feudal service obligations nor the market which restricted them, but rather absolutism's ideological censorship and network of police spies.

Consider the example of Pushkin, who might have lived comfortably on the considerable income from his estates, whose aristocratic rank even secured for him a post at court. His poems earned him only a rather dubious renown, a few amorous successes, the constant threat of banishment, and remarks like that attributed to Count Benckendorff, the head of the notorious Third Section (political police), who is said to have whispered to the poet at a ball that if he kept on he would be sent so far away that even the birds would not see his bleaching bones. So the Eastern European noble intelligentsia had to learn to speak in an enigmatic, Aesopian language, an idiom of nuance, connotation, and allusion; and their public, too, learned to read it. Reformist social criticism was thus camouflaged from the first in the metaphorical language of literature; animal fables, historical novels, and allegories were the vehicles for radical ideas. All Moscow flocked to the lectures which the historian Granovsky gave on English parliamentarianism, for even though he said not a word about Russian conditions everyone understood that a mere account of the English system was meant as a direct rebuke to Russian serfdom and autocracy.

The relative independence of the Eastern European gentry intelligentsia, and the transcendence which was its result, explain why the absolutist governments early on worked out their own official cultural policies, elaborating them into slogans and guidelines ironically reminiscent of the party directives which govern socialist culture today. The monarchs themselves watched over poetry: Nicholas I censored Pushkin's verses himself, and personally gave permission for the production of Gogol's *Inspector General*. These marks of interest from on high only intensified the excitement of the salons whenever a fashionable author like Gogol consented, after repeated entreaties, to read a few pages from his work in progress; women fainted from the excitement, and people from all around invited the penniless author to their homes for dinner. A stir went through the entire noble society of Moscow at the news that he had completed the long-awaited first volume of *Dead Souls*. Nowhere in the West did literature have such prestige and such a wide echo in society; even a snob like Balzac could never have gained admittance to social circles of the sort in which the Eastern European noble intellectuals were entirely at home. That fact among others explains, perhaps, why the heroes of the French novel of that day are careerist intellectuals struggling for wealth and success, while their Russian counterparts are noblemen of intellectual temper, conscience-stricken at the status they already enjoy in society. In Eastern Europe noble self-criticism took the place of criticism of the bourgeoisie, and the difference was by no means to the disadvantage of literature. If for a lawyer pragmatism is more useful than metaphysics, the same cannot be said for a novelist. Thus it is that the great prophetic myths of the intellectual class are to be found in the works of Tolstoy and Dostoyevsky, rather than in those of Flaubert or Thackeray.

The limits of noble transcendence

Naturally there were limits to the yearnings of a conscience-stricken nobility after Western institutions and the triumph of bourgeois democracy. In Tolstoy's story, "A Landlord's Morning," a well-meaning young landowner visits several of his peasants in turn, offering them material assistance and moral counsel; but the peasants are reticent and evasive and cling stubbornly to their old ways, perhaps suspecting that in the end their service obligations will only be increased. And they were not far wrong either: In Eastern Europe the peasants received their freedom without land, and were saddled with heavy redemption obligations. The noble intelligentsia took the part of the people and considered themselves their spokesman vis-à-vis the existing order, for they formed the only possible opposition to the coalition of Emperor and aristocracy. The peasants who made up nine-tenths of the "people," still legally subject to the jurisdiction of the village commune even when they went away to work in a factory, were incapable of formulating their interests or organizing any kind of alternative force; they might burn down a noble manor house now and then, but they still looked to the Tsar for any improvement in their fortunes. Because of its backwardness this peasantry, by contrast with the Western European bourgeoisie, could never have taken the lead in modernizing Eastern Europe, even if it had managed to overthrow the old order. This was the "people" in whose name the noble intellectuals, moderate or radical, made their appeals. Eastern Europe had its own peculiar Jacobins, who hailed Louis XVI's execution and plotted their own ruthless Terror, like the Russian Decembrist leader Pestel. But this appeal to the people, if not insincere, was not altogether consistent, for in the last analysis what did the noble intellectuals live from, to what did they owe their spiritual independence, if not the labor of their serfs?

Bourgeois transformation was all very well, but the noble intelligentsia despised the fat, uncultured bourgeois when he bowed and scraped, and even more perhaps when he luxuriated in his new palace, freshly bought from an impoverished nobleman. And if they were magnanimous enough to accept the bourgeois as a human being—even when he belonged to an alien race, German, Jewish, or Armenian—and even willing to recognize his legal equality, still they never acknowledged him as an ally in the struggle for power, never associated the idea of progress with him. They preferred to give a utopian-socialist coloring to their democratic aspirations rather than become the mouthpiece for such a bourgeoisie.

The noble intellectuals were in search of a class to ally and identify with, of masses at whose head they could achieve the democratic revolution. But they never found them, if only because both bourgeoisie and peasantry timidly, even deferentially, kept their place in a hierarchically structured, semifeudal society, or else treated the nobility with as much suspicion as they did the bureaucracy, looking on with considerable indifference while the gentlemen debated (if they looked on at all). So it was at the time of the Decembrist uprising, and during the rebellions of the Polish nobility. The Hungarian revolution and war of independence of 1848–49 was exceptional among Eastern European social movements precisely because there a liberal, nationalist noble intelligentsia succeeded at least partially in ranging behind themselves significant sections of the Hungarian-speaking population (though even there the unsolved land question overshadowed everything else).

For the Eastern European noble intelligentsia could never bring itself to free the serfs and at the same time divide the soil among them, thus pulling the foundations out from under its own economic existence. If they renounced their feudal privileges, they were unable to give up their privileges of property. They wanted to modernize their estates—and in no small measure with capital accumulated from their former serfs' redemption payments—not parcel them out among the cultivators. The Russian nobleman who carried the self-criticism of his class to its furthest extreme, Leo Tolstoy, the sworn enemy of every kind of inequality in land ownership, wrestled unsuccessfully to the end of his life with demands from within and without that he unite theory and practice by dividing his estates among the peasants who lived and worked on them.

THE INTELLIGENTSIA IN THE SECOND STAGE OF EARLY
RATIONAL REDISTRIBUTION

From liberal noble intelligentsia to state bureaucracy

To free the serfs without land it was not necessary to overturn the social and political edifice of early rational redistribution. By the middle of the nineteenth century the noble reformers had to recognize that emancipation from above and without land reform, while it meant modernization of a sort, brought with it some of the quantitative achievements of Western economic growth but without introducing the Western model of civilization. Eastern European social development took other directions. A different type of industrial growth, agricultural modernization, and state administration was in process of development there, in which the government bureaucrat would have at least as important a role as the bourgeois entrepreneur. Peasant emancipation without land distribution and the Prussian way of agricultural development stabilized early rational redistribution anew in Eastern Europe. But the Prussian solution was not favorable to middling and small-scale noble producers in quest of investment capital for their estates. It rid them of serf labor, to be sure, but without providing enough capital to mechanize their operations and convert to intensive use of wage labor. Redistribution on the Prussian model brought about a shortage of capital and an agrarian policy designed to subsidize industry, from which only large landowners could draw any benefit. The great landed proprietors were able to go on making a profit from extensive grain cultivation, using the cheap labor of a landless proletariat made up of former serfs and often paid in kind; and if the profit margins were small, still the size of these estates guaranteed that large enough sums would be made to permit modernizing investments. In addition, credit policy and such modest state subsidies as were available for agriculture favored large landed property.

Only a more intensive mode of cultivation could have helped medium-sized estates weather the crisis. But that would have required proportionally larger amounts of capital than were needed for agriculture on the large estates; and no such credits were available, as a result of the deliberate policy of the state. And so a substantial proportion of the lesser nobility was driven from the economic arena and allowed to go to rack and ruin; medium-sized landed property was redistributed among merchants, manufacturers, and prosperous peasants, men with more capital at their disposal (including, frequently, Jewish lessees), who were in a position to modernize their newly acquired land even without state subsidies, and having done so could benefit the state by paying more taxes from their increased production. For its part the state, in order to avoid social unrest, took the impoverished or bankrupt noblemen into the ranks of the rapidly expanding government administration.

The rapid expansion of the bureaucratic apparatus was spurred on from two different directions: It was demanded not only by those who needed and sought jobs, but also by the policies of the central government itself, intent on hastening the pace of economic development through increased state intervention. In general the imperial governments strove to perfect a technically

proficient, smoothly functioning administrative system, omni-
competent and directed from above, on the model of that Prussian bureaucracy which excited Hegel's enthusiasm and even
Max Weber's guarded admiration. The governments fared well
by it: They rid themselves of an opposition of noble reform
intellectuals without any violence, through the force of economic
compulsion alone, and transformed them into a loyal intelligentsia of civil servants. There appeared a veritable reserve army of
noble intellectuals, reduced in circumstances but still anxious
to maintain their noble manner of living, with a residence and
servants befitting their rank, who from now on placed above all
else a secure, well-paying government post which would rescue
them from the hazards of competitive capitalism. At one time
the nobleman had striven to withdraw from state service, in
order to live from his estate. Now the service nobility of that
earlier day gave way to a new corps of noble officials, deprived
of any other livelihood but still jealously intent on defending
their coats-of-arms, however hazily those emblems may have
distinguished their owners any longer from non-noble officials
of comparable rank and salary. Still, the noble administrative
bureaucracy did manage to extract one concession: Henceforn-
ward non-nobles would rise to higher posts in the state service
only in exceptional cases. And so the bulk of the liberal, landed
noble intellectuals were transformed into an intelligentsia of
noble officials; from being reforming critics of absolutism they
became one of its mainstays, retaining only the mildest of liberal
outlooks. The ideological needs of this new officialdom were met
by a conservative imperial patriotism, by a Pan-Slavic, Pan-
German, or even Pan-Magyar colonialism calling for expansion
at the expense of the smaller peoples of Central Asia, Eastern
Europe, and the Balkans, and by demands for further expansion
of the state apparatus, hence construction of more public buildings to house still more officials.

Social and political conflicts within the triple coalition

The once-liberal new bureaucrats no longer insisted on mean-
ingful reforms. Their vestigial liberalism aimed only to achieve
a few modest, corrective concessions, in order to allow the mod-

ernization process to go forward more smoothly—a certain rationalization of early rational redistribution, undertaken not least in
the interests of the new third partner in the power alliance, a
bourgeoisie itself too timid as yet to take an active part in government. For its part the bourgeoisie was content to enrich itself.
It made little use of its newly acquired political rights, submit-
ting respectfully to state authority. It was satisfied if government
measures guaranteed it a reliable market, while rural overpopulation assured a cheap and plentiful labor force which the police
made sure would remain unorganized. The bourgeois craved en-
noblement, a baronial title for himself, far more than he wanted
to limit the political monopoly of the old barons.

And so, with the stabilization of this new triple alliance, a
relative equilibrium of power emerged. That in itself brought
an ebbing of the revolutionary temper during the last decade of
the nineteenth century, and with it the isolation of the radical
intelligentsia. In each of the three Eastern European empires
there arose a viable system which generated rapid industrial
growth (above all in heavy industry), turned the larger towns
of Eastern Europe into great cities in short order, and kept
under arms large, modern, relatively well-equipped armies with
a large corps of officers and an abundance of recruits provided
by universal military service. It was unable, however, to make
market relations universal. Nor was it able to broaden its social
base to any appreciable extent. It could not effectively extend
the process of rationalization at the expense of the traditional,
hierarchical, feudal elements of the social system. An exclusive
ruling caste, tenaciously defending its short-run interests, narrowed the channels of upward mobility to a marked degree.
Some room was accorded to capital ownership, the principle of
achievement, as a legitimation of power, alongside the more
traditional legitimation of authority by birth; but there was no
place for the achievement-based legitimating principles of professional intellectual knowledge or ownership of labor-power.
This system was unable to introduce openly transactive relations
with the intellectuals left outside the state apparatus, or with
the working class, or with a peasantry which, though largely
frustrated in its efforts to accumulate capital, was still rapidly
becoming differentiated. The coalition of state, great landed

property, and large-scale capital carried through the process of redistributive modernization to the distinct disadvantage of the laboring masses, by depressing living standards, and thus without creating a strong internal consumer demand. For that reason it gradually turned against itself all those social forces which had an interest in extending political rights and freedoms, or in exchanging the Prussian model of agricultural development for an agrarian economy of free individual farmers, or in any other kind of land reform. In short, it made enemies of all those who, in opposition to the bureaucratic nobility—the leading force in the second phase of early rational redistribution—still demanded the long-overdue achievement of the bourgeois transformation.

The appearance of an Eastern European professional intelligentsia, and its precarious existence

Having lost its economic independence, the noble intelligentsia was obliged to bid farewell to its intellectual independence as well, and consequently to the transcendence inherent in its earlier intellectual role. By the last third of the nineteenth century noble liberalism was an object of derision; young radicals dismissed even Pushkin's poems as so much whining, fit only for young gentlewomen to read. Whence came that radical wing of the intelligentsia which, unable to reconcile itself to its historically determined situation, reemerged in the form of a creative and professional intelligentsia or as marginal revolutionaries, thus lending a new content to the transcendent role of the intellectuals? What structural position did they occupy in society? And what ideological dilemmas confronted them?

There is no question that in the last third of the nineteenth century, and especially at the beginning of the twentieth, a quasi-stratum of professionals in the Western sense appeared in Eastern Europe, however small in numbers and precarious in its existence, and however much exposed to conflicting ideological currents. It was several times larger than at the beginning of the nineteenth century; nevertheless the limitations on its absolute size are indicated by the fact that even at the end of the century the number of university students in Russia was still under 30,000, and even so most of the graduates still went into the civil service. The state was the largest employer not only of teachers and lawyers, but of doctors and engineers as well. Nonetheless there did appear, alongside the intelligentsia of officials, a small group of intellectuals working as self-employed professionals or employed in the private economy, or else selling their products on the open market. They were a relatively independent element, and in any event were determined to augment their independence.

By the end of the nineteenth century the market had begun to function more efficiently in Eastern Europe, especially in its more westerly portions, the German Empire and Austria-Hungary, thus affording scope for a group of professionals which began to form into an intellectual stratum. But if the market had broadened, it had not expanded enough to offer a secure livelihood to a rapidly growing intelligentsia, not all of whom could be accommodated in state jobs. It was a permanent feature of capitalist development in Eastern Europe that the production of intellectuals constantly ran ahead of economic growth, especially the growth of the bourgeois private economy. Doctors and lawyers suffered from a chronic scarcity of patients and clients, the public for serious artists and writers was stiflingly narrow, and industry's demand for engineers (much less research and development personnel) was small. The gap between the supply of intellectual labor and intellectual products, and the demand for them, constantly widened, even though in absolute terms both supply and demand were growing.

Thus it was easy for educated professionals to become intellectual proletarians: Their livelihood was uncertain, their market shifting and unstable. The intelligentsia could not support its own creative artists and scholars, and the stratum of the bourgeoisie that was willing to pay for culture was exceptionally small. A captain of industry or wealthy banker might subsidize a review or conservatory, or buy paintings by a contemporary artist, in order to indulge his own aesthetic inclinations; but what was needed was a cultivated and growing middle-class stratum which would create an influential model of cultural consumption and become the core of a public for intellectual products, and that was precisely what was lacking. The whole situation was peculiarly tinged by the existence of a stratum of noble officials who strove above all to preserve the traditional way of life of their elite, though on a reduced income, rather than to base their prestige and way of life on their new intellectual status: They spent considerably more on servants, gambling, and hunting than on books, theater, music, and art.

Slender social basis of the professional intelligentsia;
absence of a bourgeoisie risen from the peasantry

The economic structure itself did not permit a more rapid expansion of one possible social basis of a broader culture, the bourgeoisie. Owing to the Prussian way of agricultural development, the failure of land reform, and a one-sided industrialization, a disproportionately large share of the peasantry remained mired in agriculture. The nonagricultural sectors of the economy did not grow fast enough to draw the surplus rural population off into industry, which would have created a labor shortage favorable to mechanization and intensive cultivation of the soil and brought about an expansion of peasant property, as happened in Western Europe. The practice of dividing peasant holdings equally among the heirs swelled the number of dwarf-holders who, with the landless laborers, made up an agrarian proletariat living on the very margin of existence, able to find wage work only at peak seasons. Neither migration to the towns and industry nor successive waves of emigration to America could reduce their numbers enough; indeed, the agricultural proletariat was constantly enlarged by the intensification of cultivation on the large estates, with which the peasant holding could not keep pace.

Demands for radical land reform offered a temporary, yet often illusory, solution, since land reform failed to solve the underlying problem even where it was tried (Poland, the Baltic countries, Bulgaria); for overpopulation was caused in the first instance by the underdevelopment of industry and the service sector, not by the existence of large estates. Thus the vicious circle was complete, for the greater part of the rural masses, living from hand to mouth, cut off from commodity and money relations, could consume the products of industry only to a very limited degree. Even at the end of the century the production of articles of daily use in most of Eastern Europe scarcely transcended the scale of cottage industry. And so, as a result of the absence of an internal consumer market, industry itself developed one-sidedly. Heavy industry outstripped the branches producing consumer goods; the sphere of the small and medium entrepreneur remained a narrow one alongside large-scale industry—another indication of the relative underdevelopment of the small and middle bourgeoisie. Indeed, under early rational redistribution industry did not even fill the social role which one would have expected from its statistical share in the economy. The failure of farmer-type peasant production to develop gave rise to a parallel phenomenon: No small and middle bourgeoisie could emerge from the peasantry, later to transfer its capital to urban industry. Thus the age of finance capital saw only a small, weak, petty and middle bourgeoisie, incapable of supporting a rapidly growing intelligentsia. The intellectuals had no one to rely on, no one whose ideology they could supply, no one whose organic intelligentsia they could become.

*Jewish capitalist bourgeois and Jewish communist
intellectuals. Early rational redistribution's
defensive response: Anti-Semitism*

The problem acquired its uniquely Eastern European character because of the presence and importance of a bourgeoisie and professional intelligentsia of Jewish and, in general, of ethnically alien extraction. Capitalist development owed its origins not to peasant commodity production but, in the main, to commercial capital; it went back to the stratum of Jewish grocers, innkeepers, and peddlers who streamed into the Habsburg Monarchy in particular, drawn by the emancipation of the Jews there and by the liberal temper of the age, and impelled to leave their homes by successive waves of pogroms in the Russian Pale. Once free of the ghetto, they quickly began to assimilate. Within a generation or two the Jewish bourgeoisie had emerged from its isolation and could take its place in the national culture of its new country, indeed had even come to form the basis of a consumer market for the products of that culture. The same thing happened in the professions: The peasantry could not afford higher education for its sons, the nobility flocked mainly into government service, and so as a result the free professions, lower in prestige, came to be filled primarily by the sons of the Jewish bourgeoisie. The phenomenon was somewhat akin to the entry of American blacks into the entertainment industry: Marginal groups take up precisely those trades which the traditional elite turns up its nose at. In those occupations, moreover, a feeble market demand spurred them on to display exceptionally competitive behavior, and they often attained a better than average success. Thus a cleavage set in within the intelligentsia, with an unfolding ethnic rivalry lending a special tone to the conflict between professionals and bureaucratic intellectuals.

If the first generations of Jews were happy to be allowed to sink roots at all, and remained uniformly loyal to the social and political system of their new country, their sons turned against the system of early rational redistribution as soon as they realized that their situation, though a distinct improvement on the earlier, near-outcast status of the Jews, was still a narrowly circumscribed one. Theirs was a social ghetto whose walls were indicated not by legal restrictions but by the attitudes and ideologies of a traditional, feudal social structure slowly undergoing modernization in the "Prussian way." In that society the Jews inevitably became the target of the animosity of the most diverse strata of an incompletely industrialized and bourgeoisified society. The landowners were bound to see in the better-financed Jewish leaseholder an enemy or at least a rival, not only in a social sense but also in an ethnic one; the governmental and ecclesiastical intelligentsia regarded the Jewish free professional in the same light, as did the peasant and worker the exploitative Jewish employer and merchant. While in the West capitalist development was an organic process, not a privilege of the Jews, in Eastern Europe it was above all the Jewry who represented capitalism in a social order which, in the process of modernization, still preserved its traditional authority structure. Although this conflict underwent significant modifications when socialism appeared in Eastern Europe as an alternative to "feudal" capitalism, the fact remained that whether as capitalists or as socialists Jews by the very nature of their interests found themselves in opposition to the existing social and political structure. Thus every social conflict came of necessity to be colored by ideologies of ethnic conflict and especially, as the crisis of liberalism deepened, by anti-Semitism in its many ideological and emotional forms.

A second critical reform generation emerges from the professional intelligentsia in Eastern Europe at the beginning of the twentieth century. Its cultural creativity and political impotence

The foregoing should suffice to explain the built-in contradictions in the social situation and ideologies of the rising professional intelligentsia in the late nineteenth and early twentieth centuries; and it helps to explain the internal dilemmas which were later to issue in full-scale crisis. In Eastern Europe the free professionals represented the social force most interested in the expansion of Western-type capitalism; their ideology was necessarily a liberal one, even if, in reacting against their milieu, they called themselves radicals.

Prior to the emancipation of the serfs the liberal intellectuals of the lesser nobility, looking to capitalist development to shore up their own position, had represented a critical reforming liberalism and a capitalism which must necessarily have led to the dissolution of a system based on a combination of Asiatic redistribution and European feudalism, and which demanded, specifically, the abolition of serfdom and of centralized absolutism. Now that the descendants of the gentry had found a place as state officials in a somewhat modernized version of early rational redistribution, it was again an intellectual group, the professional intelligentsia, which in the absence of a radical bourgeoisie undertook to advocate an alternative, Western European type of development—bourgeois transformation, by revolutionary means if necessary.

The emancipation of the serfs, which marked the transition to the second phase of early rational redistribution, did not bring the social changes which the liberals of Eastern Europe had hoped for. Imperial absolutism survived in a more or less liberalized form; the centralized bureaucracy, scarcely controlled by parliament, and the police and military establishment continued to assure its sovereignty over society, with only minimal limitations. Demands for constitutionally guaranteed civil rights and liberties, government by democratic representation, a transactive labor market, and legal organization of particular interests remained to be achieved.

An intelligentsia committed to liberal democracy was bound to come into conflict with a government policy of economic and political interventionism which did more to frustrate than encourage the advance of a small and medium-sized entrepreneurial bourgeoisie. In industrializing, the state promoted only concentrated heavy industry, while in agriculture state subsidies were available primarily for large estates; both policies only strengthened the existing order. Since this intelligentsia, situated as it was outside the state bureaucracy, had little interest in strengthening the redistributive mechanism, it went on for a good while advocating a liberal capitalist economic policy against the prevailing bureaucratic centralization.

Moreover, since large-scale capital was itself divided, with important groups profiting from their alliance with the state and the great landowners (through state orders and subsidies, and a pool of cheap labor kept in line by the police), the professional intelligentsia turned more and more emphatically against finance capital as well, justifying their designation by Marxists as petty-bourgeois radicals.

Finally, since in Eastern Europe the Church not only remained an economic force (as the largest single landowner), but also had primary charge of a whole range of social services from education to public health, separation of church and state and restrictions on the social and economic power of the former also became part of the professionals' program.

But what kind of bourgeois radicals could these intellectuals be if no radical bourgeoisie stood behind them? Were they radicals at all?

They were indeed, for they loathed the "redistribution" of the casino, in which a whole village might change hands on the turn of a card, and the military reviews that cost more than the whole higher-education budget; they did not want to be tutors to the effete sons of counts and princes and sit at the lower end of the dinner table like a more genteel species of footman. The whole archaic structure of privilege and injustice which they saw around them pressed on them like an impossible, phantasmagorical reality, in which intellectual knowledge lent only a distorted consciousness, in which their precarious existence was constantly threatened by the danger of proletarianization, in which educated men and women were forced into defiant isolation, in which the whole state apparatus weighed heavily on those who knew what they wanted and advanced cogent arguments for it.

Completely hemmed in as they were, how could the intellectuals, who thought themselves more intelligent and more honest than the counts and ministers, have helped thinking that the whole system had to be overthrown? Land reform, universal suffrage, a democratic constitution, autonomy for national minorities, democratic social policies were all needed. The bourgeois revolution was ripe, but there was no one to make it. In the West a youthful intelligentsia had succeeded in overthrowing the allied power of absolutism and landed aristocracy because it had behind it the Third Estate, not just the people but a bourgeoisie emerging as a class. In Eastern Europe there was no bourgeois-democratic alternative to early rational redistribution, and so the political impact of bourgeois radicalism was slight. The members of the second reform generation came to form an elite opposition which offered a real alternative to the conservative-bureaucratic intelligentsia in the sphere of culture, but politically they represented a utopian alternative.

At the turn of the century Eastern Europe teemed with talent in the arts and sciences; movements sprang up and works appeared which have shaped the culture of our century at least as much as anything conceived in Western Europe. A veritable intellectual renaissance started out from Central and Eastern Europe, from Vienna and Berlin, from Budapest, Prague, Warsaw, Petersburg, Moscow, and Odessa. But because it was so isolated socially this movement carried little political weight; it never seriously threatened the alliance of state, latifundium, and finance capital, and perhaps this very harmlessness explains why early rational redistribution in its second stage, in the years before World War I, could permit itself a degree of cultural liberalism which creative intellectuals in Eastern Europe have wept for ever since. The independent professional intelligentsia of Eastern Europe was as impotent in politics, then, as it was creative in the sphere of culture. Nor could it have been otherwise, for the real winning alternative to the existing order was not bourgeois democracy, but the extension and universalization of rational redistribution, with its dazzling prospect of class power for the intellectuals. That, however, was not to be the accomplishment of professional men and women who dreamed of transplanting Western conditions, but of a radicalized marginal intelligentsia which found in Lenin's Bolshevism a profoundly original political vehicle.

The ideological crisis of the bourgeois-radical intelligentsia

Even had it not built on unrealistic social and political premises, the second reform generation would eventually have arrived at a crisis which called its most basic strategic objective into doubt. For why should intellectuals, naturally given to teleology and to sweeping historical solutions, have wanted the complete triumph of market economy and capital-ownership as a legitimating principle, and the emergence of a social structure in which their own aspirations to power would have to be put aside for an indefinite time? Nor did their traditional philosophy of rational, evolutionist positivism prove of any help in dealing with their situation. They could make far better use of romantic irrationalisms of the right or left, whose obvious political consequences were fascism and communism.

Thus the reform intellectuals of Eastern Europe were constantly exposed to the temptations of two different ideologies of power for the intelligentsia, each offering a distinct role for the intellectuals. One meant entering the state apparatus in order to work there for the final victory of the bureaucratic intelligentsia over the other members of early rational redistribution's triple alliance—finance capital and the landed aristocracy. That way led, after World War I, to the fascist and semifascist regimes of Eastern Europe. The other way was to reject the whole system, abandon reform altogether, and assume the role of professional revolutionary; then, eventually, to seize the commanding heights of political and economic power by revolutionary means, topple and destroy the landowning and capitalist classes and their legitimating principles, abolish every element of traditional rule, perfect the system of rational redistribution, nationalize the entire economy and society and, after joining hands with the bureaucratic apparatus (if not exactly with its former denizens), to lay the foundations for the class power of the intelligentsia. That road led through the crises that grew out of the First World War to the socialist revolutions of the Bolshevik type, and to today's Eastern European reality.

THE EASTERN EUROPEAN INTELLIGENTSIA'S RAPPROCHEMENT
WITH THE BUREAUCRATIC ETHOS

The modernizing role of the bureaucracy in the second stage of early rational redistribution

Even before the First World War the professional intelligentsia served as a permanent reserve for supplying the state bureaucracy. Many shrewd observers believed that reform and structural change were only possible, if they were possible at all, through the medium of the state, while bourgeois revolution was not in the realm of practical possibilities. Thus anyone who wanted to take an active part in modernizing the backward societies of Eastern Europe might better enter the state administration and work there in the interests of modernization. Around the turn of the century many of the most outstanding professionals in the Eastern European intelligentsia believed that a modern legal system and a developed bureaucratic state would represent real progress over traditional feudal conditions. They were convinced that in the existing situation the professionalization of the bureaucracy, still mainly noble in origin and ethos, and its conversion into a modern, rational administration, were valid objectives.

Always fearful of the possibility of proletarianization, the intellectuals strove to find a steady taker for their expertise, and they were not averse to accepting posts that offered a secure and respectable income, accompanied by paternalistic authority and a certain sense of missionary calling. Nor did they mind if their official status sometimes enhanced their influence to the point

where even industrialists and landed magnates might compete
for the favor of an ennobled and bemedaled ministerial coun-
selor who represented the ethos of a system based on expert
knowledge, and who on occasion might even turn to the police
to secure compliance with his decisions. There appeared, at
least on the ideological plane, the ideal of the government
agency standing above the whole of society, rising above market
competition and class conflict, and reconciling the interests of
all social strata in a higher synthesis. Many hoped in this way
to turn the tools of redistribution to social purposes, at least in
part, in order to combat social injustice. And in fact many rational and democratic reforms were made in Eastern Europe
around the turn of the century in the realm of social welfare,
from education and housing policy to child-welfare laws and
prison reform.

All over Europe in this period demands were raised for increased state intervention in the economy, partly as a result of
cyclical crises with their recurring business failures and bank-
ruptcies, partly in connection with the extension of local and
infrastructural services. Railway fever gave way to nationalization of the rail lines, land speculation to government urban planning; military security demanded state supervision of arms
production and sometimes even nationalization; state model
farms set an example for large-scale capitalist agriculture; the
Church was incapable of developing a modern educational system. In a word, there was no avoiding a rapid expansion of the
state bureaucracy and a spectacular growth in its power and
influence. For professionals unable to make a living in the private economy entry into the state bureaucracy represented a
welcome arrival in harbor, even if they had to make certain concessions at the expense of their spiritual independence, like the
Russian professors who were obliged to appear in uniform. The
bureaucratic ladder of promotion, perhaps leading even to a
ministerial post for those who met the technical criteria and
demonstrated the requisite discipline and an impersonal esprit
de corps, was no more repugnant a way to rise socially, in the
eyes of many intellectuals, and no less achievement-oriented a
channel of social mobility, than (say) a big killing on the stock
exchange. And if we consider that the civil and military administration still took its tone from the noble officials who con-

gregated there, with their unrelenting emphasis on their titles and prestige, and that this aristocratic atmosphere lent a special distinction to non-noble intellectuals in the bureaucracy as well, then it is easy to understand how the "star" status of a leading state official came to haunt the imagination of the whole intelligentsia of the day, overtly or tacitly. And that was true not only of the radical-liberal reformers but all the more so of the marginal revolutionary intellectuals, for the high state officials had a great deal of power while they had none. However much the radical intelligentsia may have reviled these high-ranking administrators, they secretly envied them too, as demonstrated by the way they began to imitate the behavior and life-style of their vanquished predecessors once the revolution had raised them to the same seats of power.

The incorporation of the bureaucratic ethos into socialist ideology

It was a further indication of the irresistible advance of the ethos of bureaucratic *dirigisme* that following the victory of the revolution even orthodox revolutionary Marxism, having long ago rid itself of all anarchist and syndicalist elements, could not devise any other model for building the new society than that of a comprehensive statism. In it all society, each and every economic unit, was organized into a single vast productive enterprise whose structure coincided with that of the state. Kautskyan Social Democracy no less than Bolshevism called for the elimination from the economy of all competitive and "anarchic" market elements, replacing money with labor certificates, the labor market with labor armies, the market for investment and consumer goods with central allocation, the supply-and-demand mechanism with technical planning and a system of calculating value on the basis of labor-time. However much German Social Democrats and Russian Bolsheviks may have differed on how much force and violence the dictatorship of the proletariat ought to exercise following the revolution (as on the use of violence generally), they fully agreed that the triumph of socialism was synonymous with the nationalization of the whole economy and the transfer of total authority to a scientific, rational bureaucracy (now said to embody the authority of the working class).

That circumstance also explains why, at every critical juncture, it was so easy for the Bolsheviks and their left Social Democratic allies to demand that the Social Democrats act according to their own principles. For socialization—i.e., nationalization—was after all a program common to them all; the Social Democratic leaders of the Second International could not object to it in principle; at most they might dispute tactical questions of tempo and degree. But no one could hold to any alternative model of socialism, the ultimate strategic goal, except that of rational redistribution. Half a century had to pass before Bernsteinian revisionism could become any more than a delaying tactic; only then could a new party program openly abandon the demand for nationalization of capitalist property, replacing it with proposals for a technocratic mixed economy in which redistribution through fiscal and monetary measures would be limited to the sphere of social-welfare policy. The end result of the process is that the socialism of today's Western Social Democratic parties means no more than a welfare neocapitalism governed by parliamentary means.

Around the turn of the century, however, rejecting capitalism and proposing any kind of socialism was tantamount to a demand that bureaucratic relations be made universal and total. That explains why one of the greatest admirers of the German Empire's war economy, Lenin, defined the dictatorship of the proletariat as state capitalism plus soviet power, or in other words a totally bureaucratized economy plus a Communist Party with a monopoly of power. Thus the idea of technocratic and bureaucratic power gained ground, either in the form of early rational redistribution with its structure of divided powers, or in the alternative form of socialist ideology; and both drew the intellectuals closer to the ideology of rational redistribution as the prime alternative to liberal capitalism.

The rising bureaucratic intelligentsia's new alliance with finance capital and the great landowners. The third stage of early rational redistribution: Fascist-type redistribution

That was not the only alternative, however. In the more liberal parts of Eastern Europe the professional intelligentsia were stronger and less proletarianized than in Russia, and their outlook was predominantly reformist; all this stood in the way of their being radicalized into an intelligentsia of revolutionary socialists. There such unresolved national problems as the repressed nationalisms of the polyglot Habsburg Empire made it more likely that when the crisis of liberal reformism struck the professional intelligentsia would transfer their allegiance to the national bureaucracies rather than to the illegal revolutionary movement. German nationalism too was so inflamed by the peace treaty that a significant social foundation for national radicalism evolved. At the same time a more limited version of the intellectuals' strategy appeared on the horizon: the rebellion of a state bureaucracy swollen in numbers and power by the growth of the war economy against the compromise of early rational redistribution, in which it had been obliged to settle for the role of a third partner alongside finance capital and the great landed estate. A program for a new type of alliance emerged, demanding hegemony for the interventionist state's bureaucratic intelligentsia, which would induce capitalists and landowners fearful of socialist revolution to accept certain restrictions in their own long-range interests, subordinating their narrower interests to an expanding nationalistic war economy. In this new alliance, which typifies the fascist-type systems that emerged from the crisis of defeat, revolution, and counter-revolution that followed World War I, we can see the third stage in the evolution of early rational redistribution. The fascist bureaucratic intelligentsia did not need to nationalize the factories, for it nationalized the manufacturers themselves. It managed to pump new life into the old redistributive system by monopolizing political power, by constructing a one-party system (or at the very least restricting parliamentary oversight severely in favor of the executive and the police and military), by politicizing both society and economy, and by releasing masses of workers and peasants, organized into nationalistic, militaristic, and even paramilitary movements, into elaborately staged forums of public life.

Once again the bureaucracy was able to redistribute the national income, channeled now through an even larger state budget, in favor of a heavy industry working to fill government orders, supervised by the state and benefited additionally by the decline of small and medium-sized capital, and on behalf of a transportation and communications infrastructure suitable for military as well as civilian use. Keynesian interventionism was unabashedly put to work to build up the industrial potential needed for military expansion. Military and bureaucratic methods of direction and control were extended to every sector of social life, from culture to the labor market. The result was a coordinated *(gleichgeschaltet)* economy; the structures of state and society came to coincide ever more closely.

In preserving the traditional ruling element, however—and, indeed, by centralizing power even more in a conservative defense of their interests—fascism was able to raise only one intellectual group to a position of hegemonic authority: the same noble-military-elitist bureaucracy which had exercised power before. It could not integrate the whole intelligentsia; not enough managerial posts could be created in the non-nationalized sectors of the economy, and so power could not be secured for the intelligentsia as a whole. For that reason fascist-type societies always contain groups of radical intellectuals excluded or forcibly driven from power, and often subject to persecution; they represent a potential political menace to the regime's traditional and authoritarian elements, and may even become organized eventually into an underground resistance. They may come forward as the organic intelligentsia of the working class or bourgeoisie; simply by defending the values of political democracy they may destabilize the whole fascist-bureaucratic redistributive system, which in turn is driven to ever more brutal police measures in order to maintain itself.

We would certainly not contend that this third stage of early rational redistribution represents a social and political model with no long-term viability. There are too many analogous systems in the Third World today, though usually on a lower plane of economic development—all manner of military-bureaucratic, one-party, or quasi-constitutional dictatorships dedicated to economic development—and as a rule all of them have in common the fact that the traditional landowners and the national bourgeoisie enjoy some share of economic power under the political aegis of the civil and military bureaucracy. We would still maintain, however, that these fascist-type systems retain the ambiguous character of early rational redistribution. In them the intelligentsia can never coalesce into a class; on the contrary, those intellectuals who exercise power from within the bureaucracy must constantly contend with opposition movements of other groups of intellectuals who cannot be integrated into the power structure and whose opposition may be radicalized even to the point of guerrilla warfare. Amid the resulting political instability the regime may even be overthrown, leading either to the establishment of a capitalist market economy and a multiparty parliamentary system, or to a rational-redistributive socialism which opens the way to the integration of the entire intelligentsia and to the emergence of the intelligentsia as a class.

THE RADICAL INTELLIGENTSIA'S ROAD TO POWER IN
EASTERN EUROPE

The knights of totality: Notes from underground

It would be the rankest kind of apologetics to stamp victorious movements with the seal of historical necessity, while purporting to show that the others were always condemned to defeat; still, later historical events invariably revise our estimate of the relative importance of the tendencies of earlier epochs, highlighting those which found fulfillment and became determining factors in their own turn, and relegating to secondary importance those which were defeated, or interrupted, or which had no consequences. The weight of the facts alone compels even an immanent analysis to devote more attention to what has come to pass, seeking to explain the reasons for its triumph, than to those foreclosed alternatives which have been rejected in practice. The general diffusion of socialist revolution in Eastern Europe, and the gradual demonstration of its viability there, prove not only that during the second stage of early rational redistribution no real liberal-democratic alternative existed in Eastern Europe, since the intelligentsia could not by itself substitute for a laggard bourgeoisie; it also demonstrates that at the time the only possible alternative to Bolshevik-type rational redistribution was the fascistic hegemony of a nationalistic, military-bureaucratic intelligentsia, or else a more limited kind of central redistribution with the emphasis still on war production but unable, by reason of its compromises with the traditional elements of power, to carry through any radical modernization of society and economy.

As we have said before, it was easier for the prophets of Western technocracy: They could afford to wait for the depersonalization of private property, the expansion of administrative-intellectual functions, the shunting aside of the classical bourgeoisie and the triumph of a planning rationale; meanwhile their power would ripen from one stage to the next, and they would be well paid all the while. But the Eastern European intellectual who could not market his skills in the private economy, and who lacked the pliability which might have raised him to the policy-making levels of a cautiously modernizing state, had no choice but to settle for a minor official's post. No wonder that in his proletarianized situation he thirsted after power, or that he craved it all the more fiercely because his rival, the bourgeois, scarcely made a move to claim it.

The section of the pre-1917 Eastern European intelligentsia which was to prove of fateful importance historically was not outstanding either by its numbers, or its intellectual level, or its creative powers; on the contrary, the life of an underground sect which its members led half-hid them from the eyes of their contemporaries. And yet it was they who prepared the program of class power for the intelligentsia and the revolution of October 1917, which Gramsci rightly called an event of metaphysical importance. This wing of the intelligentsia was made up of radical-revolutionary intellectuals. It was they who tried out for the role which Nietzsche had designated for the elite, that of being the "knights of totality"; and that is why they so quickly made the transition from ethical principles to the categorical imperative of the gun. They were most in evidence in Russia, where the proletarianization of the intelligentsia had gone furthest and where the reformism of a narrow stratum of professionals could not divert the radicalized sons and daughters of shopkeepers, priests, and ruined noblemen, many of whom had been expelled from university, from thoughts of revolution. The radical Russian intellectuals astonished Western observers by their verbal delirium, by the exalted dogmatism with which they debated, whether in intimate discussion groups or in prison, in the wooden shanties of their Siberian exile or the émigré cafés of Western Europe. Dostoyevsky called them the great vagabonds of Russian life, and there was good reason for him to take notice of them. Within the space of a few decades they traversed the road leading from the Narodnik anarchist to the Bolshevik commissar and so, symbolically, to class power for the Eastern European intellectuals.

The first proposal to bypass capitalism: Russian populist (Narodnik) ideology

A singular new type of left radicalism appeared in the middle of the nineteenth century in Eastern Europe, above all in Russia, in the political vacuum created by the collapse of noble liberalism. The failure of the European revolutionary movements of 1848 brought about an ideological crisis: Disenchanted with the course of developments in the West, the Russian critical intelligentsia became anticapitalist, turned away from the Russian and Western European bourgeoisie alike, and ceased to demand for themselves a role akin to that of the Western professionals. They wanted more: Condemning capitalism as a painful and unnecessary detour, they strove now to bypass it altogether. In doing so they put their faith in the historical peculiarities of Russian society's development, in particular the legacy of the village commune, which still had not been dissolved by the advance of private property.

Before 1848 a predominantly enlightened, rationalist, antifeudal intelligentsia had been relatively little affected by Slavophilism, with its religious and feudal-romantic tone, its idealization of pre-Petrine Russia, and its program of idyllic cooperation between pious serfs and paternalistic masters. But under the impact of the events of 1848 Slavophil thought took on new implications. The Slavophils too considered Russia's isolation from the mainstream of capitalist development a special advantage, and now the radical left-wing intellectuals were prepared to agree with them on that score. Thus they no longer called for the dissolution of the village commune and the proletarianization of the Russian peasantry; on the contrary, they appealed to the instinctive socialism of a peasantry still untouched by the spirit of capitalism, lauding the collectivist discipline of the commune as a unique cultural value. By contrast with the early Slavophils they were antifeudal, however, and wished to transfer the landlords' estates to the collective ownership of the village communes. But to achieve that the alliance between Tsarist autocracy and an aristocracy which retained most of its lands even after emancipation had to be overthrown by revolutionary means.

The populist intellectuals saw their mission as the enlightenment and spiritual leadership of the Russian people, around whom they built up a well-nigh mystical cult. At first "leadership" was interpreted as service: The young intellectuals who went out among the people went as teachers, doctors and nurses, handicraftsmen—anything that could meet the tangible needs of the peasantry—and their work of political enlightenment was carried out in that context. But when the peasants proved to be indifferent to their teachings (especially to atheistic propaganda), or even turned the young agitators in to the police (among other reasons because the peasants could hardly distinguish a young intellectual in his costume-wardrobe peasant dress from a country gentleman's son), the conclusion became inescapable that (as Herzen put it) the peasant wanted potatoes and didn't care a damn for a constitution. From that point on the original populism of the Narodniki gave way increasingly to various forms of elitist revolutionism, from Tkachev's pre-Bolshevism to Bakunin's anarchism, and represented most typically perhaps in the figure of the cynical and heroic Nechaev. The young intellectuals who organized Narodnaya Volya (The People's Will) no longer expected that as a result of their educational activities the peasantry, awakened to political consciousness, would rise in rebellion. Instead they took upon themselves the planning of an organized, conspiratorial uprising. The succession of terrorist acts perpetrated by the nihilists were meant as signals to the masses, sparks to touch off the powder-keg of popular discontent. But when bombings and assassination attempts made as little impact on the masses as propaganda booklets distributed among the peasants, it became clear that the revolutionary intelligentsia would have to organize itself into a strictly centralized vanguard. Such a conspiratorial elite, they hoped, might by concentrating its assault be able to seize power and, placing itself at the head of the state apparatus, establish a revolutionary dictatorship in the name of the people, which would then transform all society.

Narodnik ideology was never sufficiently worked out to uncover the complex conflicts of interest in actual society, and for lack of any economic theory it could not offer an economic program. As time went on it became more and more problematic in view of the ongoing development of capitalism in Russia; in a new situation its abstract demand for a seizure of power could not be filled with any rational content. Nor could its ideology indicate with whom the vanguard of revolutionary intellectuals might form alliances and whom it had to treat as enemies, or what they should do with power if it should ever fall into their laps. This abstract, mystical, voluntaristic revolutionism had to come into contact with Marxism before it could acquire real social relevance or meet the theoretical needs of the intelligentsia in the scientific atmosphere of a new age.

Russian Marxism's counterproposal: Indirect acceptance of capitalism in the interest of the empirical working class

Georgi Plekhanov's personal odyssey was typical of the evolution of the Russian revolutionary intelligentsia. Originally a member of the terrorist People's Will, he soon came to see the futility of its tactics; disillusioned with its brand of elitist thinking, he openly questioned the sense of seizing power for its own sake. Marxism found a ready soil because it offered substantive guidance on such matters as: What were the real social forces and interests which by their very nature transcended the existing order? And what should the revolutionaries do with power once it was within their grasp? In a series of acerbic debates with the populists and anarchists Plekhanov denied that the village commune had any progressive merits and declared that the development of capitalism was inevitable in Russia, and with it the conversion of the bulk of the peasantry into wageworkers. Only the evolution of a large, organized, and educated proletariat could provide a real social basis for any kind of socialist strategy. From that it followed that in Russia socialist revolution

was a long-term prospect, and had to be preceded by a bourgeois-democratic revolution which would create the institutional
framework within which the modernization of Russian society
could be carried through. The proletariat, meanwhile, trained
in struggle within a legal, organized labor movement and impregnated with the ideas of Marxism, would acquire the ability
to carry out the socialist revolution, which Plekhanov envisaged
as a movement of the masses rather than of an intellectual elite.
To that extent Plekhanov, and Eastern European social-democracy in general, were the heirs of earlier Western liberalism (as
against the Narodniki), except that they did not see capitalist
development as an end in itself but merely as the necessary
transitional stage to socialism. Plekhanov set the radical Russian
intelligentsia two concrete tasks: To study the Marxist theory of
scientific socialism and apply it theoretically to Russian conditions, and to take up the empirical interests of the still small
and backward Russian working class by building a democrati-
cally organized mass workers' party. Illusory notions of an immediate seizure of power were to be abandoned. Plekhanov
dismissed anarchism, terrorism, and conspiracy with contempt,
flatly declaring Bakunin a throwback to Stenka Razin, the eighteenth-century Cossack rebel leader.

Plekhanov's program had two inherent weaknesses, however.
Its scientific determinism and economism postponed the prospect
of socialist revolution into an indefinite future, which would
have imposed an intolerable period of waiting on an intelligentsia which had grown accustomed to a more radical role
during the heyday of anarchism and nihilism, and which was
attracted to Marxism rather because of its revolutionary mes-
sianism. The latter found expression in the symbolic question
which Vera Zasulich, herself a one-time terrorist, addressed to
Marx himself in a letter: Should the Russian revolutionaries
dismantle their bombs and go out to build factories instead? A
difficult question, to which Marx himself could give only an
uncertain and evasive answer.

In fact the radical Russian intellectual had psychologically
outgrown the posture of the bourgeois social scientist which made
so many of the Western European labor movement's Marxist
intellectuals virtually indistinguishable from other professionals.

Moreover, there was an objective basis for their radicalism in the structural conflict common to agrarian societies which had developed on the Prussian model—the land question. The most elementary demand of a largely impoverished peasantry emancipated without land and able to enter industry in only limited numbers was for ownership of the land they already cultivated, even if that meant taking it away from the landlords by force. The Russian socialists who joined the Second International took over from the Western European social-democratic parties a mistrust of the peasant which was rooted in the fact that in the West the peasantry was developing into a class of small farmers and expanding the size and technical equipment of their holdings within the context of commodity production; and so, as independent small producers, they were more interested in democratizing capitalism than in abolishing it, and did not join the socialist labor movement in any great numbers. By contrast, the Russian peasantry was made into a potential revolutionary force by the fact that its most basic demand, for distribution of land, could not be achieved by reformist means within the power structure of early rational redistribution. Whenever the Russian radical intelligentsia turned to the unsolved land question it saw there a justification for its revolutionary impatience. The time was ripe for the Russian radical intelligentsia to work out a Marxism which would serve its revolutionary intransigence, a Marxism which would furnish a scientific analysis of the social structure and at the same time yield the conclusion that in Russia conditions were ripe for a democratic revolution which might lead directly into socialist revolution. A synthesis of Plekhanov and Tkachev was needed, and it was Lenin who with his Bolshevism offered that synthesis.

The Bolshevik program relieves the intellectuals of the need to represent the working class, and shows the most direct road to power

The first step on the road to Bolshevism was the recognition that the radical intellectuals need not, and indeed could not, content themselves with representing the interests of the working class exclusively. In Russia capitalism was enjoying boom times at the turn of the century; it seemed inconceivable that in the foreseeable future the internal contradictions of Russian capitalism would issue in proletarian revolution, and so there appeared to be little chance that the radical intelligentsia could climb to power on the shoulders of the working class. Still, it would have been a mistake for it to abandon its preparations to seize power altogether, especially as Russian society was in a state of political crisis. The triple alliance of bureaucratic state, great landed property, and finance capital was no longer capable of containing mounting social conflicts. To deal with them a fundamental transformation would have been required in the system of early rational redistribution. It was quite conceivable that the political and governmental structure of early rational redistribution might collapse even without proletarian revolution, and if it did the moment would be at hand when a well-prepared and well-organized minority might seize political power. Thus for Lenin the function of the workers' party was not to represent workers' interests, but to prepare for the seizure of power and to serve as the organizational prototype of a new form of state power.

That is why the question of the party's organization became a matter of such exceptional importance for Lenin. It was no accident that the birth of Bolshevism was connected with a dispute over so apparently trivial an issue as: Was it enough, to be a party member, to pay one's dues and accept the party's program, or must one work full-time as well in one of the party's organizations? And yet the importance of this debate can hardly be overemphasized, because in winning acceptance of the Bolshevik principle of party organization from one section of Russian social-democracy Lenin effectively sacrificed all prospects of making the Bolshevik faction into a mass party of the working class, by almost automatically excluding from membership the masses of workers who could not carry out regular party work in an organization driven underground because of its declared intention of seizing power forcibly, since to do so meant embracing the life of a professional revolutionary. The Bolshevik party was a vanguard of militants, well-schooled theoretically, well-disciplined, voluntarily subordinating themselves to a hierarchical chain of command; sooner or later they had to decide to make political work their exclusive calling in life, and as such they were either intellectuals to begin with or became intellectuals in the course of their rise through the party hierarchy. It was a school which prepared its graduates to fill the leading positions in a new kind of government, not so much by reason of their technical ability as because of their ideological education and their unswerving obedience to the Central Committee.

In order to take power the Bolshevik party did not need a parliamentary majority, only a political vacuum of the kind which followed the collapse of Tsarism, and enough reliable party members to fill the leading positions in the state apparatus which they had overthrown and would now set about rebuilding. They had no trouble finding that many followers in the political turmoil that ensued after the February revolution. The Bolshevik party represented not a shadow .government but a shadow state which after the coup that overthrew the Provisional Government had only to be lifted into the place which the Tsarist autocracy had occupied before.

Bolshevism enabled the intellectuals to rid themselves of the ideological ballast which they had been obliged to carry as representatives of the working class. For in treating the proletarian state as the *sine qua non* of socialism the Bolsheviks made an end of socialism as a political, economic, and social problem, simplifying it to a mere matter of organizing state and economy. The Bolshevik intellectuals did not ask in what sort of institutional order the associated producers would find maximum political and economic freedom, but only: How can state and economy be organized so that every decision-making position will be monopolized by the party's trained cadres, and in such a way that those power positions cannot be limited in scope by other kinds of legitimations (be it tradition, capital ownership, or political representation)?

The historical originality of Bolshevism lies in the fact that it substituted for the interests of the real working class the historic mission of the working class—the achievement of the dictatorship of the proletariat, or more precisely the dictatorship of a centralized Bolshevik party leadership. It could not have attained that objective by relying on the real working class alone, however. For that reason it had to proclaim, during the revolutionary years, an alliance of workers and peasants, promising immediate distribution of the soil in order to take advantage of the peasantry's land-hunger, and leading them to believe that free rein would be given to small-scale commodity production in agriculture. Indeed, from the very outset this singular alliance contained within itself the possibility that, once power was consolidated, the Bolsheviks would make themselves independent of the historically given interests of these two classes of toilers and would subject them to the interests of a new type of state power. Following the consolidation of power they were not long in taking the land away from its cultivators again, converting the peasants themselves from independent small producers to kolkhoz workers, their labor at the disposition of the state; while the soviets, institutions of self-management set up by the workers before the Bolsheviks came to power, were absorbed into the state apparatus and, having become transmission belts for party directives, soon ceased to exercise working-class control over a bureaucratic executive power.

Bolshevism, then, offered the intellectuals a program for freeing themselves of the duty of representing particular interests once power had been secured, and it used particular interests simply as a means of acquiring power. With the expropriation of the expropriators—that is, with the transfer of the right to dispose over the surplus product from landlords and capitalists to intellectuals in power, or to worker cadres whose political positions and functions made intellectuals of them—and with the destruction of the immediate producers' organs of management and control, the Bolsheviks traced the outlines of a new rational-redistributive system and, within it, indicated the position of the teleological redistributors, called to represent the interests of all society expertly and professionally.

IV

---

*The Evolution of the Intelligentsia
into a Class in the Socialist Societies
of Eastern Europe*

10

Power, Its Nature and Institutions under Rational Redistribution

THE CHARACTERISTICS OF REDISTRIBUTIVE POWER

The social structure of early socialism is organized in keeping with the principle of rational redistribution. In line with the rational principle on which its economy is based, we regard this as a class structure, and indeed a dichotomous one. At one pole is an evolving class of intellectuals who occupy the position of redistributors, at the other a working class which produces the social surplus but has no right of disposition over it. This dichotomous model of a class structure is not sufficient for purposes of classifying everyone in the society (just as the dichotomy of capitalist and proletarian is not in itself sufficient for purposes of assigning a status to every single person in capitalist society); an ever larger fraction of the population must be assigned to the intermediate strata.

We consider as belonging to the middle strata those who neither possess redistributive power nor engage in direct productive labor themselves; those who occupy low-level supervisory positions in which they communicate redistributive decisions to the workers but which carry no orienting or cross-contextual functions and so do not involve intellectual knowledge; and those who partake of society's goods on the basis of some other legitimating principle, such as the few remaining small owners (who even still employ wageworkers occasionally), small craftsmen and shopkeepers, and private peasants. Despite their apparent heterogeneity the middle strata have in common their "feudal" character: They are the vassals of the intellectual class. Compared to the working class they all enjoy some privileges, be it a larger income, a taste of executive authority, or simply exemption from fatiguing physical labor. Then there are those intellectual dropouts and ambitious workers who land in the middle strata on their own initiative—the economist who throws up his job and opens a tobacconist's shop, the engineer who sets up an auto repair shop, the worker who leaves the plant to grow vegetables on a rented plot and sells his produce at the market. But they are exceptions. For the most part middle-stratum status is a reward given by the intelligentsia (whether in the form of a job, a craftsman's permit, or what have you), in recognition of their loyalty, to those whom it wishes to elevate above the working class but is unwilling or unable to raise to intellectual status. The aging Olympic champion who for lack of higher education cannot attain to an intellectual position may receive a license to run a restaurant. A worker who speaks up often at production conferences (without ever contradicting the management's point of view), who joins the "workers' guard" or volunteers to become an informer, or signs up for ideological training courses, can fairly easily become a supervisor or inspector, or even a lower-level police investigator. An unpaid party secretary in a small village, if he needs a job, may be recommended to take over the management of a small brewery nearby. Thus most members of the middle strata get there only because they enjoy the confidence of someone in power. The most typical representatives of this status can be seen in the train of secretaries, personal aides, and chauffeurs, often better versed in their way in the workings of an operation than the assigned intellectual personnel itself, whom a rising leader carries along with him and whom his successor will quickly replace if he falls from power; if they forfeit the confidence of their boss they can be dismissed at any time because they owe their jobs to their reliability, not to any special technical knowledge. It follows from this vassal status that the bulk of those who belong to the middle strata are oriented toward the intellectual class, share its ethos, values, and interests, snobbishly and pedantically ape the intelligentsia's way of life, and have no higher aspiration than to get

their children admitted into the intellectual class—as illustrated
by the common observation that the children of the middle
strata are the ones who study hardest in secondary school. Another factor in the growth of the middle strata is the fact that
the ruling elite (and in a way the intellectual class in general)
see the middle strata as their social base and use them as a kind
of buffer between themselves and the working class. Or it may
use them to isolate and control marginal groups of intellectuals,
through them reminding the latter of the norms of conformity.
It is the secretaries who tell the marginal intellectuals to shave
off their beards, put on a tie, get to the office on time, and be
sure to show up at nonobligatory meetings; they are the gentle
guardians of the conformist spirit of the bureaucracy

In modern redistributive systems it is the rationality of the
redistributors' activity which legitimates their authority. The
power of the social group which exercises a monopoly over
the redistributive process has a class character; it is the power
of the intellectual class. We say "intellectual class" even though
the functions of central redistribution in the strict sense are carried out not by the intelligentsia as a whole but by a narrower
segment of it—the state and party bureaucracy, which we shall
call the ruling or governing elite, since the criteria for admission
to it are those of a status-group rather than a class.

Modern redistribution replaces the decisions of the market
with official administrative decisions which, in the aggregate,
call into being a bureaucratic organization that tends to become
highly centralized and monolithic, and to encompass the whole
of society. Important political and economic decisions are made
on the upper levels of the elite bureaucracy, and these upper-
level positions must be occupied by intellectual-officials. Not
every intellectual takes part in making important redistributive
decisions, but every major decision is made by the intelligentsia
of office.

It is a further important characteristic of rational-redistributive
society that it does away with the separation of economic, political, and cultural power, a division of powers which is taken for
granted, almost like a constitutional principle, in societies with
market economies. Thus the powers of the redistributors are far
more than just economic powers. Redistribution creates a whole

model of civilization, in which three partners of equal importance participate: The stratum of economists and technocrats,
which actually carries out the work of central redistribution; the
administrative and political bureaucracy, which guarantees the
undisturbed functioning of the redistributive process, by police
measures if necessary; and finally the ideological, scientific, and
artistic intelligentsia, which produces, perpetuates, and dissemi-
nates the culture and ethos of rational redistribution. The ideologue, the policeman, and the technocrat are mutually dependent
on one another and are impregnated with one another's logic.
The political policeman is also an ideologue and on occasion
may even lay claim to the title of an expert on the economy.
The manager not only expects his subordinates to perform their
assigned tasks; he also participates in their political education
and may at times use police methods to check on their reliability.
The same may be said of the ideologues, those who formulate
the guidelines of cultural policy, right down to the level of the
elementary-school principal: They have to translate the general
guidelines of economic policy into practical cultural work, or
in other cases, must call to the attention of the police any individuals or works which deviate from the prevailing ethos. In
sum, then, the intelligentsia is the class par excellence of a social
order based on technical expertise.

Thus the emergence of the intelligentsia as a class is synonymous with the intellectuals' acceptance of the logic of redistribution, strictly or broadly defined. We believe it is justified to speak
of the possibility, in rational-redistributive systems, of a class
taking form around the position of the teleological redistributors.
The class position of the redistributors as it is evolving under
rational redistribution differs qualitatively, however, from the
position of the expert manager in market economies. The latter
may appear to have the same decision-making powers as the
redistributor, but his structural position is fundamentally different. He may decide upon the redistribution of some portion
of the surplus product (as defined by the market), but in principle and to some extent in practice he is under the political
control of the owners wherever the various spheres of power are
still separated. Thus a class of intellectuals does not form around
the technocratic intelligentsia of market economies.

THE CHARACTERISTICS OF THE RATIONAL-REDISTRIBUTIVE
BUREAUCRACY

The development of the intellectual class under early socialism can only be understood if we examine the special characteristics of rational redistribution's bureaucratic structure, for the
transformation of the bureaucratic structure according to the
ethos of rational redistribution is perhaps the chief means toward the formation of the intelligentsia into a class.

The bureaucracies of market and rational-redistributive systems have in common the fact that, in both cases, technical
knowledge legitimates bureaucratic power. But bureaucracies
in market economies are always subject in principle to the
separation of power spheres and to the distinction between
policy-making and executive functions. The management and
trade-union structures of a large modern factory are both bureaucratized, but the two bureaucratic hierarchies do not coalesce
into a single common hierarchy; the two bureaucratic structures
pursue different goals, and their relationship to each other is
characterized by transactive dealings. In both, moreover, an independent political control mechanism can be identified. The
board of directors oversees management on behalf of the stock-
holders and sets policy in its broad outlines. Union members
exercise a comparable sort of influence and oversight over their
trade unions. It was a fundamental tenet of Weber's theory of
bureaucracy that policy making is in principle distinct from the
executive functions, strictly speaking, of bureaucracies. Today,
of course, one has to ask whether in modern capitalist societies
it is not possible to observe the interpenetration of bureaucratic
structures, or that other portentous phenomenon, the usurpation
of policy-making functions by the bureaucracy. But in any event
these phenomena, when they appear, are interpreted in market
economies as distortions of bureaucracy's proper function, as an
anomalous "bureaucratism."

The interweaving of bureaucratic structures

It is an inherent property of rational redistribution, on the
other hand, that goal-setting activity turns into technical activity;

there is no longer any distinction between the political and economic spheres (or any division of power spheres at all), no dualism of policy making and execution, no pluralism of ends. Under rational redistribution a variety of bureaucracies organized on functional lines interpenetrate one another until they come to form a single unified hierarchy. The various bureaucracies are woven together by a fundamental identity of goals and arranged into a hierarchy; the higher organs and officials, those vested with decision-making powers, are always the ones which by reason of their functions have the most long-range perspective and must weigh alternatives from the standpoint of the whole society. Under rational redistribution it is precisely the interweaving of the bureaucracies which is deemed natural, while independence on the part of bureaucratic organs is condemned as an anomaly that interferes with the pursuit of unitary goals. These conjoined bureaucratic structures raise the intellectual above his narrow and partial technical orientation, converting him into a teleological agent.

Thus a unique Eastern European socialist bureaucracy is developing, characterized by both vertical and horizontal continuity and by a hierarchical structure rising to a single apex. Everyone, from the First Secretary of the party to the engineer employed in the planning office, is an officer in the service of the state. The Party Secretary is paid to represent the state as a whole, the engineer the planning office alone; but in the last analysis both represent the whole state-society (for state and society are one). Everyone, wherever he works, knows on which level of the state-society he is situated. The manager of a small enterprise ranks with a department head in a large enterprise, who in turn ranks with a section chief in a ministry. It is possible to know with precision whether a transfer between two organizations, enterprises, or institutes means a promotion, a demotion, or a case of someone's being "kicked upstairs." There is no bureaucratic organization which does not fit into the state apparatus, none which lacks a superior organ to lend legitimacy to its operations.

Under these conditions there appears the circulation of the bureaucratic elite, an important indication that the intelligentsia is being formed into a class. For those who acquire a university degree a multiplicity of positions opens, including some whose knowledge-requirements do not correspond to the curriculum of the degree-granting university; for the diploma is rather a warrant that its holder is capable of mastering the knowledge pertaining to a given post, regardless of his specific training. Every degree-holder who observes certain rules of conduct carries a marshal's baton in his pack. The diploma is a kind of ticket of admission to the realm of opportunity, which opens before the graduate like a gambling casino. It does not in itself guarantee him success against the other players; every future rise and fall depends on how he minds his step in the gaming room, but without it he cannot even set foot there to try his chances of success and failure.

What makes all this possible is the fact that intellectual knowledge is not interpreted narrowly, as technical skill; the teleological element in it is decisive, and that is why it is so easily convertible. As a result this knowledge is almost as neutral as capital itself; just as owners have no difficulty transferring capital from one sector of the economy to another, so too in the bureaucracy of rational redistribution the intellectual can easily change his position: His knowledge serves as a kind of bureaucratic medium of exchange. Once he has demonstrated that he is sufficiently conversant with intellectual knowledge (that is, with the ethos of redistribution), and has perhaps acquired some experience in its application, then it is assumed that he can easily acquire the specialized knowledge needed to carry out any new duties that may be entrusted to him. That is the reason why the teaching of the ideology of scientific socialism occupies such a prominent place in the education of the intellectuals. Indeed, this shift in emphasis in the makeup of intellectual knowledge has been carried to such a bizarre extreme that the pure ideology offered by the higher party schools, quite devoid of any substantive content, has become the most negotiable kind of intellectual knowledge—so much so that diplomas acquired there entitle their holders to assume any kind of leadership position. From one day to the next a general can become a publishing executive, a political policeman an aesthetician or, vice versa, a newspaperman a colonel, and a bishop Foreign Minister or the chief political commentator of the state radio network.

*The apex of the bureaucracy represents the
collective interest*

The bureaucratic structure of rational redistribution must guarantee that conflicts do not arise among the various organs or, if they do, that they will be brought before a higher authority empowered to sit in judgment and capable of issuing directives that will settle the conflict. Even economic organs generally have no way and no right of their own to contract with one another for exchanges based on mutual advantage or to compete economically with one another; their powers derive exclusively from higher authority. Consensus must be reached between branches of industry, too; "chauvinism" must be avoided at branch level as well as at enterprise level. Capital does not go, and on principle cannot go, where it will earn a return most quickly and most efficiently; it goes and must go wherever the teleological redistributors allocate it.

The redistributive system is a many-storied edifice, with a hierarchical structure built on the strict lines of a military chain of command. An official entrusted with the functions of one component of this system will carry out his duties correctly, "politically," if he subordinates his decisions to the interest of the overall redistributive process, the "interests of the people's economy." This system of interests is not always incorporated in concrete directives, but a good administrator knows even without them "what the line is" and where the overall redistributive process is tending at any time, and voluntarily subordinates the interests of his own organization to the higher interests of the whole, which he can discern from reading between the lines of successive party resolutions. The ideal administrator, then, is one who senses almost intuitively the governing principles of redistribution, and who acts in accordance with them. Such, for example, is the chairman of a town council who does not even ask for a larger capital budget because he knows that his town is not one of those singled out for development in the national plan, and so its inhabitants are not even due an average level of municipal services.

The total redistributive process is, then, an entity abstracted from practice, from an enormous number of concrete, hierarchically ordered decisions, unsurveyable as a whole. As a result lower-ranking decision-makers, in order to justify their decisions, must operate with an ever more vaguely defined concept of "the interests of the people's economy," that unapprehensible deity of socialist economy which daily becomes less teleological than theological.

The redistributor cannot be content with the role of expert planner and administrator. He must assume an ideological role as well, for he represents the interests of the whole community vis-à-vis his subordinates, the bearers of particular interests, and he must constantly appeal directly to higher interests and considerations. He must act like a kind of intellectual augur, who knows something that others cannot know, and the more ill-defined the higher interests to which he appeals the more often he must draw on his store of emotional and ideological arguments, hinting occasionally at the confidential disclosures which have come down to him from higher powers. The technical expert too must constantly reconcile technical and economic parameters with ideological considerations, becoming thereby not just an administrative official but a "professional revolutionary," which in his case means simply that he will decide unhesitatingly in favor of the overall interests of redistribution to the detriment of professional or technical demands. Having thus won the confidence of his superiors for faithfully reflecting their wishes, he can look down with an almost feudal hauteur on those of his colleagues who in their work are still guided primarily by technical considerations.

Conflicts still arise between individual bureaucracies

Although particular interests are theoretically impossible in the single, pyramidal bureaucracy of rational redistribution—at most we can speak of the interests of different levels—still individual organs on the same level of the hierarchy have their own interests, and agreement between them does not come about of its own accord; it has to be created. Any bureaucratic organization inevitably develops its own special interest, which leads to demands for expansion and for increases in its powers and range of jurisdiction. The organization's special interests coincide with the personal interests of its members: The power and income of the office-holders depend on what positions they occupy in the organization. They will receive a larger salary only if they get better jobs, and in order for them to do that the whole organization must grow in size. In this respect the head of the organization has a community of interests with his employees. Their numbers must be increased, they must be promoted from time to time, thus incidentally increasing their chief's power, his range of influence, and his income. But of course other institutions on the same level stand in the way of the growth of any one organization. In the economic sector, for example, everyone competes for a larger share of the social capital to be redistributed. Even a leadership with a firm and disciplined ideological commitment to rational redistribution cannot free itself altogether from the influence of these organizational special interests. In market economies, where the corporate bureaucracies are independent of one another and are not arranged in any hierarchical order, each one of them can grow only so far as efficiency permits; but under rational redistribution there are in principle no limits to the tendency of the bureaucratic apparatus to expand. Competition is the only thing that sets temporary bounds to these tendencies—more precisely, the constant effort of higher organs representing higher interests to regulate organizational competition and to settle conflicts by compromise.

This clash of bureaucratic interests may come into conflict with the basic interests of the redistributive system, even though it follows from the logic of redistribution. The fundamental principle of rational redistribution is the maximization of the power to redistribute. A redistributive decision is rational if its result is a maximal increase in the size of the surplus product appropriated for redistribution.

On the empirical level that means that redistribution is budget-centered. Its rationality is measured by the rate of growth of the state budget, for that figure reflects the proportion of the national income which enters into the budget and so becomes available for redistribution. The principle of maximizing the amount of surplus product which flows into the redistributive process is altogether different from the principle of profit maximization. Given a choice of two productive investments which promise an identical return, the redistributive system will in all probability prefer one that expands the investment-goods market over one that expands the consumer market. This preference will have further implications for the budget, demanding more investment subsidies later on; but that consequence is not at all unwelcome to the redistributors, for expansion of the consumer market increases the personal income of the population in the first instance, while enlarging the investment-goods market first and foremost increases the budget's share of national income.

The same tendency is evident with respect to investments in the economic infrastructure. Here again it is the interest of the redistributor to promote infrastructural investments financed through the state budget irrespective of the actual benefits to be derived from the proposed improvements. Thus if it takes X billion to build N number of cooperative apartments when the X billion is saved from their wages by the prospective tenants, while only N-minus-V number of flats will be built if they are financed by the state, the redistributors will prefer the second alternative so long as V does not represent a politically intolerable number of dwelling units lost.

The conflicts of interest which we described a little earlier are not really in contradiction with this overall rationality. For what in fact happens is that each individual redistributor seeks to maximize his own power to redistribute in the belief that the overall effectiveness of the redistributive system will grow the more his own power grows. But since the state budget is finite, as is the patience of the population at the share of the value they produce which is withheld from them, restricting their personal consumption, the tendencies we have been discussing may theoretically lead, in the last analysis, to political or economic crisis.

Political crisis may erupt in popular demonstrations, or even in armed uprisings of the working class, whose personal consumption is restricted the most. Economic crisis would most likely take the form of an overheated, inflationary investment-goods market, which with the exhaustion of credit sources would lead to a critical increase in the number of uncompleted investment projects. Just as, in capitalist societies, the interests of capital as a whole demand that the state place certain restrictions on the efforts of individual concerns to maximize their profits, so too under rational redistribution the individual redistributors must be restrained in the interest of the survival and relative stability of the total system of redistribution. If in capitalist economies a technocratic state bureaucracy exercises oversight over the owners of capital, under rational redistribution a political bureaucracy exercises control over technocratic redistributors who strive to maximize their own power.

THE ROLE AND STRUCTURE OF THE PARTY: THE MASTER
CONTROL OVER THE COMPONENT BUREAUCRACIES

Thus a ruling elite emerges from the intellectual class to become the ultimate repository of the redistributive ethos and, as such, to give final sanction to all redistributive decisions. The instrument of this ruling elite is the party. The members of the elite occupy the key positions in the party and represent the policies of the party, as formulated by the ruling elite, in a variety of national organizations.

Bourgeois parties and particular interests in society

In capitalist society the spheres of economics and politics are, in principle, separate, and the principle has some actual validity even under modern state-monopoly capitalism. Despite the state's growing propensity to intervene, the economic sphere still retains a certain autonomy of its own. Similarly, the machinery of political power has a relative freedom of movement independent of the operation of the economy. No single, unequivocal hierarchy of social interest can develop under these conditions, and so separate arenas are needed to accommodate the clash of particular interests. The market provides an economic mechanism for the conflict of interests, while the competition of parties offers a political one.

Bourgeois parties never really act as the representatives of society as a whole; even in their professed ideologies they only go so far as to enunciate certain concrete particular interests in society in more or less universal terms. The same party cannot argue simultaneously for nationalization and free enterprise, and so long as the growth of the state sector versus the growth of the private sector is a genuine alternative in society, with distinct social groups lining up behind one or the other objective, the most a party can do is to create a consensus (or rather a compromise) in a bloc of particular interests. Yet by doing that it only exacerbates the conflict with other interests which cannot be included in the compromise.

Bourgeois parties can legitimize their power only by the number of votes they can muster. They do not urge the acceptance of their political goals by contending that some ideology, even a "scientific" ideology, demonstrates that those goals alone are correct. They are content with the persuasive power which the votes cast for them confer. Indeed, their goals may become relativized to a point where small parties which at times hold the balance of power, like the Liberal parties of England and Germany, can come forward as representatives of interests that cannot hope to acquire an electoral majority. They strive only to deprive the major parties of an absolute majority and so, by entering into coalition with one of them, to win a more effective voice for the interest they represent through compromises in the formation of a government.

Right down to the present day bourgeois parties have been vote-getting machines, and parliaments are the obvious institutional premise and arena for their functioning in bourgeois democracies. This operating principle of capitalist society's political system is so decisive and the mechanism of parliamentary elections itself works with such compelling force that even parties with an antiparliamentary ideology, which seek to expose electoral freedoms as a fig leaf for capitalist rule—like the socialist parties once and the communist parties today—eventually develop into great vote-getting machines themselves. That in turn has necessarily entailed a reformulation of their strategic goals. Those goals themselves have become relative: Revolutionary transformation of every institution of society has given way to a program of structural reforms, a program which, recognizing the plurality of interests and goals in society, has in principle accepted a pluralistic political system. Strategic goals derived from the ideology of scientific socialism have been replaced by a tactic of seeking compromise between inherently conflicting interests. The Communist parties can only hope to achieve parliamentary successes if they give up representing exclusively the broad social goals of the most conscious vanguard of the working class (a vanguard composed not so much of actual workers as of radical intellectuals), and strive instead to broaden their mass base, embracing the historically given, pragmatic interests of the empirical working class (a tactic which would have been dismissed before as petty and diversionary in the light of history). Indeed, they have expanded the range of their constituency to take in the interests of other groups, such as peasants, small businessmen and shopkeepers, and national and religious minorities; alliances with them (which would once have been rejected as unprincipled and opportunistic) are dictated purely by electoral tactics, not by any coherent confluence of interests. In the arena of bourgeois democracy the political contestants have grudgingly had to accept one another's existence. The Communist parties too have been forced to abandon the temple and descend into the profane marketplace of votes; they know they will go further if, rather than espousing the cause of History (that tribunal to which Lenin in his polemics so often appealed) they embrace instead the interests of pensioners and dairy farmers, or of those who want to be able to get a divorce.

In capitalist societies the economic and governmental bureaucracies are supposed to form separate hierarchical structures, but the power aspirations of the techno-bureaucracy lead to a constant interweaving of the two, until the professional administrative apparatus, originally vested with purely executive authority, begins to appropriate policy-making functions as well. Max Weber, studying the state bureaucracies of the turn of the century, could still point only to the German Empire as an example of an administrative apparatus independent of the legislature; by contrast he cited the United States, where the executive machinery was subordinated to the two houses of Congress and where, moreover, after every presidential election, thousands of followers of the new President were given government jobs, replacing the previous President's men, as if to assure through changes in personnel that the executive machinery would be responsive to the interests which had triumphed at the polls, and to avoid the possibility that the bureaucracy, appealing to its professional knowledge, might put its own objectives above those legitimized by a majority of the voters. Seven decades later the executive branch was making war and deciding all important foreign-policy questions without asking Congressional approval, and it appeared likely that the executive would become completely dominant in domestic matters as well. So sharp had the conflict between the legislative and executive branches become that Congress decided on the drastic step of starting impeachment proceedings against the head of the administration, the President. Impeachment was a symbolic gesture, expressive of the attachment of democratic societies to the principle of separation of powers and to the notion that political decisions should be made by a legislature separate and distinct from the executive bureaucracy, and representing a plurality of social interests as expressed in the contest of parties. It is a distinctive feature of bourgeois democracy that it constantly resists the efforts of its bureaucracies to merge into a single pyramid and subordinate everything to a single bureaucratically defined value-system, thus appropriating the right to make political decisions and with it the authority to represent the interest of society as a whole. A bourgeois democracy with a one-party system would be a contradiction in terms, for the parties act like a wedge to keep apart the various technical and professional bureaucracies, which constantly tend to coalesce and to acquire collectively a decisive policy-making position.

The ruling Communist Party as the exponent of the collective interest

When parties are replaced by the Party a change takes place so profound as to make ridiculous even the etymological suggestion that something which by its very conception represents the whole could be associated with only a "part" of anything. In rational-redistributive societies the spheres of politics and economics, state and society, policy making and execution are interconnected on principle. When individual bureaucracies are arrayed into a single hierarchy, any conflicts that appear among them are labeled "bureaucratism," a functional anomaly; at that point the party steps in as arbiter among feuding ministries and branches of industry, trade unions and local administrative bodies, each of which thinks its interests just as important as any other and, under the influence of the redistributive ethos, depicts them as identical with the collective interests of the whole society. The party is the repository of the unity of society; as the embodiment of society's teleology it acts as supreme judge in the profane squabbles of the various bureaucratic organs.

Technocracy, by presenting value-free alternatives and by striving to measure rather than evaluate possible outcomes, indirectly and involuntarily relativizes values. In the principle of efficiency technocracies have discovered a neutral yardstick stripped of all other values, and hence useless in making value-judgments between competing technical rationalities, since every technical rationale appeals to some kind of efficiency (to whatever serves its own interests, in fact). For that reason the technocratic mentality is unable to arrange competing interests into any kind of hierarchy and must willy-nilly fall into a system of transactive conflicts and pragmatic compromises. Techno-bureaucracies tend to replace the principle of hierarchical organization with one of parallel organization, without being aware that in so doing they conjure up the danger of a divorce between politics and economics and of the development of a separate and pluralist political system. The technocracy urges economic reforms without noticing that values plucked from the sky of teleology and reduced to a neutral common denominator would, if implemented, bring social and political reform after them as the next logical step.

The technocratic mentality does not prefer any particular activities or products over any others, and so it does not consider industry more valuable or more socialist than agriculture. Thus if it does not see the necessity of transferring capital from agriculture to industry, in accordance with the ideologically formulated "basic economic laws" of socialism, it must accept as legitimate a situation in which all the interests connected with the development of agriculture will find formulation and will begin to make alliances with one another, creating within the various bureaucracies an interconnected agricultural lobby which will speak in relative unison on investment and pricing policy, foreign and domestic trade, engineering, transportation, labor and land-use policy, even cultural and social policy. This lobby will function as a latent agrarian party, demanding, sooner or later, that agriculture receive a share of foreign-exchange earnings proportional to its share of exports, that agricultural prices be raised and industrial prices lowered to world-market level, that the development of the best growing areas not be held back for ideological reasons, that the productive functions and organizational forms of agricultural units not be restricted through administrative measures, that no restrictions be placed on family farms, that no upper limit be set on wages payable in agriculture (thus bureaucratically hobbling agricultural producers in the competition for labor), that all workers in agriculture receive the same pension and health-insurance benefits, and so on.

But if (for example) the handicaps imposed on agriculture by ideology were removed, then the whole logic of a politicized, value-laden hierarchy of interests would melt away; redistributive decisions based on the ideology of scientific socialism would lose all objective meaning and would give way to a very concrete struggle of inherent interests, which in turn would demand a separate and, in fact, a pluralistic political mechanism. Technocracy by its very functions is not perceptive enough to recognize what political dangers accompany its technical rationality. By itself it cannot see when efforts to maximize redistributive authority and make it more efficient come into conflict with the ethos of rational redistribution.

That is why the party is essential, a political organization distinct from the individual bureaucracies yet interlacing with all of them. The party stands guard over socialism's highest achievement, the political coordination of the economy and the consequent integration of individual bureaucracies. It makes certain that economic and technical decisions will always be primarily political decisions and that these politicized decisions will always be correlated with a unitary socialist ideology, even if that can only be done by pragmatically reinterpreting the ideology from time to time; the leaders' speeches provide a running exegesis of the classic Marxist texts which changes constantly yet is the only valid and authoritative one at any given time. The Party is above the parts, the Party is above parties; it is not one factor in the political mechanism, it *is* the political mechanism. In countries building socialism the party, according to its own program and as defined in the constitution, is the leading force in society, the bearer of its ideological and political unity, the vanguard of the most politically conscious of the working people, and the motive force of economic development, pointing the way to the construction of socialism. That is why it cannot recognize any legitimate political alternative to itself and its policies, and cannot submit to any popular representative body. Even if it comes to power through parliamentary elections it must shake off parliamentary control as soon as it is in power, ceasing to be a parliamentary party—as is demonstrated by the fact that in the socialist countries it is the various people's front organizations, not the Communist Party, whose representatives sit in parliament.

The party's representatives meet not in parliament but at the sessions of the party's own elected bodies, the Party Congress and the Central Committee; in practice the party's political line and the composition of its leadership can be debated only in these forums. The party, or rather its leadership, legitimizes its authority by professing to be the party of the working class, the leading class in society, though it attributes an axiomatic rather than an empirical validity to this claim.

The Western Communist parties, operating on the treacherous terrain of parliamentary democracy, are forced to represent the empirical interests of the working class, for they must prove through the actual votes of real workers that they are indeed the parties of the working class. In the bourgeois democracies public opinion would see in a loss of the workers' vote a repudiation of the axiom that "the Communist Party is the party of the working class"—a petty, positivistic conclusion from the standpoint of the logic of rational redistribution. The Communist parties that have come to power have made it their first order of business to free themselves from the obligation, so unworthy of their historic mission, of participating in the vote-getting carnival of bourgeois-democratic elections. The workers' votes were replaced by a new conception of the working class in which the latter, rising to the level of its own historic mission, frees itself from its own empirical interests, which henceforward are branded as petty-bourgeois or lumpenproletarian traits.

In this new situation both parliamentary elections and the institution of parliament itself acquire a new content. Gone are the strident electioneering, the mutual recriminations of the parties, the appeals to a confused and ideologically defenseless electorate uncertain of its long-range interests and hence easy prey to a demagogy which panders to its narrow immediate concerns. Under the leadership of the party the state apparatus, relieved of the political instability caused by elections, can go on building socialism undisturbed. Elections become grand but still heartfelt demonstrations of the unity of the toiling masses. The candidates share the proud good humor of their electors, for in these festive rites of substantive democracy they, unlike the candidates in the formal democracies, cannot lose their seats. At most they must learn to accept the loss of ten to twenty percent of the votes cast, for there are always a stubborn few clever enough to figure out (without any help from the voting instructions or the ballot itself) how to vote "no."

The party's power monopoly, and its relationship to the various bureaucracies and representative organs

It is not the business of deputies ceremonially elected in the name of unity to debate alternative political goals in parliament. They do not and cannot promise the voters that in discussing national affairs they will pursue an independent political course; their role is merely to approve the budget proposals laid before them by the party and government, thus giving them legal sanction. The most they can do with those proposals is to contribute to their drafting in final form by taking part in the work of the specialized committees of parliament. There, however, they do not exercise control over a decision-making executive as elected representatives, but rather assist it in the capacity of expert advisors; and since their influence in these committees is legitimized not by their representative character but by their expert knowledge their activity in committee remains confidential, for publicity is the hallmark of authority based on direct representation.

In rational-redistributive societies, as we have said, expert knowledge is authority's prime principle of legitimation. In the institution of parliament, however, redistribution too accepts representation as a justification of authority; but nothing remains for these bodies to do except give ceremonial approval to decisions made by experts in the executive branch. Critics of socialist parliamentary systems may think they have no function except to serve as a useless ornament to rule by executive decree; but since rational redistribution—unlike fascist forms of government —is not avowedly rule by an elite but, on the contrary, appeals unceasingly to the interests and political unity of the working masses, the representative authority expressed in parliament does have an independent function of its own: It secures the consensual approval of a society as a whole, in ceremonial form, for measures worked out by the party and government organs of the intellectual class.

Although socialist deputies stand above the class or group interests which form around the key positions in the social structure, they are not altogether exempt from representing certain kinds of particular interests, in their case the interests of the district from which they have been elected. The parliamentary deputy acts as a go-between in the handling of the petty problems of his district in the redistributive economy of the larger region. The purpose of a parliamentary interpellation, for example, is not to modify the outlook of the executive on some national issue, but to obtain a remedy for some local grievance. No deputy will ever ask for school reform, only for a new school in a certain community; no one asks for a change in transportation policy, only that a station on a branch rail line not be closed. And if the appropriate minister, after consultation with his experts, grants the request, then the interpellator can return home to his election district happy; he is not a puppet, but a representative in the true sense of the word. Granting these local requests a hearing is a kind of gift which the redistributors bestow in exchange for the consent of the population and their representatives to redistributive decisions of national significance.

Parliament's ceremonial unanimity in exercising this ratifying function is only possible because the interests behind different political alternatives have already had their struggles out in advance. Only the final decision comes before parliament, and by that time it represents the consensus of the various expert bureaucracies. That consensus does not come about spontaneously, however; the party's leadership forums pass final judgment on the rival claims of bureaucratic authorities of equal rank. At times a bitter struggle rages over the division of redistributive authority between branch and functional ministries, and within each of these categories between the finance ministry and the planning office, the ministry of agriculture and the ministries with jurisdiction over the different branches of industry, the ministry of housing and construction, representing local interests, and the ministries responsible for the various productive branches. In the minutes of departmental conferences and the mutually contradictory analytical studies of the most diverse groups of experts—all meant strictly for official use, of course—the historian of the age will one day discover the real dimensions of these clashes of interest, which he will learn nothing about from the parliamentary journals.

The party, through its own central staff of technically qualified experts, acts as the final court of appeal in the rivalries of the individual bureaucracies. In order to do so it must, so to speak, crowd the headquarters of twenty or thirty ministries into party headquarters, creating within its own organization a miniature replica of the whole state apparatus. Thus the party's section chief in charge of economic policy, who represents the finance ministry, the planning office, and various other economic portfolios, needs in the last analysis to reach agreement with no one but himself when he sits down to reconcile the differences between contending particular interests. The headquarters apparatus, with the secretariat at its head, makes routine political decisions, settling day-by-day conflicts of interest between the specialized bureaucracies. The party's central administrative machinery has no power to make political decisions of strategic significance or to decide on possible changes in the party line; it can only formulate the issues for decision by the Central Committee at its next session.

The relationship between the Central Committee and parliament illustrates more clearly than anything else the relationship of party and state. Every representative member of the ruling elite takes part in the sessions of the Central Committee. Every secretary and section chief at party headquarters is a member almost automatically, as are the heads of all the larger regional administrative organs of party and state, the heads of every ministry and administrative organ of national scope (from the president of the National Bank and the director of the Statistical Office to the secretary of the Academy), the editor-in-chief of every daily, the directors of the state radio and television, the heads of the larger enterprises, and not least the chiefs of the army and police; all those are present who by reason of their office dispose of significant power and for that reason can take part in redistributive decisions of national significance. Thus the whole governing elite is on hand at the expanded plenums of the Central Committee—the general staff of the ruling system, the magnates.

Here, then, you will find the heads of every important decision-making center, and they are present because of their bureaucratic sphere of competence, not in any representative capacity. The Central Committee derives its power from the basic legitimating principle of rational redistribution; if its members are not the country's foremost technical experts they are in any event the bosses of those experts, and so they are all intellectuals; there is not a man or woman among them who is not an intellectual. In order to take part in a plenum of the Central Committee it is not enough just to be an intellectual, however. One must also become an outstanding representative of the ruling elite, just as in the upper house of a constitutional monarchy everyone is noble, but only those who also have magnate status can take their seats here. Thus the princes and counts of rational redistribution are qualified by their official rank to attend the sessions of the Central Committee.

The Central Committee's business is not to give demonstrations of national unity or ratify decisions already arrived at, but to make real decisions, at times amid sharp debate. In these discussions semiorganized factions sometimes attack one another almost like separate parties, even though the debate is steeped in the phraseology of consensus; it would require an observer trained in the content-analysis of Communist political language, in the deciphering of hidden meanings, ulterior motives, and veiled threats to do justice to the barbs that fly, just as it takes a regular devotee of water-polo matches to imagine, from the suddenly contorted face of a player, what underwater offense to his manhood he has just suffered.

Since this is the place where real decisions are made, there is no room here for such decorative marionette figures as the collective-farm milkmaid or the bishop who sit in parliament and decide nothing, except to validate the principle of representation by their mere presence. The relationship of Central Committee and parliament bears some resemblance to that of Commons and Lords in the English Parliament. Real decisions are made in the first of each pair. While the authority of the House of Commons is guaranteed by bourgeois democracy's chief principle of political legitimation, that of representation, the authority of the Eastern European Central Committee plenums is assured by the main legitimating principle of rational redistribution—expert knowledge in the service of the ruling elite. Formal ratification of real decisions is left to the Lords in England and to the parliaments in the Eastern European countries. The English upper house stands for the long-lost principle of legitimation by feudal position, while the Eastern European parliaments represent the equally lost principle of legitimation by representation.

We do not wish to stretch the analogy too far, however. Once an English M. P. has voted for a law he has no more to do with it; others will attend to its execution. But when a Communist Central Committee member votes for a proposal he also accepts responsibility, as a high-ranking official in the executive apparatus of party and state, for seeing that his legislative decision is implemented. Thus it is that the highest party organs, though essentially legislative in character, can content themselves formally with issuing statements of position, guidelines, or at most resolutions, in the knowledge that virtually all of them will become law almost word for word. In the case of policy-making party organs and executive state organs the separation of decision-making and executive functions is a merely relative one, since in the leading bodies of the party and especially in the Central Committee plenum it is the heads of the executive departments who make the political decisions. Indeed, even in the

case of lower-ranking party officials and state officials who perform parallel functions the separation is not absolute, for the
party bureaucracy participates regularly in public administration
in a kind of consular capacity, and if it does not take actual
executive measures it nevertheless still exercises pressure to bring
them about.

The party, distinct from the technical bureaucracies and superior to them, secures its hold on the bureaucratic structure
through an elaborate (indeed, sometimes overelaborate) network of interlocking roles. As a rule only party members can
hold high state posts; they are bound not only by official discipline but also, and first and foremost, by party discipline. If that
does not prove strong enough and a party member in his capacity
of a public official begins to interpret his duties in too autonomous a fashion, giving too free rein to purely technical interests
and to the apolitical experts beneath him, then the party secretary at his workplace, who may rank well below him in both
the state and party hierarchy, has the responsibility of demanding from him a stricter adherence to the party's wishes. It may
happen that a distinguished magnate of the ruling elite, grown
overconfident and careless, will fall victim to the intrigues of a
"squire" of a party secretary. Leaders learn from such instances
to have their party secretaries chosen from members of their
own entourage or, if the post is already filled, to bind the existing party secretary to their own persons through all kinds of
favors.

To avoid this sort of "family relationship" and to assure that
political controls will not be evaded, an inestimable importance
is accorded the political police with its many-tiered, sophisticated,
and highly efficient network of agents. Every high administrator
is obliged to report to a liaison officer officially delegated to him
by the political police, in whose selection the administrator has
no voice whatever and with whom he is bound to be all the
more honest since the same agent also collects information from
an unknown number of his subordinates, who are likewise obliged
to supply information about their chief to the police. Thus it is
inconceivable that any important decision, from the selection
of a midlevel manager to the consideration of a passport application, could be made by a department head or university dean

on his own authority, without the prior concurrence of this double set of controls. Directly or indirectly the same multiple controls are effective in other areas as well, indeed in every technical decision which has the slightest political relevance.

This interpenetration within a framework of relative separation of legislative, executive, and control powers—or rather this moving, reciprocal dialectic of separation and integration, which distinguishes socialist political systems from both the simplified, one-dimensional fascist state and from bourgeois democracy, with its principled separation of powers—lends the political and economic machinery of rational redistribution an unusual flexibility and effectiveness by comparison with other political systems. This effectiveness is found above all in the fact that the executive machinery as it were internalizes the guiding principles of the legislative organs described above and so can depart from them to only a limited extent in the name of its own administrative authority. On the other hand these executive legislators, in making their routine decisions, constantly acquire experience of the difficulties which stand in the way of implementing their policies, and can keep the inner policy-making circles (to which they sometimes belong) regularly informed on them.

Thus there arises an internal circuit of information feedback, which on principle precludes any sort of publicity. In the socialist countries the average citizen remains almost totally ignorant of the pressing problems of domestic politics. The system spares him the worry that might accompany publication of news of social conflicts, economic difficulties and defeats, or political crises and scandals, so that he can spend his days carrying out the party's resolutions undisturbed, cheerfully and apolitically. It is inconceivable that the citizens of a socialist society should be occupied for months on end with any domestic political crisis, as brought to them by the news media, even though the ruling elite in the socialist countries is not immune to them. The population learns of them only afterward, from the Central Committee's final communiqué reporting the solution of the crisis, but in such a form that the facts of the crisis cannot be discerned; at most they can be inferred from shifts in emphasis in the conventional phraseology and from the laconic report of resulting transfers of personnel. These crises do in fact compare with the noisy government crises of the bourgeois democracies, but public opinion has no influence whatever on their course; at most they give rise after the fact to a store of anecdotes derived from the verbal confidences of party members and circulated by the intellectuals, whose class situation is affected by these crises, in large part because of their personal consequences. These effects are felt both by those who belong to the ruling elite and those who are outside it, and often even by those who have been forced into a marginal situation; one may be affected by losing a hoped-for promotion or academic appointment, another may have to delete several poems from his new book of verse, while a third may have to prepare for renewed house searches or a prolongation of existing police surveillance, all depending on whether the regime as a whole has become more liberal as a result of the crisis, or more stringent.

The exclusion of public opinion from any kind of control function protects the power structure from shifts in the political temper of the public. Restricting political opinion to the inner circles of the ruling elite and the penumbra of intellectuals surrounding it serves effectively to hold down those short-term waves of crisis which the bourgeois media at times blow up to almost apocalyptic proportions, sometimes even after the outlines of a solution to the economic and technical problems underlying the crisis have begun to appear, as happened in the energy crisis of late 1973. This compression of the public arena lends the system an impressive stability, yet at the same time it is a cause of instability too, for it makes it more difficult to recognize and deal with the conflicts which constantly arise from structural changes in economy and society. As a result these overlooked and unaddressed problems may become envenomed and can even break out in political explosions.

However essential the system of multiple controls may be to the effective functioning of the executive apparatus, it simultaneously jeopardizes that same effectiveness by very largely discouraging bold, dynamic leadership. Sooner or later it winnows such men out, replacing them with cautious, gray record keepers, characterless apparatchiks. It slows down the making of decisions and leads sometimes to a near paralysis of the decision-making process, which in certain situations can produce disastrous consequences. It is a structural paradox of rational redistribution that it controls the executive techno-bureaucracy too closely, while at the same time it is unable to control the party and police apparatus closely enough. Thus relatively brief periods of liberal reform marked by a recession of the control apparatus alternate with relatively long political ice ages in which the control mechanism expands again.

The meaning of the dictatorship of the proletariat under rational redistribution

According to the ideology of the Communist parties socialism is the social system in which the working class is the ruling class; socialism means the dictatorship of the proletariat. What is there to support this cardinal tenet of all Communist theory? What empirical facts point to the rule of the working class under socialism? Do workers receive the highest pay? Hardly; the average intellectual's earnings are considerably higher than the average worker's, and the differential between the maximum an intellectual can earn and the maximum worker's wage is as great if not greater than in the market economies. Are the workers able to take greater advantage of state-subsidized benefits over and above wages? No; white-collar people live in larger and more comfortable dwellings in pleasanter neighborhoods, and they have a far better chance than workers do of getting an apartment in a building being constructed with the aid of state subsidies. Even the right to settle in town is a class privilege: It is easier for intellectuals to get permission to settle in the cities with their superior services, and so they can live relatively close to their places of work, while a good part of the working class—in some countries as much as half—is obliged to commute to work from the ill-served villages where they live. The children of the intelligentsia go on to university-level studies in far higher proportion; even earlier, they gain admittance to better schools more easily than do workers' children. Only intellectuals and their dependents are admitted to the special hospitals and clinics which provide outstanding care for ranking state and party officials. The cafeterias of institutions employing mostly intellectuals offer better and more varied meals than do the factory canteens. An engineer can vacation at his enterprise's or trade-union's vacation resort more readily than a machinist can; indeed, he will probably go to a more pleasant resort, in season, while the latter settles for a more modest one after the season is over. It is easier for intellectuals to travel abroad, especially in the West; they are the only ones to receive grants from state funds for study abroad; only they can accumulate foreign currency as a result of their missions abroad or from the sale of their works, and so only they can shop in the special stores which sell goods not otherwise available, in exchange for hard currency. Thanks to a variety of special advantages and credits intellectuals are the first to acquire cars and building plots for summer cottages, prime symbols in Eastern Europe of a higher standard of living. Finally, they have ways and means of supplementing their incomes in not altogether regular and sometimes even indictable ways. They can build themselves homes using materials and labor belonging to their enterprises. They are in a position to accept bribes in the course of foreign-trade negotiations. They are the ones who can buy themselves women through the allocation of an apartment or a soft, well-paid job. It is they who, capitalizing on the customary unwieldiness of the bureaucracy, can solicit gifts for themselves in exchange for guaranteeing timely delivery of otherwise perfectly legal orders. The scarcity economy of socialism, which manifests itself in the form of excess demand for producer and consumer goods alike, makes the satisfaction of the needs of both individuals and institutions dependent upon favors. These favors cost money, and so there appears an area of half-legal incomes which grows ever larger as the people who do the favors rise in social position. With respect to these semilegal incomes the difference between the intellectual and the worker is simply that the former can often pocket large sums in exchange for a signature or a favorable consulting opinion, while the latter has to toil outside of his regular hours for relatively small amounts and, in addition, runs a greater risk of discovery. A truck driver can lose his job or even go to prison for using an official vehicle to make a private delivery outside of working hours, yet it earns him little and he still has to work for it. But if a well-known engineer or economist gives a positive opinion in some matter of investment policy (having perhaps arranged in advance to do so with the agency that wants to make the investment), he can come by a large extra sum of money perfectly legally and with very little work, sometimes merely by lending his prestigious name—a fair return on the secure capital of his reputation or rank, and all with no more risk than that of a few pangs of professional conscience.

As a result of all these perquisites the differentials between the living standards of workers and intellectuals are far greater than their official earnings alone would indicate. For that reason one must be cautious in using those statistical analyses which claim to measure the inequalities between social strata on the basis of the relatively modest differences in official earnings.

If the leading role of the working class cannot be demonstrated from any tangible aspect of material life, such as income or living standard, are the workers compensated perhaps by a greater voice in the making of decisions? Does the leading role of the working class mean that actual workers have a little more to say than others do in deciding essential economic issues or even just the shop-floor technical questions that arise in their factories? In fact the worker, for all his alleged "leading role," has just as little to say in the high- or low-level decisions of his enterprise as the worker in a capitalist plant. He has no voice in deciding whether operations will be expanded or cut back, what will be produced, what kind of equipment he will use and what direction (if any) technical development will take, whether he will work for piece rates or receive an hourly wage, how performance will be measured and production norms calculated, how workers' wages will evolve relative to the profitability of the enterprise, or how the authority structure of the plant, from managing director to shop foreman, will operate.

Those forums whose purpose it is to bring the workers face to face with management—production conferences, plant meetings—do not even in law guarantee the workers anything more than the right to hear management present selected information and to present their own requests and grievances. But since the workers know of enough instances where valid criticism has led to reprisals from management—assignment to poorly paid work or to inconvenient shifts, unjustified withholding of premiums, discrimination in profit-sharing, transfer or even dismissal—when

they do speak up they at most complain about the sanitary condition of the locker room or the monotony of the food in the
canteen. Then, after a few such mournful comments followed
by some good-natured, paternal reassurances from management,
these scenes of worker participation in public life generally break
up, and the workers' contributions to the policies of the enterprise cease until the next annual or semiannual production conference.

Workers, as workers, cannot intervene in the policies of their
enterprises because in the socialist countries there are no real
workers' organizations. The Communist parties, after coming to
power, quickly dissolved or transformed every organization in
which only workers participated, from workers' councils, factory
committees, and trade unions to workers' singing societies,
theatrical groups, and sports clubs. In the socialist countries only
corporative organizations exist, and workers belong to them only
in company with the administrative personnel and technical intelligentsia of their enterprise or branch. Thus the general manager and the common laborer are members of the same trade-
union local, and it is hardly likely that the worker will have as
much voice in the affairs of the local as his boss does.

In the last decades of the nineteenth century one of the
fundamental objectives of the Western European labor movement was the creation of unions independent of the employers,
a goal achieved in the more liberal countries by around 1900.
Even earlier, of course, during the era of the most brutal domination of capital, workers won the right to organize their own
social and cultural associations. Capitalist class rule permitted
the workers to have their own organizations. The class rule of
the intelligentsia has never made this concession. It is noteworthy that the reform programs of the intellectuals, even the
most radical opposition ones, never demand that the workers be
allowed to transform their organizations into bodies independent
of the intelligentsia, even though they are replete with demands
for the creation of all sorts of organizations of intellectuals, from
university student associations to societies to defend the interests
of intellectuals imprisoned under Stalinism.

It is hardly a coincidence that whenever a political upheaval
culminates in a workers' rebellion—which always comes just as

unexpectedly and just as terrifyingly for the opposition intelligentsia as for the ruling elite, as in Budapest in 1956 or Gdańsk in 1970—the first order of business for the workers is to form their own, noncorporative organizations: workers' councils or soviets. Nor was it any accident that after the defeat of the Hungarian uprising of 1956 the workers' councils, formed without the participation of intellectuals, were the first to be dissolved; and even though the retrospective "white books" containing the official ideological evaluation of the event speak only of the leaders of the intellectual opposition, the great majority of the death sentences imposed (apart from those on armed rebels) fell on members of the workers' councils, who in general took no part in the armed uprising.

But even without any efforts to organize or take up arms the working class would still have felt the weight of the ruling elite's punitive measures in far greater degree than did the intelligentsia, and the peasants were indeed allied with them in suffering the cruelty of the regime. From the October Revolution to our own day the number of workers and peasants executed or imprisoned in internment or forced-labor camps has been immeasurably greater than the number of intellectuals, and at least as great proportionally. Stalin's mass persecution of intellectuals had hardly begun at a time when the peasantry was already being decimated in the course of the collectivization drive; in two years' time more peasants perished than the total number of intellectuals then living in the Soviet Union. And the same phenomenon was repeated in the Eastern European countries, where a peasant could go to prison for years for cutting down a fruit tree in his front yard, for slaughtering a pig without permission, for being late with a compulsory delivery of a few dozen eggs, or for concealing a sack of grain from his harvest so as to have enough left over after fulfilling his delivery obligation to make bread or perhaps use as seed; a worker could be imprisoned for an outburst in a tavern or a political joke, for protesting against demands to subscribe to a compulsory government loan, or for a factory accident that could be interpreted as an act of sabotage.

But the intellectuals who have chronicled the prison universe —with the sole exception of Solzhenitsyn, perhaps—have taken far greater note of the names of imprisoned intellectuals, friends once prominent in the regime from whom they have learned personally the dark mythology of the gulag universe, than they have of the names of imprisoned workers and peasants, unnoticed, unsung, preserved only in the files of the secret police. Those who acquainted the Western world with these events were also intellectuals and former bourgeois, and so it is no wonder if their accounts of the persecution of intellectuals and bourgeois have come to be seen by the Western bourgeoisie as part of the dark tragedy of the dictatorship of the proletariat, and by leftist intellectuals in the West as regrettable excesses of proletarian power.

Why should the axiom of proletarian dictatorship not appear self-evident when, after the Communist seizure of power, thousands of men and women who the day before had been factory workers (even though in the aggregate they still represented only a small fraction of the working class) took up leading positions overnight in the governing elite? How did nationalization take place? One day a thousand workers were called together at party headquarters and told that starting the next day they would be the heads of the thousand biggest enterprises; into their hands were thrust the decrees of nationalization with which they would occupy the offices of management in the morning. No wonder the plant engineers, trembling before the uncouth, ill-spoken new general manager, saw in these measures a proof of proletarian dictatorship. These workers, elevated from one day to the next to ministerial office, to the general staff, to university party secretaryships, even to the diplomatic service, bore the marks of their class in the most graphic manner. Unfamiliar with the rules of protocol, they signed their names with clumsy hands; they knew no foreign languages, not even words of foreign origin current in their own, they spoke in dialect, with sovereign disregard for the rules of grammar, they talked with plebeian heartiness; they wore shirts with open collars. Their proletarian roughness provoked alarm or (behind their backs) mockery, not only from the Western diplomats and trading partners who came in contact with them, but also among their employees of bourgeois or intellectual origin. The more adaptable of the latter put their best suits away in the bottoms of their trunks in those days, bade farewell, to all appearances, to their books and neck-ties, kept it a secret if they spoke a foreign language, even ex-perimented with a few dialect expressions themselves. How could these forced-draft proletarians ever have imagined that in less than a decade their one-time "worker" bosses would send them home to change if they dared to come to an important meeting without a tie or wearing a checked shirt, or that the boss would be grateful for their advice on which French perfume to bring back from abroad as a gift for the secretary who in the meantime has taken his wife's place in his affections?

So long as the title "worker" or "peasant" could appear be-side the names of party secretaries and heads of great industrial combines in the Central Committee's roster, or on the roll of members of parliament, without appearing absurd in light of their actual functions or by the addition of "Dr." before the name, no very ingenious theoretical constructs were needed to make these party and state leaders appear to be living proof of the dictatorship of the proletariat. But soon the intellectual character of these leaders became obvious: A majority of them presently acquired advanced degrees, while many who could not dropped out of the ruling elite; they acquired the intellectual knowledge which their functions demanded, and in their every-day lives they did not act any differently from any other intel-lectual in a similar position. It soon became apparent, too, that their managerial functions demanded a kind of intellectual knowl-edge which was more conveniently obtained by hiring and promoting new university graduates, so that the proportion of leaders who had risen from the working class inside of one generation grew smaller, while there were more of those who could claim at best worker or peasant parents. Finally, as the new and the old intelligentsia grew not only to resemble each other in their mode of life but even to recognize their community of interests in identical situations, it became evident to the great majority of society (even if sociological theory did not formulate it explicitly) that by their functions these party and state leaders were intellectuals, and it became problematical how this power of the intellectuals could possibly serve as a proof of the leading role of the working class.

In these circumstances the Western notion of a new working

class came as an unexpected boon to apologists in Eastern Europe, even though they had to perform plastic surgery on it to make it serve their purposes: In their version the working class was extended to take in, not the technical intelligentsia involved directly in production, but rather the members of the state and party bureaucracy and the officers of the armed services, who were now characterized as workers in a political if not economic sense, by reason of their functions rather than their origins. And so now a general, a government minister, or a city party secretary qualified as a worker even if he had never done physical labor and even if his parents had not been workers, simply because he was a general, a minister, or a party secretary. Thus there emerged an unimpeachable tautology, as devoid of heuristic value as it was of empirical content: Under the dictatorship of the proletariat proletarians are supposed to exercise power; since we claim this is a dictatorship of the proletariat those who wield power here must be proletarians; but if those who wield power are proletarians, then this must indisputably be the dictatorship of the proletariat.

It would be easy to use this arbitrary, empty, and unverifiable syllogism to dismiss without further ado the ideological axiom that socialism means the rule of the working class. But in order to understand the class basis of the power relationships of rational redistribution in all their nuances we must look more closely at Lenin's assertion that the party's supremacy guarantees the rule of the working class, and that the working class exercises power through the medium of its own vanguard, the Communist Party. It follows from that notion that there is no need to declare the party's leaders to be workers in order to see in the party the incarnation of working-class power. And so we must go on to ask what is the real class basis for the power of the ruling Communist Parties.

The class basis of the ruling Communist Parties

In the course of our earlier functional analysis we came to the conclusion that the party is a kind of master control joining the technical bureaucracies together into a single structure, holding their particular interests in balance, and guarding against the

whole mechanism falling apart into separate bureaucratic structures. Constant party supervision draws policy-making and executive functions together into a unified whole and safeguards
the primacy of politics over economics and administration, thus
holding in check a technical intelligentsia eager to increase its
own power. The party strives to vindicate the interests of redistribution as a whole over the special interests of the several
redistributive technocracies, and defends the social consensus
against technocratic rule by appealing to the interests of the
working class. To that extent the party by its very function keeps
technocratic tendencies in check. Party control is by no means
welcome to the technocrats, who try to evade it whenever they
can.

The party's dictatorial control over technical administration
is an undisputed fact, even though its rigor varies considerably
over time; in stricter periods it is represented by the political
police, sniffing out sabotage everywhere, in laxer periods by
the more enlightened base organizations of the party.

The question of how far the party can be regarded as the instrument of proletarian dictatorship can only be answered, however, through an analysis of the party's structure. In our view
the ruling Communist Parties have a dual class base: They are
at one and the same time mass parties of the intellectual class
and cadre parties of the working class. In this respect they differ
markedly from Communist Parties contending for power by
parliamentary means and from those which have been driven
into illegality. The legal minority parties—most conspicuously
the French and Italian Communist Parties—are indeed (by contrast with the ruling parties) mass parties of the working class
and cadre parties of the intellectuals; the illegal parties, again,
are cadre parties of the intellectuals so far as the bulk of their
membership is concerned. These differences are explained by
the social composition of the membership and of the party's
officials.

Intellectuals in the party

Even though they consider themselves parties of the working
class, the ruling Communist Parties draw upon the intelligentsia

for the bulk of their membership; in general intellectuals make up a higher percentage of the party membership than any other social group, including workers. In the party bureaucracy, however, the proportion of officials who were once workers or whose parents were workers is much higher; indeed, there is no other intellectual occupational group in the socialist countries with so high a percentage of people of working-class origin. The party, in other words, is the prime channel of upward mobility for workers and educated children of workers; once drawn into the party bureaucracy they become intellectuals. Indeed, there is a strong probability that if a worker joins the party at all it will make an intellectual out of him. But the difference between cadre party and mass party is evident not only in the difference between the membership and the bureaucracy, but also in the fact that the party means different things to the intellectual class and the working class. For the intellectuals the ruling Communist Party has more of the character of a political movement, while for workers who do not belong to the paid bureaucracy this aspect is considerably attenuated; the life of their base organizations is emptier and more formalistic. Nothing illustrates this more graphically than the fact that while intellectuals are most often expelled from the party for their ideological vagaries (or at any rate for political reasons) workers generally suffer expulsion (and in fairly substantial numbers, too) because of failure to pay their dues, or because they have lost their membership books or have not been attending meetings regularly —that is, because they have not been taking an active enough share in the activities of the party as part of the Communist movement.

In mass Communist parties competing legally for parliamentary majorities, on the other hand, worker membership is much higher; the role of the intellectuals is largely restricted to the party bureaucracy. Most intellectuals never join the party, and of those who do many do not remain party members permanently. Considerable numbers of the intellectual elite do turn up in the party at one time or another, but critical shifts in the party line, or a general organizational atmosphere that is far from congenial to theoretical discussion, prompt them after a relatively short while to resolve their crises of conscience by turning in their party books. Having broken with the mass party of the workers these intellectuals, jealous of their independence, either form little dissident elite parties or else give up left-wing political activity altogether. Those who stay on through everything, styling themselves professional revolutionaries, will in all probability advance to the leadership echelons of the party, eventually crowning their political careers with election to a parliamentary seat or membership on the Central Committee; thanks to the Communist Party they will become respected public figures. Intellectuals are probably to be found in the ranks of the Western Communist Parties' parliamentary deputies and leading functionaries in numbers disproportionate to their overall strength in the general membership; the percentage of workers who have risen to become professional politicians is probably no greater than in the Social Democratic parties—a situation glaringly apparent in the government of the Hungarian soviet republic of 1919, whose Communist commissars were intellectuals while those drawn from the Social Democratic party were workers. For the workers, however, the Western Communist Parties are genuine workers' parties, in part because of the integrating role of the trade unions, in part because the hard core of the party is composed of veritable dynasties of workers for whom the party has been for generations not just an organizer of strikes and demonstrations but also a forum for self-improvement, collective social and cultural life, and leisure activities generally; in that respect the French and Italian Communist Parties fill the same workers' needs as did the Socialist parties of the turn of the century for the proletariat of that day.

Illegal Communist Parties are intellectual cadre parties made up of professional revolutionaries. They maintain their links with the actual working class only under the cover of the legal trade unions. When they take power, their memberships swell rapidly. In Russia in the spring of 1917 the party's membership numbered in the tens of thousands, but within a short time it had risen to one million. In Hungary during the Second World War the underground Communist Party had fewer than a thousand members, but five years later, when it enjoyed exclusive sway, it too had grown into a party of a million members. This rapid growth in numbers was due in good part to the fact that in both cases large numbers of intellectuals flocked to join the party. There were ideological reasons for this phenomenon, for the non-Communist intelligentsia were open intellectually to the ethos of rational redistribution, and quickly realized that the role awaiting them in the new society was by no means a disadvantageous one. There was, however, a more mundane and practical reason for this influx into the party. The intellectual soon learned that he could be sure of holding on to his job only if he had a party membership book and, even more, that he could get ahead in his career only with the help of a boost from his party book. In the new situation intellectuals had double reason to cling to their social status: Every other avenue of success in society had been closed, while on the other hand the direction of a nationalized economy offered intellectual knowledge a power which earlier generations of intellectuals had never even dreamed of.

As membership grew the party's bureaucracy grew even more rapidly and, having climbed to the top of the social pyramid, promptly sought to set itself off from the throngs of intellectuals clamoring to join the party, and even more so from the intellectuals who remained outside. And so there emerged at the top of the party bureaucracy a ruling elite whose members were indeed intellectuals; but to be admitted to it it was not enough simply to be an intellectual. As we have said, the function of the ruling elite is to guarantee the authority of the overall redistributive process over the various individual technocracies, the primacy of *telos* over *techné*. But since scientific rationality plays a much smaller part in setting and justifying goals than in the solution of technical questions, it is especially important for those who define society's goals to be well-organized and well-disciplined and for their ranks to remain unbroken by any ideological disputes. That is why the upper strata of the party bureaucracy function as an organized elite group, why it is not enough in those quarters to possess a certain level of technical knowledge, why the members of this elite all strive to resemble one another in everything, right down to their dress and bearing.

The ruling elite reserves to itself the right to make decisions; in general, decisions can only be taken by someone who has a party book and sits behind a desk, connected by direct telephone lines with the rest of the functional hierarchy. Anyone with a direct phone line can make decisions with relative autonomy in the area of responsibility assigned to him; there he has a monopoly of decisions affecting the lives of others, and he need not turn to his superiors unless he is uncertain in a particular case what the interests of the ruling elite demand. In his every gesture the successful member of the ruling elite combines with instinctive flair a smooth pliability and a forceful independence. He can even sense when to contradict his superiors, which may bring down their anger on him for a time, of course, but he will be vindicated when it turns out that his obstinacy has served the interests of the ruling elite over the long run. To find your bearings in this way you must have a special internal compass; you must have the ethos of the ruling elite under your skin, must be able to give the right answers even when the phone wakes you up in the middle of the night. If you are to advance rapidly your superiors must be convinced that you would put your hand in the fire for them.

The ideology of scientific socialism functions (and with very few errors) like a fine gauge to measure not so much the heuristic value or technical rationality of an innovation in thought or practice, but rather its potential usefulness or danger to the ruling elite. Confronted with a new philosophical proposition, a member of the elite will not get excited over its elegance or originality; he would be guilty of a lapse from duty and would be denying his entire historical role if he did not first ask: Does this proposition fit in with the accepted tenets of scientific socialism? Does it have any antecedents which might serve as a precedent for it in the corpus of safe, legitimized doctrinal theses? Is it useful from the standpoint of the interests of the ruling elite? What will party opinion say about it (meaning, of course, the frank private opinion of high-ranking party functionaries)? If I tolerate it will I be called down by my superiors for being too lenient, or reported by my subordinates?

An intellectual can belong to the ruling elite of his class only if he unfailingly upholds the redistributive ethos at every tactical juncture. If he does he will succeed in attaining a share in power, promotion in the hierarchy of important positions, and eventually a key policy-making post. The loyal member of the ruling

elite does not just influence decisions; he has the power to make
them himself. By comparison any other social advantages or
privileges he may enjoy are secondary. In any event his material
rewards and prestige (manifested perhaps in advanced academic
degrees) will be higher than the average for the intellectual
class. On the other hand it is not always certain that he will be
accorded the same professional respect as the independent intellectual. The members of the ruling elite are compensated for
their sometimes lower prestige or income by the greater power
they wield. For less talented or less well-educated members of
the intellectual class (among them many party members who
have risen from the working class) it is worth it to accept rules
of elite conduct which would be stifling for independent intellectuals, because in that way they can not only compete with
them in one of the main dimensions of social inequality—power—
but can have a virtual guarantee of coming out ahead of them in
the end.

11

The Struggle for Power within the Intelligentsia

In the Soviet Union it was Stalin who, in the early 1920s,
carried through the arduous task of organizing the ruling elite.
In building up a party apparatus, in his capacity as General
Secretary, he brought into being those cadres whose loyalty
would in future be measured by their devotion to him personally.
From the very beginning the creation of a party apparatus entailed a system of keeping dossiers on all party members, and it
was no accident that the Communist system began by collecting
data on every aspect of the personal lives of the members of the
ruling party itself, for that was an essential part of the method
of selection by which less-dedicated party members were excluded from the ruling elite. As soon as Stalin felt that the new

elite was solidly behind him, he launched the campaign to elevate it above the intellectual class and above the party as a
whole. Winning supremacy for the new elite was no easy task,
however, if only because the old leaders of the party possessed
few of the characteristics desired in the new elite. And so Stalin
and his followers turned on old party members who did not
conform to the requirements of the new elite, launching a drive
to purge them from the ruling elite. Henceforward only those
would be tolerated who had no minds of their own, who were
most dependent on the General Secretary, who could be relied
upon not to try to put across any policies of their own, who had
no capacity to innovate in the sphere of ideology, and who lacked
the kind of colorful, striking personality around which factions
could form. Obviously, then, fewer and fewer of the outstanding
representatives of the intelligentsia were fit for continued membership in the ruling elite. So Stalin had to settle accounts with
Trotsky and the others, and indeed it is clear that from the
standpoint of the new elite Stalin, by reason of his personal characteristics alone, was better qualified than Trotsky or Bukharin
to be the leader of the Bolshevik party.

Earlier, in the years immediately following the revolution,
anti-intellectualism had been directed primarily against the
bourgeois intelligentsia and others outside the Bolshevik party
(Menshevik, Socialist-Revolutionary, and anarchist intellectuals),
with the aim of creating a new Communist intelligentsia of the
proletariat; that was one reason why the intellectuals took refuge
en masse inside the Communist Party, in the hope that there
they might be accepted as this sought-after new type of intelligentsia. Now, however, in a party swollen by the adhesion of
intellectuals, it was precisely the intelligentsia which became the
target of the purges. The campaign took two directions. On
one hand the elite had to assure its supremacy over the techno-
bureaucracy, and its struggle against them surfaced even in the
1920s, when the party bureaucracy turned against the technical
elite of the state planning office. Nevertheless, the class power of
the intellectuals was still very real in the Soviet Union in the
1920s, making possible the many noteworthy intellectual achievements of the decade in every field from economics and physical
science to literature and film. The vast, bloody purges of the

1930s were needed to make the intellectuals understand that early socialism did not mean their direct class rule: The power of the intellectual class could be exercised only through the medium of the ruling elite. But the more forcefully the elite proceeded against the technical and economic intelligentsia, the more ruthlessly the logic of the purges recoiled on their own heads as well. For the purges created a frighteningly powerful political police who soon exceeded the responsibilities delegated to them and went on to look for ever larger tasks for themselves, and in that they were aided by a public mood of mutual suspicion in which the members of the ruling elite vied in seeing who could denounce the other first. Soon the "eggheads" among the ruling elite began to roll; only blockheads could be certain of remaining securely affixed to their necks. Within the elite, meanwhile, purely formal criteria of membership became more and more important, until before long they were reduced to the sole requirement of absolute, unthinking loyalty to the leader. One might even say that within the elite there emerged an inner circle of the most reliable, an elite of the elite, which even the ruling elite itself could not keep under control—we mean the political police, which soon extended the atmosphere of insecurity and terror in the party to the ruling elite itself.

THE FORMATION OF THE RULING ELITE AND ITS STRUGGLE
FOR POWER

*The evolution of the ruling elite and the character
of its absolute power*

In both the Soviet Union and the other socialist countries of Eastern Europe the ruling elite acquired a monopoly of power during the Stalinist years. In arrogating all power to itself, however, the ruling elite internalized the conflicts existing within the intellectual class; as its original aim in starting the purges was to assure its own stability by acquiring a monopoly of power, it was hardly prepared to see a new conflict break out between the political police and the elite as a whole, which in fact led to a new instability within the ruling elite. The elite had to recognize—though not openly until the Khrushchev era, after Stalin's death—that if it wished to stabilize its power it must reach a compromise with the intellectual class, give up its power monopoly, and settle for a hegemony of power within a system of shared rule. With this historic compromise the ruling elite in fact assured itself of a new and stabilized supremacy, for thereby it rid itself of the conflict between the elite as a whole and the elite within the elite, a conflict that threatened to consume the elite itself by deepening the loyalty-treason cleavage within the inner circles and even within the schizoid consciousness of its members; and it converted this conflict into a regulated and rationally controlled system of conflicts between the intellectual class and the ruling elite.

The period during which the elite monopolized power was one of transition, in both senses of the word: On one hand it represented a passage, a bridge between two social situations, while on the other it was a temporary state of affairs which had to pass because by its very nature it prevented the consolidation of the social order which it had called into being. For society as a whole its basic purpose was to destroy traditional forms of social organization, hierarchical structures, and cultural regulatory systems, and to create a new social structure appropriate to the emerging economic system of early rational redistribution. It extended commodity relations to the entire potential work force, dissolving the family as a productive unit and radically modifying the peasant family's consumption of its own product; in this way it was able to extract a maximum amount of labor and surplus product from agriculture for purposes of industrialization. It assigned an absolute primacy to industrial investment as against the consumption needs of the population and against other forms of public and infrastructural investment. Fifty million people fled from the exhausted villages to the towns during the course of this period.

The Stalinist era saw a colossal redistribution which consciously and systematically defied all the laws of organic industrial and economic growth and of technical rationality in general, and partially realized a fantastic dream of converting a poor, devastated agrarian country into the world's strongest military and industrial power. In the midst of so radical and headlong a transformation of the social and economic structure the leader-

ship of the ruling elite, and the charismatic tyrant who dominated
them all, could not pay any heed to the misgivings of the technical experts, or the ability of the population to bear further
burdens, or the technical capacities of an industry being developed at such a forced tempo; nor did they lay much stress
on economic efficiency. Technical rationality had to be subordinated to a pure ideology which from now on would totally
pervade social life, and which was soon reduced to an unquestioning devotion to the ruling elite (or rather to its leader).
From the technocrats it demanded not professional scruples but
a faith willing to take on anything. At the same time, the period
of the elite's monopoly rule assured that the workers, and the
peasants who were more and more becoming workers, would be
converted into dispositive wage-laborers, and that the intellectual
class would accept the supremacy of the ruling elite.

Nevertheless, this period was only a temporary one. Compulsory labor that at times reached mass dimensions, a system of
wage-labor completely subject to administrative regulation, and
industrial armies (in the form of both actual military forced labor
and ostensibly civilian industrial work, half-militarized by the
use of such positive compulsions as wage premiums and "socialist
emulation") turned out to be alarmingly inefficient economically.
But it also turned out that the technocrats themselves, in meeting
the demands of the ruling elite, overcame their professional
scruples so well that they too came to believe that faith rather
than rational technique moves mountains; having abandoned
their professional consciences, fearful for their very safety, the
technocrats became so prodigal in both planning and execution
that their actual output did not even approach the rate of growth
anticipated from so severe a curtailment of consumption and
so drastic a maximization of the surplus product devoted to investment. Indeed, because of the extremely low rate of return
on invested capital, real output was perhaps not even as high
as might have been achieved if growth had been more organic
and if more tolerable living standards had been accorded the
population.

For all these reasons, instability soon appeared outside the
ranks of the ruling elite as well. The population wearied of the
incomprehensible and unattainable rationality of the elite's (or

rather the leader's) dictatorship. Thus even in the days of its unlimited power the ruling elite was obliged to make concessions to the technical experts, as demonstrated by the way the Soviet party leadership, after the blunders that accompanied the outbreak of war with Germany, had to recall significant numbers of military and technical experts—as many as could still be found alive—from the concentration camps, and restore them to leading positions in industry and the army. In the late 1950s began the process—not uniform in all the Eastern European societies but everywhere describable in terms of a regular alternation of easing, tightening, and easing restrictions—by which the ruling elite, having relinquished its power monopoly, has made structural concessions to the intellectual class and especially to the technical experts. We might call this period the second stage of early socialism, which leads on to the third period of rational redistribution, the achievement of class power by the intellectuals, or what might be termed developed socialism.

The most lasting accomplishment of the Stalin era is the ruling elite itself and its institutions. The replacement of its monopoly situation with a hegemony of power has scarcely affected the elite's composition, recruitment methods, and organizational forms. It was a virtual precondition for the unlimited power of the elite that its ranks had to be purged of all those intellectuals who were inspired by any kind of personal motive—scientific, cultural, or technical prestige, the authority of the old revolutionary, or what have you—to display any kind of independent behavior. Those who enjoyed such prestige but were pliable enough to survive the purges were obliged, on the other hand, to give up all creative activity, and had to adopt the mentality of the apparatchik. The example of intellectuals stripped of their autonomy and creativity, treated by the elite with more suspicion than honor, and unceremoniously expelled from the party for the slightest wavering, did not hold much attraction for the more able members of the rising generation of young educated professionals. In light of the elite's compromise with the technocracy they preferred to pursue nonparty careers offering greater security and prestige, and sometimes even more income—as engineers, perhaps, or university professors—rather than try to struggle upwards in the party apparatus.

It is true of course that a significant number of these expert intellectuals do join the party and indeed, as we said before, the party is a mass party of the intellectuals; but that is quite a different matter. The reason they join is simply so as not to be hindered in their rise through the technical hierarchy by the taint of nonparty status—a status which, in intellectual careers at least, is easily associated with political unreliability. These intellectuals join the party not in order to advance within it, but in order to acquire (or keep) the status which their professional achievements entitle them to and which in any nonpolitical competition they would attain in any case. It is not so much that party members are privileged in intellectual careers; rather, nonparty intellectuals are underprivileged. In the end that still means that intellectuals with party membership are privileged; they run in an artificially restricted field and not necessarily against the ablest competitors. Many of the most able choose to rely on their abilities alone, hoping to succeed without benefit of a party book, a hope that is not always borne out by their actual progress.

Those who join the party receive advantages. Those who do not must struggle to make their professional accomplishments offset the magic power of the party book. It is "irregular" to entrust a nonparty man or woman with a position of confidence. One must perform exceptional services in order to get one. Of course there are always "show" nonparty people, in reality secret party members who cannot join openly because they are supposed to stand as living proof that one can get somewhere without being in the party. There are also genuine nonparty people who receive appointments to important posts, and then are left to decide for themselves whether they will join or not. Most probably they will, thus bringing their political status into line with their professional standing; only thus can they become leaders in the full sense, with access to inside information of the kind that only party members can know. The party member is a nobleman. Whenever a key position comes open, there are always people whom professional opinion unanimously regards as well qualified for it by their knowledge and personal abilities. Yet their names never come up, even among those who do not share the selection criteria of the ruling elite, for they too take into consideration only those who have a chance because of their political acceptability. A successful choice is made when the party intelligentsia and the professional intelligentsia reach agreement on a party member who also has some professional reputation. In the narrow area where these two sets of qualifications overlap a little group of favorites appears, pluralists of jobholding. Anyone lucky enough to possess this double seal of approval can be as secure as a person with dual citizenship. If the political horizon darkens and the ideological pressure on technical circles grows heavier, he need only fall back on the political aspect of his job; when a period of liberalization sets in he will be spared, in traveling abroad or moving in professional circles, the rather condescending criticism which awaits those who are distinguished solely by their ideological reliability. However the political weather may change, the dual citizen of party and profession will always have the wind at his back.

Not every party member belongs to the ruling elite; not even every intellectual who belongs to the party can belong to the elite. But it is clear that no one can be a member of the elite who is not both a party member and an intellectual. The intellectual who enjoys professional esteem but lacks the passport of a party book can rise, it is true, but only along a circumscribed path, and there are positions to which he cannot aspire. He may become a prize-winning artist or scholar, or an outstanding technical expert; he may live to see his works published in many large editions; party leaders will be eager to be photographed in his company and will frequently cite him as an example of the success of their cultural policies; the highest political leaders will willingly receive him when he calls and will gladly attend to requests of his, as a favor—finding an apartment for a son about to be married or seeing to a passport for a young colleague whom the police have refused one. But he has to show gratitude for such personal acts of grace, even though he will probably be proud that for his faithfulness in performing little services in return he has been received at court, as a kind of baron of intellect. The other side of the coin is that for him nothing works of its own accord; he has to ask the intervention of his friend on the Central Committee not only if he wants to accept an invitation from abroad, but even if he wants merely to have a telephone installed in his new apartment or to have his name put at the head of the list for buying a car. For that very reason, of course, the satisfaction of even his most mundane requests fills the prominent nonparty intellectual with a sense of his own exceptionalness and importance. With his telephone he also acquires a feeling of security: Somebody up there likes him, no serious ill can befall him, at least not in the near future. But if next week or next month the political police should happen to call on him and ask in the politest way possible for information about a young and apparently thoughtless friend, student, or colleague, and if he should hesitate to cooperate in a confidential inquiry, then he will soon learn from a series of little signs that his optimism was premature: Nobody up there likes him that much after all, and he had best prepare for unanticipated setbacks, because the people up there know everything there is to know about him; he is in their hands. That is how far the power of favor has gotten him, and he has no other power. He can no longer even think of asking, much less expecting to receive, something which is his professional due and which is perfectly legal. He can still intercede with his high-ranking protectors on behalf of others, but it is inconceivable that he will ever be made editor-in-chief of a periodical or publishing house or the head of a scholarly institute, and it will arouse surprise if he is even appointed to head a university department. He will never, in other words, achieve any position in which he could make decisions on his own responsibility in matters of political importance.

The ruling elite in the Stalinist and post-Stalinist eras

It is obvious to all that the more than half-century history of socialism falls into two distinct periods. In the common parlance of political journalism (which the social sciences have taken over for lack of anything better) these are the era of Stalinism and the post-Stalinist period, which is still with us today. Various political and economic differences are cited to distinguish the two eras, and in its ideology the post-Stalinist ruling elite claims it has left behind the policies of Stalin's day and corrected his errors.

The hallmarks of Stalinism, as subjected to criticism after his death, include:

1. The autocratic rule of the General Secretary of the party, and the development of a cult surrounding his person. In general, an excessive centralization of the state and political bureaucracy.

2. The primacy of the police apparatus over the party and the judiciary. The police have the right to detain or banish citizens for an indefinite period. The minister of justice has no control over the organs of state security, which are thus able to torture and even kill citizens in the course of their interrogations. On the contrary, the security organs have power over prosecutors and judges to such an extent that their accusations, drawn up while the accused are in their sole and uncontrolled power, are virtually binding orders on the courts; no prosecutor, judge, or defense attorney dares to question testimony extracted from the accused and the witnesses by force and interpreted according to preconceived political aims. Thus the citizen feels himself completely at the mercy of the authorities, particularly the security police.

3. In the realm of economic policy the post-Stalinist period condemns its predecessor for violating the principles of balanced development and for many other excesses—such purely quantitative errors as the excessive exploitation of agriculture for the benefit of industry, exaggerated preference for investment in heavy industry and producer goods, and overrestriction of consumption leading at times to violation of the recently promulgated basic law of socialist political economy that living standards must gradually and constantly rise. Other targets of criticism include an excessive centralism in managing the economy, with too much restriction of the economic autonomy of individual enterprises and cooperatives, and a one-sidedly quantitative view of economic planning manifested in the fact that the planning office ran the enterprises by direct command, using overdetailed and natural (rather than money) plan indexes. Other manifestations of the same error included insufficient attention to economy, technical development, and the quality and variety of products, and to the material incentives which are indispensable to achieve all three.

4. A dogmatic subjectivism prevails in cultural and intellectual life. In its Stalinist interpretation Marxism-Leninism shrinks to

a few dozen propositions which are decisive in all scientific and cultural questions, making concrete research superfluous or twisting it to its own ends in every field, from cosmogony to plant breeding, from linguistics to political economy, from atomic physics to aesthetics. As a result the philosophical values of Marxism, originally meant to guide the historical strategy of communism, sink to the level of tactical slogans. Scientific and artistic cognition are divorced from facts, which cease to be objects of knowledge and are treated as illustrations of dogmatic propositions.

5. One scene repeated itself almost daily in the life of one or another average man of the Stalin era. The personnel director calls him in and asks, "Comrade, do you love Comrade Stalin?" "Of course I do," he replies. "Do you love Comrade Stalin enough?" the personnel man continues. He hesitates; if he says he loves him enough the personnel man will think him conceited, if he says he does not love him enough he will give proof of political weakness. Either way he may be in trouble. This banal dilemma indicates the total politicization of the daily life of the average citizen of a quarter of a century ago. There was no sphere of private life; in every aspect of his life he was compelled to profess his faith in the political system. He had to be at work before the regular working day began to discuss the leading article in last evening's party newspaper, the working day was interrupted by impromptu political meetings, and the walls of factories and offices were decorated with pictures of the leaders and slogans drawn from their speeches. Mass political meetings were a daily occurrence, at which workers had to present petitions asking for higher prices or a raising of production norms. At lunch or in the locker room correct answers had to be given to the trick questions of the agitator. One had to take part in ideological seminars; Sundays you had to go somewhere to do "social labor" or agitational work; you could not stay away from mass rallies, and if you were unwilling to subscribe a month's pay to the state loan campaign, you might have to face the most unpleasant consequences. When you left work you did not step back into private life, for in your apartment-house tenant meetings once again discussed the same political questions which had just been gone over a few hours

before at work. "Social work" might involve collecting scrap metal, editing a wall newspaper for the apartment-house lobby, or getting together with friends to march under the red flag singing movement songs. The more zealous set up little red corner shrines in their homes, complete with bunting, pictures of the leaders, works of Stalin, and candles. Even those who to be on the safe side hung a picture of Stalin over their marriage bed, thus linking the most intimate events of their lives with the course of world history, could hardly be accused of overzealousness. Many were the opportunities for testing the citizen's loyalty, and many the pitfalls. Anyone who tried to evade these tests immediately drew suspicion on himself and might eventually find himself labeled politically unreliable, with unforeseeable consequences. To be sure, the Western ideal of the separation of public and private life had sunk deep enough roots in Eastern European society so that, with a few exceptions (as when husband and wife called each other "comrade," or children reported their fathers for uttering incorrect opinions), politics did not penetrate into everyday family life. Thus even in the heyday of Stalinism the campaign against privatism never achieved such glowing results as in China, where the family unit became an integral part of the political mechanism. That is why Eastern European Stalinism, though it would very much have liked to, never won as much admiration as China did from Western radicals struggling against alienation and for personal fulfillment and an end to social frustration.

What changes can be described in the post-Stalin era, by comparison with the earlier period?

1. In the highest organs of the party the principle of collective leadership has triumphed. The First Secretary of the party shares power with the other members of the Politburo, and they divide up their duties among themselves, thus giving greater independence to the government, whose head is generally one of the more influential members of the Politburo. The First Secretary and the Politburo allow genuine debate to take place at the meetings of the Central Committee, and with that consider that they have fulfilled the requirement of assuring democracy within the party. More than that, indeed, the much-cited Leninist norms of party life scarcely demand.

Though the prestige of the First Secretary remains high, his cultic veneration ceases. Today the Communist First Secretaries of Eastern Europe are surrounded by the same sort of obligatory respect as a paternal constitutional monarch or the president of an important bourgeois democracy like the United States. Here and there one can find in offices a picture of the First Secretary, or the monarch or president, and one is expected to speak of him in a respectful way; but a crude remark about him can still bring a prison term in the Communist countries, while in the monarchies and presidential democracies it draws down no heavier sanctions than the disapproval of all right-thinking citizens. We hardly need add that kings and presidents can be freely criticized in polite language without any grievous consequences at all, while First Secretaries cannot be publicly criticized at all.

The collective leadership itself relies more heavily in its decision-making on the professional administration and on the heads of the technical bureaucracies, and for its own part recognizes as binding the formal rules of government administration. It respects the desire of the bureaucracy to have its sphere of activity and chain of command fixed and regularized through formal rules and regulations.

2. The party leadership has succeeded in bringing the police apparatus under its control and restricting it to its proper role in the judicial system. During the investigative process the police must observe the law. They may not arrest anyone or search anyone's home without first securing a warrant from the public prosecutor's office. They may not extort testimony by physical means. Witnesses and accused are no longer completely at the mercy of the prosecution; depending on their intelligence and knowledge of the law they can to some extent joust with the authorities. If they feel there have been procedural irregularities in the handling of their case they can turn to the public prosecutor for redress and will sometimes even find it.

The courts have a considerable degree of independence from the police; they are somewhat less independent of the party. In criminal proceedings the evidence collected by the police is subjected to careful scrutiny and genuine argument by the prosecution, defense counsel, and court. Convicts serve out their sentences in prisons under the jurisdiction of the Ministry of

Justice, not the Interior Ministry (to which the police are assigned), and insofar as prison regulations are observed they enjoy the full protection of the law.

All this to some extent rationalizes the citizen's relationship to the organs of public coercion. He cannot bring suit against the police for violating his constitutional rights by refusing him a passport, tapping his phone, opening his mail, or bugging his home, but if he abides by the letter of the law he will probably not wind up in jail. And if he does break the law he should be able more or less to estimate in advance the probable extent of his punishment.

On the other hand, the laws dealing with the rights of citizens almost invariably contain clauses giving the prosecuting authorities or other administrative organs the discretionary right to declare someone guilty or to restrict him in the exercise of his civil rights. In Hungarian law, for example, the prosecution does not have to prove that a critical remark or writing actually subverted anyone. To send someone to prison for subversion it is enough for the prosecution to show that the statements in question are of a sort that could be subversive. Thus the law has relinquished the only objective criterion for distinguishing legitimate criticism from antistate agitation. And since there is probably not a single citizen who has not at one time or another made fun of the official ideology or of important state institutions, we owe it only to the forbearance of the investigative and prosecuting authorities that we have not all been put in prison before now for subversion.

According to Hungarian law everyone is entitled to a passport, but the passport regulations allow the police to refuse anyone a passport on no further grounds than the bare statement that his travel abroad would be "harmful to the public interest"; and their decision cannot be appealed. Thus there is really no point in having passport laws and regulations, for the police still issue and deny passports just as they please.

The constitution guarantees the basic civil rights of citizens, such as the right of free speech, of assembly, of association, and the like, but in every case with the elastic proviso "in conformity with the interests of the working people," and those interests are left to the authorities to interpret. Thus the criminal authorities are empowered to mete out criminal sentences running to several years for a joke in a tavern, participation in a harmless demonstration, or a small private gathering of friends to discuss ideas for political reform. This nearly unlimited freedom of the authorities in interpreting constitutional rights and related legislation is sufficient to deter the citizen from making any practical use of the rights formally accorded him by law.

Still, relatively few go to prison for political reasons. By comparison with the Western bourgeois democracies the number of political prisoners is not unusually high in the Eastern European countries, the police are not conspicuous for brutality, and the prison regimen is not radically more stringent. But there is still an enormous gulf between paper rights and the practical options open to the citizenry, and the police are free to decide just how wide that gulf will be; the citizen meanwhile has no legal or political means of limiting their power to do so. For that reason these countries are still police states by comparison with the Western bourgeois democracies, although they are without doubt relatively mild police states.

3. The post-Stalin era has brought about a better-balanced development of the economy, liberalized agricultural policy, toned down the preference for heavy industry, given more attention to the development of the infrastructure and the service sector generally, and taken care to see that the standard of living rises gradually, by three or four percent a year. Through a variety of reform measures the direction of the economy has become somewhat more decentralized, and the autonomy of the individual enterprise has increased.

More modern methods of planning have been introduced, and even if planning directives have not been done away with they have been partly replaced by indirect price, tax, and credit regulators, and the number and importance of binding natural planning indicators has been reduced. As a result increased productivity, stemming from technical development, now plays a larger role in economic growth. The consumer market is better supplied with goods than formerly. More effective wage policies, geared more closely to actual work processes, have been introduced, and attempts have even been made (though rather timidly) to introduce various forms of profit-sharing.

4. As an alternative to Stalinist dogmatism Georg Lukács out-

lined a program for a "creative Marxism" around two basic demands: "back to the facts, and back to the values of Marxism." Science has been released from ideological service. It is no longer conceivable that a conference of atomic physicists and astronomers should declare—at party request—that the universe is not expanding, something which was not only quite thinkable twenty years ago in Eastern Europe but which actually happened at one university. Although fairly strict ideological controls have generally been maintained over the social sciences, there is at the same time a widespread recognition that there are many questions in history, anthropology, demography, sociology, linguistics, and psychology which can only be answered empirically. Today ideological control is exercised only over research topics or findings which touch on fundamental issues of Eastern European social structure, or which have some topical political relevance. Ideological interpretation has changed fundamentally: Where Stalinism was a simplistic distillate of a few works by Marx, post-Stalin Eastern European Marxism offers a sophisticated interpretation of Marx's entire oeuvre, and strives to incorporate the achievements of such non-Soviet Marxist thinkers as Lukács, Gramsci, and Althusser as well. From there, however, it is an easy and alluring, but dangerous, step to go on and try to integrate portions of the work of less-orthodox Western Marxists—Bloch and Korsch, Adorno and Habermas, Marcuse and Bettelheim; for broadening the legitimate basis of Marxism in that way leads inevitably to a critical threshold where one must affirm that different, equally legitimate schools of thought are possible within the basic value-range and methodology of Marxism, and that the same question can have several different Marxist answers, among which only scholarly debate can decide (if anything can), not the dictates of higher authority. The leaders of the Communist Parties have recognized, however, that this notion, so modest from the standpoint of scientific method and so banal for the reader unaccustomed to communism's inner debates, represents a mortal danger to the ideological leading role of the party, and for that reason they have cracked down on exponents of a plurality of Marxisms just as heavily as on empirical social scientists whose findings call into question the party's basic social and economic policies.

5. In the post-Stalin era politics no longer comes in through

the citizen's front door; the doorbell-ringing agitator has given way to the television screen. The total politicization of daily life has come to an end, and the sanctity of private life has been restored. Working hours are for working, not politics, and in your free time you can do what you like. You can still get into trouble easily enough if you talk politics in your private life, but no harm will befall you if instead of politicking you take an interest in football, music, stamp-collecting, or pigeon-raising. One sign of this change is the proliferation in recent years of completely depoliticized hobby-clubs, in which the citizen may freely exercise his right of association. Collective sports have given way to family camping, movement choruses to disk-jockey clubs and pop-music festivals. Enterprises no longer organize political rallies every week; one or two events a year, on important occasions, are enough. At these the main speaker is expected to talk no more than ten minutes and the listeners are no longer required to respond with cheers and applause, but may even nod off occasionally, awakening after the speeches, when management announces the award of wage premiums. Politics is a vanishing topic of conversation; after one or two jokes or anecdotes about the latest corruption scandal the talk turns to more important subjects, like one's summer house, vacation travel plans, matters of personal and domestic fashion, last night's TV movie, and marital problems. In fact the life of the average Polish, Czech, or Hungarian citizen is more rather than less privatized than that of the average Frenchman or Englishman. While the latter are even a bit apologetic about their consumption-oriented private lives, the former take hedonistic delight in knocking at the peasant's door on Sunday, not as agitators, but to seek out old pitchers for the new folk-art collections that grace their summer cottages. They no longer ransack the villagers' attics for hidden bacon, in an official capacity; now they are in search of dusty pots for which they will pay handsomely, with the self-respect which a solid bank balance confers and without any nostalgia for their earlier role of instructors of the people. The ideologues of the post-Stalin era are hard put to discern the revolutionary in this socialist private man and to demonstrate how he is the new human being of the new society, qualitatively different from every earlier type of personality. Their answer is the "revolutionary of everyday life," to whom all radical or negative criticism is foreign, a constructive revolutionary distinguished from the average citizen by his steadiness and sense of responsibility in every area of life. He works harder, is more exemplary in his family life, drives his car more carefully, cultivates his garden more conscientiously, studies to get ahead, and never forgets that everything he has he owes to society; indeed, if others forget that, he will be quick to remind them of it. The Western leftist might easily mistake this revolutionary of everyday life for the ideal of the good Christian, but we can assure him that there he would be wrong. For even though he may not know it the model Eastern European citizen, in shunning adultery and keeping the grass in his backyard mown, is actually strengthening the foundations of the family of socialist peoples. And if Western leftists cannot be content with that we can only grieve at their incomprehension.

In comparing the Stalinist and post-Stalinist periods of Eastern European socialism we have simply summarized in brief what these systems say about themselves and what the Western press generally writes or might write about them. But however striking the differences that emerge, a purely political and economic comparison of the two eras, couched in descriptive terms alone, still does not disclose any fundamental changes in the structure of Eastern European society. Yet, as we suggested earlier, the two periods do in fact differ from each other structurally. The first is characterized by the power monopoly of the ruling elite, the second by a joint exercise of power on the part of the ruling elite and the intellectual class, within which the hegemony still lies with the former. It is as if an absolute autocracy had given way to a constitutional monarchy.

Though the ideologies woven about them dwell on the growing democratization of the system, the economic reforms and social changes of the post-Stalin era have not affected its basic structure. The role of redistribution has not been reduced in the least; on the contrary, its rationalization has increased the power of the redistributors. As a result, those social interests which crystallize around the position of the redistributors, forming a potential class regime of the intellectuals, have become even more pronounced. The post-Stalinist period's attempts at economic and social reform, its thaws and freezes, reflect conflicts within the intellectual class. The issue in these struggles is always how far the circle of intellectuals empowered to make redistributive decisions should be broadened. The reformers generally do not dispute the logic of redistribution; they seek merely to secure more autonomy, and more power, for various sectors of the intellectual class within a more widely extended process of redistribution. The structure of the system has never been called into doubt by successive measures of decentralization or by the greater scope which they have in fact given to the interests of particular strata of intellectuals.

The intellectuals may argue over how far they should be subordinated to one another, but the very nature of intellectual class-consciousness does not permit them to envisage circumstances in which intellectuals are subordinated to nonintellectuals. The factory manager may be happy to acquire more autonomy vis-à-vis his ministry, but he would gladly give most of it back if it meant that simultaneously his workers were gaining more autonomy vis-à-vis him. In redistributive society order must prevail, and keeping order is the business of the intellectuals: Thus we might summarize most succinctly the ethos of the intellectual class. One may argue, while still remaining within the logic of the system, about who should tell people where they can build houses—the ministry, the planning office, or the municipality—but no one can question that *somebody has to tell them* where they can build without betraying the whole class ethos. Casting doubt on that qualifies at best as petty-bourgeois spontaneity; taken in a less charitable vein, as anarchy or incitement against authority.

The fundamental dichotomy in the social structure between the intellectual class and the working class has not changed in the least; if anything it has been brought into even sharper relief than during the Stalinist years. That is so largely because the intellectuals have been freed from the danger of persecution and from any sense of personal insecurity generally, and can confidently give expression to their awareness that "we" are in charge; they can use the first person plural in criticizing the errors of the past, among whose victims they were numbered, and in going about perfecting the social and political practice of the present, in which they are substantial partners. With that the Eastern European socialist societies have moved closer to their real essence. The period of the autocratic rule of the elite turned out, as we have seen, to be a costly but indispensable detour; now that it is past, the intellectuals have at last taken over permanently the social position which they foresaw for themselves in socialist society in the years after the revolution, and which the repression of the Stalin era so traumatically and inexplicably deprived them of for a time.

In Eastern Europe the personnel needed to run a system of socialist redistribution was recruited from two different intellectual groups. The first was the early technocracy which had already, in the course of managing a bureaucratic war economy, begun to display some of the earmarks of the class rule of the intelligentsia. The other was that prophetic revolutionary intelligentsia which among other things furnished the cadres of the narrow Communist Party elite. Both groups willingly undertook to occupy the command posts of the new state apparatus and of the nationalized economy. If Stalinism came to view the intellectuals with suspicion and hostility, thrusting most of them into the background where it did not deprive them of intellectual status altogether, that was no fault of the intelligentsia, who were eager to serve; it was only the consequence of the aspirations of the emerging ruling elite to a monopoly of power.

The readiness of the Eastern European intelligentsia, especially the technical intelligentsia, to accept the role awaiting them in socialist redistribution did not mean that they early on embraced the ideology of Bolshevism. It was not so much their political ideas as their social situation that made the professional intelligentsia receptive to Bolshevism and to the prospects which the socialist state offered. The Eastern European intellectuals did not "become socialists" because a reading of *Das Kapital* had convinced them of the validity of Marxism, but rather because in the position they occupied in society they had developed over the years an ethos which could easily find expression in the language of teleological redistribution. They offered their loyalty and their services to the new social system because they were profoundly excited by the opportunities which it seemed to offer them.

A scientifically ordered society held great attractions for the Eastern European intelligentsia, as did the fact that intellectuals were being called upon for their expert knowledge in the construction of the new social order. They were exhilarated at the opportunity to help eliminate the obstacles which had hitherto prevented the creation of a new society, whether they were obsolete feudal privileges or the first chaotic features of an emerging capitalism; once these were overcome the age of planned rationality would open before them. That was why socialist society was able to rely from the first on the loyalty of the technical intelligentsia, even though they did not for a moment pretend to be adherents of Communist doctrine or of the dictatorship of the proletariat. They sensed that socialist redistribution placed in their hands a power incomparably greater than any they had ever had before. An engineer from a small factory could advance to a position where he might supervise the investment of billions. An architect accustomed to designing private villas could go on to draw the plans for giant industrial complexes or whole sections of cities. An economist who once had to be content with a well-paid but not very influential consular post, or at best a university professorship, could now be the head of a planning office with a budget in the billions. A poet who once paid for the publication of his verses out of the proceeds of a clerical job could now live in a one-time chocolate manufacturer's villa, and see his poems published in editions of tens of thousands and recited on revolutionary holidays in hundreds of factory and village houses of culture. A librarian who used to rejoice if he could interest a few readers in his favorite books could now command from his post high in the ministry that libraries be organized in every factory and village with funds from his budget, and could determine their contents, at the same time removing from existing collections not only books which offended ideologically but also any which went against his literary taste.

The humanist intellectuals felt themselves just as much called to disseminate the cultural values of socialism as the economists and technicians did to redistribute the national income. On the eve of the socialist revolution the Eastern European intellectuals longed for the chance to free themselves from the control of laymen, the humiliating necessity of serving untutored landowners and manufacturers. From now on the people with the requisite professional knowledge would be the ones to make the decisions. It gratified them to think that knowledge, not property, would legitimize the right to make decisions. They saw in socialism the advent of a society more genuinely based on the performance principle than bourgeois society had turned out to be. The intellectuals hailed their new situation as the realization of their own transcendence. They could finally rise above the service of particular interests, the role assigned to them in bourgeois society, and undertake to serve the universal interests of the new collective owners, the whole working people, and ultimately even the goals of world history. And even where their actual work did not change, it still acquired a transcendent meaning: It was ennobled, elevated from a money-making profession into a calling.

These characteristics of the Eastern European intelligentsia help explain why in most of those countries the socialist revolution was not heralded by peasant seizures of land or worker occupation of factories, nor enforced by waves of strikes; on the contrary, Communist and other left intellectuals divided the land among the peasants and explained to the workers that nationalization was a good thing. On the eve of the socialist revolutions the intellectuals lined up en masse behind the Communist parties. The older technocrats, after soberly weighing their interests, accepted their new status with a dignity befitting expert professionals; the radicalized young, organized into militant shock troops under charismatic leaders, lent to events the appearance of a broad revolutionary upheaval. They streamed into the party, and once there rose rapidly through the ranks of a greatly expanded officialdom, eventually reaching the comfortably upholstered seats of power, where like their older colleagues they could hurry from conference to conference in black limousines. Thus the scene of revolutionary conflict shifted with almost magical rapidity from the streets to the conference tables of the ministries.

It was this high-hearted intelligentsia which was now forced to submit to the cathartic experience of the political elite's monopolistic rule. It had to learn that the road to class power was longer and more painful than it at first believed. The ruling elite which had formed in the meantime, just as quickly and almost imperceptibly, ousted large numbers of intellectuals from power. Those who remained were converted from revolutionaries or technical experts into apparatchiks. Intellectuals who realized in time which way the wind was blowing were allowed to go on working in peripheral, low-ranking positions, where they languished under onerous political controls and under the authority of technically inept superiors. Those who gave any sign of not accepting the ruling elite's monopoly of power were declassed, expelled from the ranks of the intellectual class.

This rapid turn of events, almost too rapid to follow, did not of course manifest its dramatic logic in the life of every single individual. Who wound up where was in many cases a matter of sheer luck, the work of a sometimes comically absurd combination of circumstances. One man would be expelled from the party and lose his job because his father had owned an apartment house, another because his half-brother was an officer in the American army or because he had been too friendly with a superior convicted of treason, because his correspondence with a French friend put him under suspicion of treason, because an ambitious informer turned him in for some innocent remark, or because he spoke admiringly of Freud, Mondrian, or Camus (or slightingly of a celebrated Soviet novel). It was not their fault that they were excluded from their class; they came to that end not because of any criticism they made of the ruling elite, but simply because circumstances quite beyond their control made it possible to suppose that they were not unwaveringly committed to the interests of the elite.

Shouldered aside from political power, the intellectuals once again began to regard their work less as a calling and more as a profession. The fiery lecturer on political economy became a careful econometrician, the empire-building academic administrator a laboratory researcher, the university party secretary a solid historian. The great majority of the intellectual class saw that there was no place for them in the ruling elite, gave up their political ambitions, and acknowledged the political leadership of the ruling elite. If at heart they did not accept the elite's monopoly of power and only waited for the first opportunity to question it, for the time being they had no desire to enter the elite either, or even to replace it, but simply, by throwing their gradually increasing professional weight into the balance, to arrive at a reasonable compromise with the ruling elite. By the late 1950s and early 1960s the conditions had ripened on both sides for such a compromise, at once cynical and deeply heartfelt.

THE RULING ELITE AND THE TECHNOCRACY REACH A COMPROMISE

The stability of the post-Stalin era is founded on an alliance between the technocracy and the ruling elite. The closer the alliance the more stable the system, as in the German Democratic Republic as early as the 1960s, or Czechoslovakia from the early 1970s, or for that matter the Soviet Union of Leonid Brezhnev. While not altogether happy that the ruling elite exercises a hegemonic authority over it, the technocracy is still unable to swing the balance of this unequal alliance in its favor by its own efforts alone. This compromise encompasses a protracted historical period, which forms the second stage of early socialism. Its content is determined by the mutual concessions which the ruling elite and the technocracy have incorporated into their unwritten agreement.

The ruling elite's concessions

The technocracy has succeeded in making the ruling elite give up its exclusive privileges as reflected in its standard of living and the external marks of its life-style. It has won incomes comparable with those of the elite, or close to it. It has put an end to the special stores and residential neighborhoods reserved exclusively for the elite and protected by armed guards, where the ordinary citizen could not set foot. The offices and homes of the technocrats are just as tastefully appointed today as those of the oligarchs of the ruling elite. Many domestic and foreign observers of the 1960s, taking as their basis for comparison the living standards of the working class, saw in this equalization a sign of growing inequality in Eastern Europe. What in fact happened was that within the general "equality" the number of those who were *more equal* than others actually multiplied during this period. Today a leading technocrat's life is actually more pleasant than that of a high-ranking party man. His home and income are in no way inferior, he drives a better car, travels abroad more often, can move about more freely; his authority at the office will not be undermined if he is regularly seen in public with his girl friend while his wife sits at home with the children.

Of course the life of the ruling elite and the life of the technocracy still differ considerably. The members of the elite still live largely to themselves; even in their recreations they still associate almost exclusively with one another. It strikes people as odd if the Politburo member in charge of culture makes the otherwise natural gesture of having lunch with prominent intellectuals in a restaurant, or drives his car himself when he travels abroad with his family, or goes to a concert or exhibition without a security man along. Few can afford such gestures, for members of the ruling elite who associate too freely with the intellectual class can easily fall under suspicion; their authority can always be undermined by the jealousy of passed-over comrades.

In the exclusiveness and narrow range of their social contacts the political leadership's way of life resembles that of the onetime office-holding and landed nobility. It is an ingrown style of life, characterized by private drinking bouts, indulgence in the less mentally demanding card games, ever more elaborate hunting expeditions, private parties at lodges closed to the general public, and ceremonial dinners in one another's honor, at public expense. The elite still has its own vacation resorts and vessels, and all the practices and institutions which set it apart also serve to integrate it still further, through a network of informal ties. At its social gatherings important decisions are made, of a sort which it might be painful to discuss at formal meetings. It is there that important appointments may mature, there that a senior official may casually drop a critical or laudatory remark about certain of his subordinates—the sort of thing it is important to overhear, for it reflects the political influence of the names mentioned. On such occasions nuances of ideology come out which junior members of the elite would do well to emphasize in their own speeches. Anyone who stays away from these gatherings has to have a great deal of self-confidence indeed, for he will not only miss out on important bits of information and occasionally lose the chance to influence an important decision, but he also runs the risk that in his absence he will himself become the target of critical comments which, by undermining his political credit, can even lead ultimately to his fall.

We should hasten to add that these latter traits are more characteristic of the lower-ranking members of the elite, especially provincial party and state officials and their entourage. The aristocrats of the regime, the national leaders, pay homage to these customs only when they travel about the country, and often against their better judgment. They themselves are already experimenting with a new model of conduct, that of the technocracy, which in the last analysis does not differ much from the life-style of the bourgeois intelligentsia. They would sooner read than drink, play tennis rather than hunt, play chess instead of cards. In their official dealings they like to flash their culture; appealing to the common consciousness of the intelligentsia, they wax ironic at the boorishness of the run of party members, as if to solicit sympathy at having to work with such people. They prefer to play down their undoubted superiority in power over nonparty intellectuals rather than to emphasize it; having come in contact with the more free-and-easy way of life of the intelligentsia, they are more likely to strike a note of nostalgic self-pity rather than moral superiority.

The technocracy has not been content merely to see its material and social status rise; by vindicating professional knowledge and achievement as principles which legitimate power, it has called into question the power monopoly of the ruling elite. Nor can it demand that expert knowledge and performance bring recognition for the technocrats alone. In this respect they are compelled, like it or not, to represent the interests of the whole intellectual class. No technocrat can feel secure so long as the best minds in science and art languish in prison or are forced to earn their living at menial jobs which stultify their creative powers. The technocracy will really come to trust the ruling elite, will consider its most fundamental demands fulfilled, only when the ruling elite readmits to the intellectual class all those who were declassed during the Stalinist era; and, what is

more, forbears locking them up again in times of renewed conflict but permits them to live from some kind of intellectual activity, forcing them to the fringes of the intellectual class perhaps
but not banishing them from it altogether. By extracting the
concession that critics who come into conflict with the elite will
suffer no worse fate than to become marginal intellectuals, the
technocracy has rationalized the character of punishment. It is
inclined to treat marginality as a kind of temporary quarantine
from which those momentarily silenced can emerge after a
reasonable length of time—four or five years, perhaps—to resume
their careers, after giving due indications of loyalty but without
dramatic recantations, and thence pursue their way undisturbed
as their performance warrants through the hierarchy of professional regard.

The technocracy has an interest in preventing the banishment
of those who create new values—artists, writers, and ideologues,
those who most easily blunder onto the treacherous slope of
marginality—and not only in its capacity of spokesman for the
entire intellectual class, nor merely in order to consolidate its
own status vis-à-vis the ruling elite. For undisturbed intellectual
exchange with the creative intelligentsia is indispensable to the
technocrats if they are to carry out their own functions, and
indeed they would not feel themselves to be intellectuals without
it. More specifically, the technocracy looks to these intellectuals
for its own potential ideologues, who can interpret and articulate
its own situation and stimulate its consciousness of itself. It needs
ideas, conceptions, even criticism of structural reforms designed
to strengthen its own position. Again, in their free time the
technocrats are, without further qualification, intellectuals; they
go out on the day of publication to buy the books which a latent
literary public opinion recommends even when official critics
have condemned them; they are regular concert-goers demanding classical and modern music alike; in their clubs they organize
exhibitions of avant-garde artists driven underground by official
criticism or turn the stage over to experimental theater groups;
all the more so as very often they are themselves amateur artists,
ethnographers, archaeologists, or philosophers, and they find it
unnatural if the creators and innovators they admire the most
are not permitted to create.

The technocracy and the ruling elite: The ties that bind

Many things divide the technocrats from the ruling elite, but many things tie them to it as well. The most powerful of these is fear. The technocrats learned during the Stalinist era that they could avoid trouble by conscientiously carrying out the orders of the party leadership, while no good could come of it if they began themselves to weigh the wisdom of those directives. They learned not to strive for autonomy, not to presume to judge the rationality of government policy, not to dispute the authority of their political superiors. Eastern European tradition played a part in the readiness of the technocracy to subordinate itself to the politocracy, for it was not the practice in any of the Eastern European empires, whether Romanov, Hohenzollern, or Habsburg, for officials and government experts to question central policy directives. For intellectuals, Eastern Europe over the past century has been an excellent school in the virtues of being good subjects.

Once economics and politics are integrated into a system of state interventionism which penetrates everywhere, the management of the system by administrative authorities endowed with a mantle of technical expertise does not offend the mentality of the technocrats (a mentality unique to them within the larger intellectual class). In exchange for their allegiance to the ruling elite, the technocrats' activities receive the stamp of authority. They share in the unquestioned authority of government by administrative decision. Thus it is no wonder if the humanistic and artistic intelligentsia, with their critical and antiauthoritarian inclinations, do not always enjoy the complete sympathy of the technocracy as a whole. The managers of great enterprises, the chief engineers, and the planners, empowered by the elite in the first period of socialism to run vast organizations and spend large sums of money because of their technical expertise, became the technical embodiment of higher political authority; they found their place with surprising ease in the dictatorial machinery of redistribution, whatever private reservations they may have harbored about its political aspects. The plan was law; it had to be executed, not discussed—that was the accepted doctrine of the Stalinist era. And the technocracy's obedience was undoubtedly reinforced by the fact that it was itself one of the prime beneficiaries of that doctrine. It has not been easy for technocrats trained in the apparatchik-mentality of the Stalin era to develop the habit of autonomy in the era of compromise, much less to tolerate strivings for autonomy on the part of their subordinates. The relativization of the infallibility of orders brought about a real crisis of conscience for many technocrats, demanding of them a complete transformation of their traditional system of values. There the ideologues of the intellectual class were, or could have been, of great assistance. Where they in fact undertook the task the technocracy itself became pluralized, started to acquire a taste for autonomy, and began to align itself politically with its new ally, the revisionist intelligentsia (as it is generally known in Eastern Europe). In those countries where the rise of a revisionist intelligentsia was prevented, where the party maintained its direct control over the arts and social sciences and managed to isolate or even declass dissident ideologues and artists, the technocracy has remained on the whole the obedient servant of the ruling elite, at most exacting compensation for its subordinate status in the form of a higher level of material rewards.

The technocracy is also bound to the ruling elite by the monopolies which the elite accords to its favorites among the technocrats. It does the head of a construction enterprise no harm if his organization is given a complete monopoly of building in a certain region; nor does it hurt the managers of a productive enterprise if they can double the capital they have received from state subsidies, keep all the proceeds, and use it to open new plants, bringing still more personnel under their authority —thus increasing their chances of getting still more budgetary allocations, not on account of their economic efficiency but because of their increased political influence. This process is responsible for the rise of many giant, modern-looking industrial complexes where the visitor's eye is dazzled by row upon row of the most modern machines, from the computers to the showers. Not a word is said about politics, only technical buzz-words fly, and every question will receive a crisp, precise professional reply until the visitor asks whether the products of this cathedral of technology are competitive on the world market.

It is not just the technocrats who have a stake in monopolies distributed almost in the manner of feudal benefices. Less-gifted ideologues, artists, and scholars welcome them too. It does the unimaginative researcher no harm if a certain scholarly topic can be investigated only in his institute. An incompetent director will not grieve if a state grant saves his theater from closing, while a competing university theater group is banned. Nor will the humorless humorist crack jokes about monopolies if he is the only one permitted to tell (carefully censored) political jokes on TV. Through the distribution of monopolies and subsidies, then, the ruling elite insinuates a whole fifth column of dullards into the technocracy and into the intellectual class as a whole.

While benefiting some, monopolies by definition injure others; in the present case the victims are the more able and more competitive managers who do not need to hustle for subsidies and who pride themselves not on how much state support they have succeeded in begging, but on how much profit they have made. Thus the interests of the monopoly hunters come into conflict with the interests of the technocracy as a whole. The ruling elite, by scattering alms in the form of monopolies among the technocrats, is able to divide the technocracy and so to some extent disarm its rivals for hegemony.

In exchange for the concessions accorded it the technocratic intelligentsia accepts the limits set by the ruling elite, not only for itself but also on behalf of the whole intellectual class. What are those limits? The ruling elite allows no discussion of questions relating to the political structure or, rather, of the institutionalized dogmas which deal with those questions. Among them are the following: "Socialism is morally more just and economically more efficient than capitalism." "There is only one valid model of socialism, and that is the Soviet model, although in applying it national peculiarities must be taken into account." "The Soviet Union plays the leadership role among the socialist countries." "The working class is the leading class in socialist society." "The leading force in socialist society is the Communist Party, the party of the working class." "Marxism-Leninism, the ideology of the party and its guide in building socialism, is one and indivisible; there cannot be different schools of thought within it." "Every tenet of Marxism-Leninism is true and always has been true. Any criticism of it on the basis of empirical knowledge, any historical relativization of it, any attempt to point out possible inconsistencies in its premises, constitutes revisionism, which must be fought by every means necessary."

The Eastern European technocracy tends to treat these dogmas as sacred cows—limits which, though confining, cannot be called into question. The attitude of the technocracy toward these taboos was well expressed in a recent Hungarian film, *Walls*, whose very title carried its message: Don't try to break down the walls, strive instead to extend the range of activity possible within their confines. That is also the gist of the Eastern European intelligentsia's stereotyped justification of their compromises: "Even at the risk of compromising myself I have to stay in power, because the people who would replace me would stop short long before reaching the wall, while I am ready to go all the way up to it, even though I certainly won't beat my head against it." Thus the compromise between the ruling elite and the technocracy is sublimated into a high moral duty, which tends to obscure its real significance. Any genuine analysis becomes impossible amid this haze of sentiment and self-justification; its place is taken by moralizing and by an intellectual atmosphere which in general only encourages the spread of dogma.

In liberal periods these dogmas remain sacred cows, not to be disturbed, but they do not cause much trouble. They merely hang over actual intellectual and economic practice in the shape of sanctified but relatively abstract theses. They are inviolable, but they can always be gotten around in any important matter. It is during these periods that revisionist arguments germinate, economic reforms ripen, and the technocracy screws up its courage to challenge the ruling elite. Then, however, when the elite, feeling its power ebbing away, launches a counteroffensive, it is forced to revive and give point to dogmas which meanwhile paled into abstractions. In doing so it must necessarily resuscitate the spirit of a time when every technical question was to be solved in the light of dogma. Then the technocrats have to call a halt to their rationalizing tendencies and have to cite ideological theses more frequently in order to justify their professional activities. Pure science has to give up some of its strategic gains, abandoning ideas, theories, and even technical terms which only yesterday were perfectly legitimate. Respected scholars engage in self-criticism in order to hold on to their jobs, or else bury themselves in recondite research, and the whole intelligentsia looks on uneasily while resurgent dogma inundates the columns of newspapers and the programs of conferences, and the empirical sciences shrink back into their modest role of handmaidens of doctrine. Freethinkers put on intellectual uniform again and under cover of a protective verbal camouflage wait for the ruling elite's latest ideological offensive to spend itself, for the onset of a new thaw. The regular ebb and flow of dogmatism in the second period of socialism mirrors quite precisely the play of forces in the compromise-confrontation of the technocracy and the ruling elite. The conflict may reach a point where the combatants are willing to break the basic rules of the compromise, the technocracy by challenging the hegemony of the ruling elite, the elite by trying to retract the relative degree of autonomy it has accorded the technocracy. In general, however, this seesaw contest remains within the rules of the tacit agreement between the elite and the technocracy, and does not violate the sportsmanlike rules worked out for it by the two contestants.

Over the long run it seems unlikely that this uneasy compromise-alliance can remain permanently at the level of a mere latent struggle of interests. The technocracy does not suffer the hegemony of the elite gladly; it only acquiesces in it for tactical reasons, for its fundamental values—performance, achievement—are in conflict with the organization of the elite. Even during the period of compromise, moreover, the intellectual class as a whole has begun to acquire a growing consciousness of itself, especially the marginal intelligentsia, which at times comes into open conflict with the ruling elite. At those critical junctures the technocracy must decide which it prefers to turn to for its ally.

THE ELITE'S COUNTEROFFENSIVE

The 1970s have seen the ruling elite launch its counteroffensive in almost every Eastern European country. The antecedents, extent, and presumable goals of this counteroffensive vary from country to country. So far as its antecedents are concerned, in Bulgaria, Romania, and East Germany the ruling elite never offered a compromise at all to the intellectual class (as represented by the technocracy), never lent itself to potentially risky experiments with economic reform, never made any ideological concessions to the humanist intelligentsia, even after the demise of Stalinism; it altered its strategy only to the extent of taking some of the technocrats into partnership, simultaneously moderating the excesses of a voluntaristic planning policy and so rationalizing the redistributive process to some degree. In the other countries the elite's counteroffensive grew out of its compromise with the technocracy, and was called forth by a gradual weakening of the hegemonic authority of the elite. In the Soviet Union it began as early as the mid-1960s, following the dismissal of Khrushchev, in Czechoslovakia around 1969, after the forcible liquidation of the Dubček regime. The defeat of efforts toward further liberalization in Prague was a signal to every Eastern European country that the technocracy had gone as far as it could and that any attempt to go further would bring severe reprisals. It convinced the Polish, Hungarian, and eventually even the Yugoslav leaders that the time had come to begin jettisoning their reform policies and to accommodate themselves to the Soviet elite's strategy of an Eastern European-wide counteroffensive. We cannot yet say whether that strategy is designed to overthrow the equilibrium of the compromise period (an equilibrium that has not even been achieved yet in every country) and to restore the elite's onetime power monopoly through a kind of neo-Stalinism (in which case the East Germany of the 1960s would be the model for the rest of Eastern Europe), or whether the objective is simply to stop the erosion of the ruling elite's hegemony. In the latter case the result of the counteroffensive would only be to postpone the advent of the class rule of the intellectuals for years or even decades, during which time the technocracy could gather its strength, rally the intellectuals, and prepare society through a series of gradual reforms for the class rule of the intellectuals, whose early prototype was the Yugoslavia of the 1960s.

Although the outcome of the elite's counteroffensive still cannot be predicted with any degree of certainty, it is possible on the basis of the experience of the past few years to describe the new elements in the elite's plan of attack. In broad outline, the ruling elite seeks to disrupt the class unity of the intellectuals as it has been developing around the technocracy, and to frustrate any attempt on the intelligentsia's part to form an alliance with the working class by appealing to its transactive instincts. To do so the elite has tried to split the intellectuals, integrating the economic and technical intelligentsia into a loyal technocracy which shares the privileges of the elite and is bound to think like it to some extent. The rest of the intelligentsia, in particular the humanist intellectuals, have been put under strict supervision; those who rebel against it, or even grumble too loudly about it, are once again being driven from the intellectual class. By contrast with the savage police repression of the Stalin era, however, new technocratic methods are used to control and isolate dissent. An important element in the strategy is the expansion of those groups within the working class and middle strata who enjoy various elite privileges and so, unlike the working class as a whole, have no interest in seeing genuinely transactive social and economic relations introduced. Since their fortunes depend on their dispositive status, they are content to accept the ruling elite's interpretation of the redistributive ethos. Thus the ruling elite is reinforcing its supporters in the technocracy with the silent majority of the middle strata and with an ever-growing labor aristocracy, cutting across class lines to create, within every class, strata whose interests tie them to the ruling elite at least as much as to their own class. It has rallied around itself a kind of cross-class "elite party" whose economic situation is characterized by a dispositive status and by the rewards that go with it, and whose ideological behavior is marked by an unquestioning loyalty to the elite.

The ruling elite, in other words, has taken advantage of that dual aspect of the technocracy which has permitted it all along to introduce into its ranks a fifth column loyal to the elite. The number of technocrats cut in on the privileges of the elite and bound to it by family and other personal ties is being swollen with intellectuals who are not able enough or patient enough to rise via the usual ladder of promotion and so, in exchange for more rapid advancement, demonstrate unconditional political loyalty. Thus a new type of technical expert makes his appearance, in the form of the economist willing to put mathematical methods at the service of the elite with something less than professional scrupulousness, or the psychologist who goes to work for the political police; they may use the methods of the technocracy but they have traded its outlook for the mentality of the elite. There is little that the other technocrats can do about this politico-technocracy, which has raised ambition and accommodation almost to the level of moral principle, for nobody is indispensable. If they protest against it too much they can always be replaced easily enough from the multitude of candidates for the good jobs that carry more prestige, money, and leisure time, who are particularly numerous among the victims of declining social mobility, the young.

Bolstered by this new politico-technocracy, the elite is in a position to update the economic and political methods which it employed in the days of its absolute rule. It uses them to disarm technocratic criticism of Stalinist economic policies, claiming that to eliminate the anomalies of Stalinist planning it is enough merely to introduce more scientific methods of planning and managing the economy. Thus, it contends, there is no need for a thoroughgoing reform of the economic mechanism. This was the argument used to reject Liberman's reform proposals in the Soviet Union, to block reform in East Germany, and to reverse the reform tendencies in Czechoslovakia and more recently in Hungary as well. Adopting technocratic methods of economic management has in fact enabled the elite to avoid gross blunders in economic policy and to develop the various branches of the economy in relatively balanced fashion. And so it has been able to avoid economic crises, to raise living standards steadily if not spectacularly, to assure a relative equilibrium of supply and demand, and to prevent economic dissatisfaction from breaking out in political upheaval.

Capitalizing on these achievements of the post-Stalin era, the elite uses its power over the consumption aspect of redistribution to broaden its own loyal cross-class base. That effort explains the strident new ouvrierist phraseology of its counteroffensive. In its name measures have been taken over a broad range of areas, from housing to education, which do in fact have the effect of giving workers greater opportunity to share in non-monetary, "natural" budgetary allocations. That, however, means only an expansion of the ranks of the privileged, since by reason of their very scarcity and indivisibility it is impossible to reward the *whole* working class with such benefits as new apartments and scholarships for further study; nor is it possible to distribute them in accordance with productivity, for the same reasons. Thus those who are to receive them are selected on the criterion of loyalty to the elite. This duality is clearly seen in the housing measures taken in Hungary in the 1970s, which in fact raised the quota for working-class families in the distribution of apartments built with state funds, thereby extending benefits to a small minority of the working class. But the great majority of workers were left quite untouched by them; indeed, a new tax was imposed on families building their own homes, a category composed in the main of working people. The elite's policies toward the workers have undergone a sharp differentiation since the counteroffensive began: It has granted even more favors than before to the labor aristocracy and tried at the same time to enlarge it somewhat, while taking ever stronger measures against workers who resort to transactive economic relations to better their lot. This strange ouvrierism has dropped the slogan of material incentives, tightened production norms in the name of improving the organization of labor, introduced Taylorite systems of calculating wages, made it more difficult for workers to change jobs, raised the tax burden on peasants who work their own farms, and forbidden the sale of essential equipment to them. It has brought the full weight of the propaganda media to bear against workers who earn their living outside of the bureaucratically organized labor force, making it more difficult for workers to become independent artisans and sometimes raising the tax burden on small craftsmen to almost intolerable levels. It has intervened by administrative decree to prevent higher-than-average wage increases in more profitable industries. The ruling elite uses a carrot-and-stick policy on the working class, conferring even greater favors than before on the labor aristocracy, as if to illustrate how it pays to settle for a dispositive status, while at the same time it comes down hard on workers who try to better their condition through any kind of economic transaction.

12

Some Notes on the Relationship between the Working Class and the Intellectual Class

In some of the critical ideologies of the compromise period the marginal intelligentsia has already made attempts to go beyond the ethos of rational redistribution to articulate the latent interests of other classes and strata, thus beginning to function as their organic intelligentsia. It is true, of course, that in the last analysis these interests are at variance with the interests of the technocracy and indeed of the whole intellectual class; nevertheless it seems probable that if the technocracy is to challenge the hegemony of the ruling elite it will have to allow the interests of the other classes to find a voice.

We must point once again to the parallels between the struggles of the capitalist class and the intellectual class to win power. The bourgeoisie was unable to overthrow feudalism until it ventured to ally itself with the plebeian masses, even allowing the proletariat, with which it was itself in conflict, to formulate and struggle for its own separate interests. In much the same way the intellectual class will only be able to throw off the tutelage of the elite and acquire class power if it permits some of the marginal intellectuals to articulate the interests of the working class. The technocracy, if it wishes to overcome the present disadvantageous power balance, must strengthen the unity of the intellectual class, ally itself with the marginal intelligentsia, and even allow some of the latter to act as the organic intelligentsia of the working class. It goes without saying that the technocracy is not going to agree with what these intellectuals say, but it must be content to use no more than a repressive tolerance against them, as against the repressive intolerance of the ruling elite.

The reason for this difference in methods is not that the technocracy can boast any moral superiority over the ruling elite, but simply that the technocracy has an interest in the existence of an actively functioning working-class intelligentsia. Those who wish to wield power effectively must always adopt some of the criticisms made by intellectuals acting as spokesmen for opposition interests. The technocracy is all the more capable of absorbing this criticism because the critical intelligentsia is itself Janus-faced: On the one hand it is the intelligentsia of the working class, but on the other—and this is perhaps the crucial point—it is part of the intellectual class, from which neither its structural position nor its value-system will allow it to secede.

Thus we anticipate that at some point socialism will enter a third stage, characterized by a division of power between a technocracy and a ruling elite dealing with each other through rational transactions. In that stage there will repeatedly emerge from the ranks of marginal intellectuals advocating worker interests a few individuals who, having thoroughly pondered the meaning of their own social existence, will become the direct protagonists of class power for the intellectuals. On the other side, the working class's intelligentsia will constantly be replenished by dropout intellectuals who join the working class partly because they are attracted to a marginal role, partly because they have been forced temporarily into the working class, and also by young workers situated on the boundary of working-class and intellectual life, who will not need to traverse the steps of the bureaucratic hierarchy leading out of the working class in order to become full-fledged intellectuals.

The technocracy must come to terms with the marginal intellectuals and permit some of them to articulate working-class interests if only because the ruling elite has always justified its own power largely by appealing to the interests of the workers. The elite's claim to represent the workers is not altogether unfounded. We observed earlier that the ruling Communist Parties have a dual class base: They are mass parties of the intelligentsia, but also cadre parties of the working class. We also pointed out that the elite carefully screens the intellectuals who seek to join its ranks, and that intellectuals per se do not enter the ruling elite in any great numbers. For that reason relatively few of the members of the ruling elite are professional intellectuals or children of intellectuals; even though the majority of party members are intellectuals or at least white-collar people, the members of the ruling elite proper are predominantly of working-class origin. The opportunity for workers to become intellectuals by rising through the elite makes the party function as a cadre party of the working class.

Party membership means one thing for workers, another for intellectuals. Intellectuals join the party in order to insure that they can pursue their careers undisturbed. For the worker party membership is a way to become an intellectual; it means emancipation from the worker's life (or at least from physical labor) and ascent into the middle strata. For workers the party is an express elevator of social mobility. Workers who are active in the party's base organizations rise almost automatically in the hierarchy; they become foremen, supervisors, perhaps party employees—in a word, cadres. Those who do not wish to break with the worker's life, on the other hand, will not much bother with work in the base organizations even if they should join the party, and after a time they will most probably drop their memberships. It is quite another question whether this remarkable channel of working-class mobility actually offers any guarantee that the best and most class-conscious workers will really enter the elite. But in order to form a valid opinion of the relationship between the class interests of the elite and those of the working class, and of the structural position of workers who join the elite, we must turn again to the class structure of rational redistribution and to the internal articulation of its two dichotomous classes, especially the working class.

Rational-redistributive society, as we have said, can best be described as a dichotomous class structure in which the classical antagonism of capitalist and proletarian is replaced by a new one between an intellectual class being formed around the position of the redistributors, and a working class deprived of any right to participate in redistribution. Under rational redistribution, however, social conflicts do not appear in the form of open class conflict, since in the absence of organic class intelligentsias class interests cannot be articulated openly, and no class can develop a clear consciousness of its strategic goals. Indeed, can we even say that the classes have different interests if these do not find expression in distinct ideologies? Or, going one step further: If class interests are never explicitly formulated, so that no such thing exists as a "class for itself," can we speak at all of any "class in itself"?

One possible answer is that the absence of clearly formulated class interests is only a phenomenon of intellectual and ideological life, while divergences of interest appear quite plainly at the level of everyday consciousness. The general manager always says "we" in addressing the workers, especially when he wants them to work faster; "we have to get on with it, comrades," he will say at such times. The workers, however, always speak of management in the third person, reserving "we" for themselves. For the regional planner, denying the villages the means to develop is a way of rationalizing the pattern of settlement; but the workers and peasants who live there take it amiss that even though they contribute their tax money to the state budget they get nothing for it in return. For the efficiency expert, raising the norms—norm review or revision as it is politely called—is a way to improve the organization of labor, but the workers need no subversive ideologist to understand that from now on they will get less money for the same amount of work. We might also refer to the fact that at first capitalist society too clung to the ideology of consensus; only after the bourgeoisie was firmly in the saddle did it permit workers to form organizations representing their particular interests. But the proletariat has had its own interests not just since the appearance of its own parties and ideologues, as many Communist ideologists assert, but ever since there have been proletarians, regardless of the extent to which those interests were formulated in ideological terms.

If there are two classes under rational redistribution, let us see if we can sketch in broad outline the conflicts of interest between them. Clashes of interest in society, particularly between classes, can be described in terms of conflicts between opposing principles of legitimation. To challenge the power of the class above it a subordinated class must shake the legitimacy of its authority in its own eyes and before society as a whole. Alongside (or rather beneath) the legitimating principle of the ruling class the legitimating principle of the oppressed is always to be found; though it may not pervade the culture of the age it is always empirically discoverable in the consciousness of the laboring classes. Under rational redistribution it is above all technical knowledge, intellectual knowledge, which legitimizes the right to dispose over the surplus product. That is what justifies the superior position of the redistributors and provides the ideological basis for the formation of the intelligentsia into a class. Those, on the other hand, who have been deprived of any power of disposition over the surplus product—the very people who work together to produce it—can appeal to only one alternative principle of legitimation in order to challenge the power of the intellectual class, and that is the legitimating principle of possession of labor-power.

It is the essence of that principle that those who produce the surplus product should dispose over it, not those who claim that they know better how it should be distributed. Possession of labor-power as an alternative principle of legitimation is by no means a new idea; it appeared first in capitalist society, in opposition to capital-ownership as a legitimating principle. The socialist movement was organized around it, and advanced the demand for the self-determination of the associated producers. But at a later stage of that movement, when seizure of political power had become the main goal (and in countries where the economy had been militarized and was being run by the state bureaucracy), elite parties abandoned the workers' basic principle of legitimation, limiting the self-determination of the associated producers to the symbolic fact that the state as collective owner directs production, thus substituting the political bureaucracy for the associated producers. A whole historical era had to pass before the science of sociology managed to distinguish between the political bureaucracy and the associated producers, an insight which the sailors of Kronstadt arrived at in Lenin's own day without any help from sociologists, shortly before the political bureaucracy ordered them to be wiped out.

These opposing principles of legitimation imply a different kind of economic rationality for each of the two opposing classes.

For the redistributors the economy is rational if it maximizes the size of the surplus product made available for redistributive decision; if, in other words, the percentage of the national income which is drawn into the state budget for purposes of redistribution is as large as possible. The bigger the budget, the greater the power of the officials who administer it. To maximize the size of the budget, however, everyone has to work through state-controlled trade unions and no one can be allowed to quibble about the size of his paycheck. Looking at it from the workers' point of view, that means that the producers cannot have organizations which might limit the size of the revenues which the state budget draws from the income of the productive enterprises in the form of taxes and other payments. Thus it is a fundamental interest of the redistributors that the administrative system of purchasing labor-power—which necessarily entails the enforced sale of labor—should not give way to a genuine labor-market in which the price of labor would become the subject of transactive bargaining between legally equal, autonomous contracting parties. The redistributors therefore insist on completely bureaucratizing the sale of labor, minimizing the transactive element in it and prescribing a dispositive status for the owners of labor-power. However small the concessions which the worker might achieve through bargaining, the amount of surplus product available for appropriation would still be reduced by just that much. In this connection the ruling elite is itself the most consistent representative of the redistributors' mentality, for it knows very well that its own special power is bound up with the integration of the political and economic spheres. As redistributors the technocrats, like the ruling elite itself, have an interest in keeping labor in a dispositive position. But the interests of the technocrats as owners of labor-power are precisely the opposite—to maximize their incomes by transactive means. In that respect the technocrats' interests are no different from those of the ordinary technician who, lacking elite privileges, would fare better in a transactive labor-market in which he might be able to drive up the price of his skills. The technocrats' functional outlook also demands that more faith be placed in increasing profitability through technical development, rather than by increased exploitation of the workers, particularly when they see day after day how workers respond to this exploitation with their own illicit class struggle: slowdowns, inferior-quality output, careless handling of equipment, frequent turnover. Thus the technocracy is not averse to concessions to make both the labor-market and the whole economy more transactive, which in turn arouses the political suspicions of the ruling elite. In defense of its own hegemony the elite rejects such concessions, maintaining that they would hurt the interests of the working class, for the creation of a transactive labor-market would raise the technocrats' incomes faster than the workers'. Thus, according to the elite, it is plain as day that the technocracy wants to enhance its own economic status at the expense of the working class.

The workers' interests are fundamentally different from those of the redistributors. It is the most elemental interest of the workers to raise the price of labor, removing the determination of the surplus product from the sphere of politics and changing the ratio of wages to surplus, to the advantage of wages. In order to achieve that, the purely administrative "sale" of labor must be turned into a transaction; the sale of labor-power under government compulsion must be done away with, so that workers gain the right to decide themselves whether or not to sell their labor and whether to sell their labor or some product which they have made, and the right to make the price of their labor the subject of collective bargaining in a real labor-market. The workers' interests demand the repeal of the laws which authorize the police to lock up a worker who has not had a job for more than a month. A worker should not be required to remain at the same job in order to qualify for bank credit to build a house or make an installment purchase, and to stay eligible for health insurance, family allowances, and maternity benefits. It is the worker's interest, in other words, not to be immediately classified a second-class citizen if he leaves his job, or even if he refuses altogether to sell his labor through bureaucratic organizations and chooses to live from casual labor or by turning out his own products as an independent artisan. The workers, who thought that socialism meant the abolition of exploitation, do not understand why they cannot work as independent small producers, or in family productive units, or as members of co-

operatives organized and run on a basis of free, voluntary association, in which no one is exploited and where they could still
earn more than in the great state enterprises where they must
produce four or five times their wages in order to support
(among others) an overblown administrative apparatus which
supervises them and disciplines them to achieve higher production, and which often counts one clerical employee for every two
workers. It is in the workers' interests not to be accused of political organization or agitation if they object to work norms or
price increases, state their frank opinion of the enterprise's management or its party or trade-union committee, or protest that
they are completely at the mercy of the enterprise or plant
management. It is in their interest that the political police not
be dispatched if they organize without the help of their pseudo-
protective organizations and take collective steps to raise ab-
normally low piece rates for a given job, or lay down their tools
because their machinery is unsafe, or because a fellow-worker
has been unfairly dismissed, or because the foreman has repeatedly cursed them out; if, in other words, they give any
sign of active solidarity, such as a whole crew walking off the
job together, which already counts as criminal conspiracy. Compulsory assignment of jobs is not in the workers' interests either,
nor is the practice of punishing them when they change jobs
with a freeze on their wages and loss of their paid vacation time,
nor are the labor laws which enable enterprises to join in wage
cartels which by fixing uniform pay scales make it impossible
for workers to transfer to more profitable enterprises where they
might be able to increase their incomes. Nor can the worker
understand why changing jobs, the only way he can raise his
income (and then by no more than four or five percent), is
decried by the whole propaganda apparatus of the mass media
as a grave dereliction of duty, with the suggestion that anyone
depraved enough to take such a step would probably desert his
country too, to go abroad and work for more money. Indeed,
there must be many workers who cannot understand why it is
exclusively the privilege of intellectuals loyal to the elite to
accept work abroad, while a mechanic or welder risks years in
prison if he tries to slip across the frontier illegally in order to
earn more abroad for the same work. It must occur to those

same uncomprehending workers that the soldiers who stand guard with their submachine guns in the watchtowers along the frontier are not so much defenders of their country as warders of a system where those who have to work for a living must settle for what they can get.

The logic of redistribution, reflecting the interests of the intellectual class, interprets the "basic principle of socialism"—to each according to his work—to mean that anyone having more schooling has to earn more, and it extends this rule to the whole hierarchy of work. If a factory office worker with a secondary-school diploma earns the same or less than a welder who only finished the eighth grade it is considered an anomaly to be eliminated, and in fact such anomalies are becoming increasingly rare. That is one reason why the number of office employees is constantly growing despite repeated campaigns to reduce the size of administrative staffs relative to the number of production workers, even though many office workers have little to do now but take coffee breaks, and so office staffs have grown to a degree which no capitalist enterprise would tolerate. Socialist economy may justly pride itself on how many clerks it supports from the labor of so few workers. It is no wonder that the workers, seeing their incomes peak while they are still in their twenties while those of administrative personnel rise right up to retirement, do all they can to assure that, if they can never get free of physical labor, at least their children will complete secondary school and find easier work at higher pay. In linking earnings with a hierarchy of statuses based on diplomas, irrespective of the actual amount of work done, socialist wage policy leaves open only one road to advancement: To rise from worker status to that of white-collar employee. This cult of diplomas creates a unique, status-sensitive, prestige-conscious ethos of work which filters down from the middle strata to the workers. A secondary-school graduate may refuse to type a letter because typists do not require a degree and so graduates are not supposed to be typists. The driver of a truck delivering chocolates will demand an unskilled helper, arguing that he did not go to all the trouble of learning to drive a truck just to carry boxes of candy from the truck to the store. A lathe operator expects to have a helper too, to bring him the boxes containing the parts he is to work on. Thus in the end every fifth worker is engaged simply in carrying materials from place to place, and so with uncanny consistency the productivity of labor remains low. Yet all this is only natural in a system of rewards where status is the important thing and wages are regulated not by labor supply and the demand for labor but by the possession of school diplomas.

It is in the interests of the working class that a larger share of the national income should turn up in the pay envelopes of the workers, while a smaller share goes to the state budget for redistribution. They have an interest in seeing the state spend more of the existing budget on consumer subsidies and less on weapons, and in having more state investment funds allocated to infrastructural development, especially of a sort that meets the communal needs of the population, rather than to new productive ventures of dubious value. The interests of the working class demand, further, that government subsidy of consumption should be guided by social-welfare considerations, so that those products and services which workers and low-income people in general need should receive the most support. Thus the interests of the workers are diametrically opposed to those of the redistributors not only in respect to wages and other shop-floor issues, but also in matters of macroeconomic planning as well.

By most indexes of economic trends personal consumption in the socialist economies of Eastern Europe is lower than one would expect, given their present level of development; in other words, the share of GNP going to personal income is lower, the share absorbed by the state budget higher. In the budget itself the sums set aside for investment are relatively high, the amount allocated for health, education, and other social services relatively low. In the investments column itself more is earmarked for productive investment and less for investment in the infrastructure. But even in the domain of productive investments disproportionately more is spent on unprofitable investments, as in heavy industry (particularly the arms industry), less on branches producing consumer goods. Even in the area of infrastructural investments the budget is more generous when new buildings are to be constructed for government or enterprise offices, stingier when housing, schools, and hospitals are to be built, and especially penurious when it is a matter of providing rural villages with such public services as roads and water supply. Even in such traditional areas of social policy as the provision of free or low-cost goods and services (housing, utilities, public and institutional cafeterias, vacation resorts) a disproportionately large share is redistributed to the better-educated and higher-paid strata. Thus in every single area of economic policy the rationality of redistribution, as formulated by expert intellectuals, goes against the interests of the working class. All redistributive decisions reflect the empirical interests of the redistributors and of the redistributive system as it now exists, even while appealing to the future interests of an ideal, ideologically defined working class.

After this outline of the fundamental conflicts between the working class and the intellectual class the ruling elite appears even less justified in claiming to be the representative of workers' interests vis-à-vis the technocracy. For the ruling elite is the supreme guardian of the ethos of rational redistribution and of its planning logic and social and economic policies, which, as we have seen, are diametrically opposed to the interests of the workers. The working class has a prime interest in making economic and social relations transactive and to that extent its ally during the compromise period is much likelier to be the technocracy and the marginal intelligentsia, who in their struggle against the ruling elite also have an interest in creating transactive socioeconomic relations. Strategically the interests of the working class and the technocracy lead in different directions, but in their contest with the elite they are in tactical alliance. The workers have a stake in the technocracy's reform proposals insofar as they aim to link productivity and wage scales more closely and assure that capital and labor will flow without administrative hindrance to more economically efficient branches of the economy. Such reforms would free the budget from the burden of subsidizing unprofitable plants and industries, would make investments pay a return sooner and more economically, and would give a powerful impetus to the development of the consumer-goods industries and agriculture; and they would make room in a more rational and less overextended state budget for larger and more rapid wage increases.

In the peculiar context of early socialism's economic policies, even demands that seem to Western sociologists reactionary, obsolete, and thoroughly technocratic, such as the proposal to let market relations play a larger role in meeting consumer needs (as, for example, in housing), are really closer to the workers' interests, for at present intellectuals and members of the middle strata stand a far better chance of getting state-subsidized, government-assigned housing than workers do; if a worker wants a home he now must build it himself, at his own expense, with little or no state support. In other words, the growth of a market sector at the expense of the administered sector would reduce the flow of budgetary subsidies to the intelligentsia and middle strata, put an end to hidden income supplements to the upper strata in the form of allocated housing, and thus, far from increasing, would actually reduce the social inequality between workers and the higher strata.

Both the narrower interests of the technocracy as a stratum and its wider interests as part of the intellectual class demand that ranking positions should be obtained (or lost) only on rational criteria and within a framework of formal legality. Its interests demand that its achievements be measured by formal criteria and that it not be compelled by confidential phone calls from party headquarters to make decisions contrary to its better technical judgment. Thus the technocracy is not afraid of being overseen by public opinion, because in public it can always defend its activities with rational, professional arguments, even when its ideas and decisions conflict with other, equally rational and defensible ideas and decisions representing other social interests. The technocrats' elemental craving for personal security set them against the ruling elite not only in the days of arbitrary Stalinist repressiveness, when their representatives could be killed or imprisoned; it also brings them into conflict with the new hegemonic elite's habit of making decisions behind closed doors and without giving reasons, dismissing technical experts overnight without any right of appeal or any explanation except that unnamed comrades felt a change of personnel was needed. The experience of a series of abortive economic reforms could not but convince the technocracy that only legal and constitutional guarantees can safeguard their hard-won economic achievements, for without such guarantees those achievements can be wiped out overnight with a stroke of the pen whenever there is a shift in the political balance within the innermost councils of the ruling elite.

That is why the economic reforms demand the creation of a political system in which arbitrary interpretation of the law is replaced by formal legal guarantees which will permit the legitimate expression of different interests, place the struggle of contending political forces in a legal and constitutional framework and make it visible to all, and guarantee public control over important decisions. The technocracy must accept the legitimate articulation of workers' interests even though they now conflict at times with its own interests and may do so systematically in the more remote future—up to and including worker self-management and the right to organize to defend their interests, even if such organizations may develop into rival power centers. If such legal rights are not given the workers the technocracy itself can never hope to preserve its own legal guarantees vis-à-vis the ruling elite. The technocracy's situation in the present compromise period is like that of the bourgeoisie in the late eighteenth century: In its struggle with feudalism the latter also had to come forward as the champion of equality before the law and a rational legal system, even though by doing so it gave its own potential critics and opponents the right to function legally.

If the technocracy rests content with the modest political concessions already made to it by the ruling elite, and shrinks from taking up the struggle for reforms which would legalize the workers' right to organize politically to defend their interests, then it must dispense with working-class support and will remain defenseless before any future counteroffensive on the part of the elite. Here we might mention the instructive example of Yugoslavia, where in the 1960s the intelligentsia managed to push the ruling elite into the background temporarily and at least to begin establishing its own class power. By limiting the power of the elite and extending their own, the Yugoslav intellectuals won recognition for the ideology of self-management and even succeeded to some extent in putting it into practice. But the Yugoslav ruling elite showed its political sagacity by co-opting the idea of self-administration, and soon emptied it of any real content; instead of becoming rival power centers representing real working-class interests, the "workers' councils" were charged with expressing broad general interests and functioned at most as a corrective, not a rival to the power of the redistributors (by whom, moreover, they could be institutionally manipulated). The self-management councils were set up on corporative principles, as joint organizations of workers and management, and so gave rise to a more effective, institutionalized conflict between the rationales of redistribution and self-administration, but the conflict never transcended the bounds of each individual council. When the intellectual class in Yugoslavia allowed the ruling elite to co-opt the idea of self-administration and to set up the institutions of self-management in line with its own interests it made a fatal concession, with the result that in the 1970s the intellectuals were helpless before the elite's drive to restore its power; unable to rely for support on a working class organized in its own self-managing institutions, the intellectuals had to look on impotently while the ruling elite removed the most prominent representatives of the intelligentsia one after another from their positions. Paradoxically appealing to the slogan of self-management, the ruling elite dissolved the genuinely self-administering organizations of the university intellectuals, and it was able to do so precisely because there were no real organs of worker self-management which, feeling their own autonomy threatened, might have sprung to the intellectuals' defense.

13

The Role of the Marginal Intelligentsia in the Formation of an Intellectual Class, in Articulating Workers' Interests, and in Developing a Critical Social Consciousness

The technocracy is unable to overturn the power balance of the compromise period through its own strength alone. It is un-fitted for that task not only by its inner divisions, but also by the network of particular interests described earlier, which tie it to the political hegemony of the ruling elite at least as much as its intellectual character makes it part of an intellectual class contesting power with the elite. If the technocracy wants to break the hegemony of the ruling elite and replace it with the class rule of the intelligentsia—wherein it would exercise hegemony, confronting the elite (reduced to a rationalized political bureaucracy) and other groups of intellectuals in a pluralistic, legally regulated system of conflicts—then it must consolidate the unity of the intellectual class and seek an alliance with dissident intellectuals who are capable of formulating the ideology of its struggle against the ruling elite and who, with the technocracy behind them, can even become the vanguard of such a struggle. Such marginal intellectuals are all the more important to the technocracy since, as ideologues, they can more easily penetrate the ideological bastions of the ruling elite, if only because many of them are dropouts from the elite who still enjoy a certain prestige with both the intellectual class and the ruling elite; hence they are sometimes able to detach from the main body of the elite individuals who for one reason or another can be brought to ally themselves temporarily or permanently with the technocracy (such figures, for example, as Dubček or Imre Nagy, or even, in a way, Gierek or Khrushchev himself).

NEW OPPORTUNITIES FOR THE INTELLECTUALS IN THE ERA
OF COMPROMISE: MARGINALITY FREELY CHOSEN

When the absolute rule of the elite gives way to a period of compromise in which it only exercises a hegemonic authority, an opportunity is created for the intelligentsia's ideologues to prepare themselves for their new role both theoretically and strategically. During this period wayward intellectuals are punished by being quarantined, taken out of circulation for a while; their works are not allowed to appear, they are not permitted to travel abroad, they are surrounded with a certain stigma. They may even lose good jobs which afforded them considerable free time for their own creative work; but still, they will be permitted to earn their living at some more modest intellectual task, far from the forums where public opinion is shaped. They may have to put up with police harassment at times, may even be put in prison, but their sentences will be relatively light and their lives will never be in jeopardy. During the present compromise era such quarantined intellectuals are generally not deprived either legally or materially of the means to carry on their critical activity. Where they do not do so the reason is usually that intellectuals forced to the fringes of their class often prove incapable of dealing for long with the trials of a marginal existence. Ever since the 1960s marginal intellectuals have been at liberty to choose between different courses of action, and may often behave differently from what the ruling elite had hoped to achieve in consigning them to limbo. The elite expects that intellectuals put on ice will come to their senses and return chastened after the completion of their punishment, ready to make the mandatory gestures of loyalty in exchange for being restored to fully privileged membership in the intellectual class.

In the 1960s a new type of marginal intellectual appeared all over Eastern Europe. These men and women were not thunderstruck at their banishment; their intentions included neither a return to their former positions after years of obscurity spent working on trivial side projects which could only represent a hiatus in their real careers, nor a resignation of their intellectual role accompanied by withdrawal into inner emigration. The conduct of the creative marginal intellectuals is an indication that they have accepted their situation and have tried to turn its disadvantages to advantage. Instead of attempting to wipe from their minds the generally well-pondered intellectual efforts for which the ruling elite—perhaps sensing their ultimate consequences more accurately than they—placed them under a ban of silence, they are now prepared to go on and think through, even act through, their deviations, rejecting the lure of a legality founded on compromise.

During the era of the elite's absolute rule many intellectuals became marked men and women without doing anything to deserve it; through no fault of their own their names might be entered, at the whim of an unknown police official, on the list of those to be arrested. In the compromise period the technocracy not only protects intellectuals who come into conflict with the ruling elite from that fate, it also assures them a certain freedom of choice: They can be marginal intellectuals or not, as they wish. Of course no one is born to be marginal, and there are few people who are marginal just because that role appeals to them. In fact the ruling elite thrusts marginality on many harmless intellectuals who have little desire to question dogmas that have been declared taboo and no particular dissenting urges, but who in the course of their quite unimpeachable artistic or scholarly explorations blunder into borderline areas kept under close surveillance by the guardians of doctrine, and unmarked by any warning signs to keep off the unwary. The border guards give the strayed wanderer a warning, not always very politely and sometimes with unexpected rudeness, which in itself may still not have any serious consequences. But anyone who has received a warning—be it in the form of a sharply critical article in the official party daily or in its theoretical journal, or a formal resolution of criticism from some party forum, or a friendly and not yet formal admonition from the police—has already fallen under the shadow of suspicion; more circumspect party members will tactfully avoid him, and the chattering of the sensation-hungry vultures who surround the marginal intellectual will ring all

around him. They will lift him into the limelight of a spurious
notoriety and, if he accepts the offer of marginality, will accompany him to the very threshold of quarantine where, suddenly
changing their attitude, they will bid him farewell in a tone of
pity not unmixed with blame, and turn their backs on him to
wait for the next victim.

There is hardly a creative intellectual who at some time in his
career has not found himself, as a result of his originality, in this
select predicament. But in the compromise period it is largely
up to him whether he will heed the warning signs and quickly
leave the ideological danger zone, never to stray there again, or
persevere in spite of all warning on paths that promise to be
intellectually productive for him. In general he does not go on
because he is a dissident; rather, he becomes a dissident because
he chooses to go on, and soon coming to recognize his situation,
he accepts his banishment. For its part, the ruling elite, in order
to consolidate itself and create an impression of momentum,
must constantly invent phantom ideological opposition, which it
can then use as an official scapegoat. Indeed, the apparatus reinforces its own unity by designating as public enemies intellectuals who have somehow acquired the reputation of being
critical-minded. If people who give voice to conflicts were not
driven out and branded as enemies, the unanimity of the apparatus itself would soon begin to erode. The ruling elite is constantly sniffing out opposition groups and ideological factions,
for, after all, such required reading as the *History of the Communist Party of the Soviet Union* clearly demonstrates that the
party's history is a story of the continual rise and exposure of
factions, and the elite cannot conceive that artistic and scholarly
life can follow any other pattern. Deviation, as the elite defines
it, lumps into a single category intellectuals who, apart from
their dissent, have little in common, although sooner or later the
pressure of the elite's punitive sanctions does indeed forge them
into actual groups.

If they can avoid it, why do some intellectuals accept a marginal role, with all the unpleasantness that after all accompanies
it? We must confess that for Eastern European intellectuals the
temptation to forge ahead on forbidden paths is very strong.
Imagine an ardent hunter who after prowling around for ages

in potato fields suddenly stumbles onto a game preserve whose keepers have not allowed anyone in living memory to hunt or even photograph the game. He can be certain that even without a crack rifle and a peerless eye he can still acquire there trophies which will give him the reputation of a matchless nimrod and make him the toast of every field-and-stream show. Similarly, the intellectual who sets out to explore the reservation of ideological taboos is drawn to forbidden territory not so much by an indomitable heroism which shrinks from no danger as by the prospect of an easy bag, and by the reward not only of the abstract joy of intellectual discovery but of domestic and even international acclaim for his original achievement.

THE MARGINAL INTELLIGENTSIA AND POWER

In its basic social strategy and range of possible goals the Eastern European marginal intelligentsia of the present compromise period differs fundamentally from today's Western marginal intelligentsia, and even more radically from the revolutionary Eastern European intelligentsia of the turn of the century. The two latter groups did not slip back into marginality from a position of class power; for them the years of marginal existence served as a base from which to launch an offensive to seize power (leaving aside the groups which, with every ebbing of the revolutionary tide, gave up organized political activity and with it, often, all creative intellectual activity, congregating together for mutual warmth on society's fringes, like the hippie communities of the late 1960s). Radical left groups must organize, acquire the conspiratorial techniques needed for violent struggle outside the confines of legal political activity, develop a combative, partisan spirit, and formulate and adopt norms of revolutionary discipline, so that they will no longer be defined as marginal because each individual goes his own artistic or intellectual way, but because they are all confronted with a power organized on principles alien to their own, which they must destroy or capture if they are ever to come to share in a new kind of power themselves. In this respect the road which the Western New Left has to travel resembles in many ways the road already covered by the radical revolutionaries of turn-of-the-century Eastern Europe. In both eras the marginal intelligentsia had to learn from their defeats that they could not penetrate the ramparts of power through verbal criticism or individual acts of terrorism, and that if they wanted to take effective action disciplined organization was necessary, of a sort best provided by Communist parties on the Leninist model. That explains why so many New Leftists who consider themselves more radical than the Communists, after first organizing in little elite groups or taking part in mass movements whose strength lay in their very lack of organization, have come to recognize that the Communist Parties, still oriented primarily toward intellectuals, offer the most effective organizational format for achieving goals which lie beyond the confines of the existing order.

For today's Eastern European intelligentsia, on the other hand, marginality represents not a road to power but one leading away from it. They are confronted not with the power of an alien class but with the power of their own class. It is precisely the organizational leading strings of the class rule of the intelligentsia that they are trying to escape from, and if they should finally succeed why would they want to organize again? They feel little urge to play at political parties again, to attend party meetings and practice criticism and self-criticism, to submit to sectarian discipline; they have no motive to lay violent siege to the stronghold of power when its gates stand open before them and they can saunter in at any time if they will only accept its discipline as binding on themselves. The party bureaucracy, not yet accustomed to the marginal intelligentsia and always inclined to view it in the light of its own illegal past, does not understand what the marginal intellectuals are all about. It always imagines organized, conspiratorial political factions lurking behind them, and cannot understand that someone might accept marginal status because he wants to write good books, not because he wants to become a cabinet minister. An Eastern European intellectual would have to be harebrained indeed if he did not understand, after fifty years of historical experience, that in the socialist system anyone who aspires to political power must avoid even the suspicion of marginality and at most can only maneuver within the limits of the current party line. There are many roads leading out of marginality, but not one of them leads to political power.

In the course of our earlier historical survey of the structural role of the intelligentsia we did not come upon a single intellectual group to which the notion of influencing society, directly or indirectly, was completely foreign; in the last analysis all aspired to some kind of power. It would be an ideological and, indeed, a narcissistic exaggeration to describe the Eastern European marginal intelligentsia as totally different in this respect, willing to renounce on principle all prospect of power of any kind. The marginal intellectual has only dropped out of the gravitational field of the power of the redistributors and the intellectual class; he is thus able to bring to the surface conflicts of interest which are muted by the ideology of consensus and the paternalistic atmosphere of the compromise period. He is the actual or potential ideologue of the various actors in the struggles within the intellectual class, and so at critical junctures he is in a position to acquire significant influence, sometimes by formulating the issues in a sharper and more critical way than usual, at other times with economic, social, and cultural theories which have political implications. Indeed, it is even conceivable that at times, when crisis deepens into revolution, he may have to emerge from marginality. If he is not careful onrushing events may even force him to accept a ministerial portfolio, as Georg Lukács did in 1956; although in the history of Eastern European Communist systems such political comebacks have proved to be short-lived indeed.

TWO TYPES OF MARGINAL INTELLECTUALS: TELEOLOGICAL AND EMPIRICAL REVISIONISTS

The Eastern European marginal intellectuals are divided into clearly distinguishable groups by differences in their values and ideological strategies. These groups can be understood in terms of the basic internal conflicts in the intellectual class, even where their ideas and the topics and language of the debates which they inspire do not directly reflect the issues within the intellectual class, requiring some ideological analysis to link them with conflicting interest relationships. The marginal intellectuals are bound together nonetheless by the similar situation into which repression has thrust them, although this fragile unity can easily break up as soon as the pressure is reduced or a shift occurs in political power relations.

An ideological analysis would sort the marginal intellectuals into two basic categories. The first takes in those artists and ideologues who do not wish to see the balance of power shift away from the ruling elite, to the advantage of the technocracy. These critics take the elite to task for making too many concessions to the technocrats, for abandoning the long-range goals of socialism, for substituting economic growth for the humanization of social relations, and for giving undue importance to overtaking the developed capitalist countries at the expense of the specific goals of socialism, which inevitably brings with it the introduction into the socialist countries of the values and habits of the consumer society. These critics of the ruling elite demand a greater equality of living standards instead of increasing differentiation of incomes; promotion of collective rather than individual consumption; development of collective forms of community life rather than a privatized life-style; training for political activism in genuine movement organizations rather than sanction for competitive, achievement-oriented behavior; and continuation of the cultural revolution in place of an apolitical cultural policy tailored to consumer wishes—a radical separation of culture and market. These critics oppose the technocracy, its interests, and its kind of rationality, on every important social issue. They offer as an alternative a policy of putting *telos* before *techné*—a program which could only be carried out by the ruling elite, but not by the elite as it is, bureaucratized, unrevolutionary, petty, pragmatic, "realistic," and compromising. They call for a renewed and reorganized vanguard of professional revolutionaries which would place the strategic perspectives of socialism above all tactical considerations and which, thus purified, would in all probability call these uncompromising critics back into the fold again.

The most conspicuous of the ideologues who call for a renewal of the ruling elite are the neo-Marxists. Influenced by the Western New Left, they place their hopes in the possibility of a renaissance of Marxism; in the interest of achieving it, they have transferred their emphasis from the tenets of Marxism to its values. The early work of Marx, the theory of alienation and the problem of humanizing society, occupy the forefront of their theoretical attention, and their philosophical position is one of a transcendent anthropology. Hence they seek to go beyond both Stalinism, with its vulgar historiosophic determinism, and the technocratic economism and revisionism of the post-Stalin era (a revisionism akin to that of Bernstein and later Social Democracy). Stressing the historical role of man as a subjective agent realizing himself by choosing among alternatives, and rejecting any kind of economic or sociological reductionism, they place the category of a goal-oriented human totality in the center of their thought, and trace the contours of a Marxist phenomenology.

The demands of these teleological critics for a renewal of the elite do not enjoy much popularity in Eastern European political and bureaucratic circles. But it does not take much theoretical acuteness on the part of the ruling elite's ideologists to see that in vulgarized form these demands, critical overtones and all, can be used to keep the technocrats in check and even to force them back from their current positions. Crudely oversimplified, these abstract arguments can be used to demand a closer integration of politics and economics, with politics in command, and to strengthen the position of the redistributors generally and of the ruling elite specifically. We have here, in other words, an ideology of the intellectual class which is able to envisage the class rule of the intelligentsia only in terms of the stable hegemony of an intellectual elite. The ruling elite has dealt its teleological critics a double blow: Angered at their demand that it renew itself, it has driven them into marginality, while at the same time using bits and pieces of their ideology, if only in a rather primitive form, to defend its own very real existence and interests. From this teleological critique, in other words, it has fashioned the tools of an immanent apologetics.

This development has driven the teleological critics into an ever-deepening theoretical crisis. They have tried to defend themselves against the elite's co-optation of their ideas by formulating their values in increasingly abstract and—one might almost say—elegiac terms. A kind of philosophical resignation has replaced the analysis of broad economic and social conflicts. The most striking proof of that is the fact that because of its feudal, antidemocratic political traditions they no longer accept socialism as it now exists—the social systems of the Communist countries—as being genuinely socialist, despite the degree of economic and cultural progress they have achieved. From the strategic perspectives of a genuine socialism they are declared to be a historical blind alley, upon whose economic, social, and political reform it would be useless to waste any serious analysis. Hence these critics have transferred their theoretical interest from these social formations, which they feel lack any value as models, and from macrostructural problems in general, and now proceed on the assumption that in our time the values of socialism are to be sought not in whole societies but only in individuals who have made the true ideals of socialism their own, or in elite, avant-garde communities of such people. If a genuinely creative socialism is to be developed, they believe, it can only be done by concentrating on this new type of individual personality, its structure of needs and interpersonal and community relationships. Social and political radicalism has here given way to a sociopsychological radicalism dedicated to the analysis of radical needs.

The other section of the Eastern European marginal intelligentsia, much more heterogeneous in its composition and diffuse in its theoretical objectives, is that of the empirical revisionists. By that term we mean all those who, against the doctrines of the ruling elite, appeal to empirical experience of any kind, to the facts as they see, experience, and understand them. Their relationship to society is far more cognitive than normative, and for that reason—and irrespective of whether or not they individually ever shared the orthodox Soviet Marxism of the elite—they are compelled to reexamine, directly or indirectly, the cardinal principles of that hitherto monopolistic ideology whose declared scientific validity, unity, and irreplaceability legitimate the hegemony of the ruling elite over the intellectual class, including the technocracy. Consequently the work of the empirical revisionists, in its ideological implications, supports the aspirations of the technocracy to increase its power at the expense of the ruling elite. The more radical of the empirical revisionists go on, however, to criticize the technocracy itself insofar as its narrow stratum interests lead it to accept the hegemony of the elite, rather than championing the class rule of the intelligentsia more vigorously against the elite's interpretation of the ethos of rational redistribution.

As it happened, the spirit of empirical revisionism first appeared in Eastern Europe in the arts, over the issue of the kinds of subject matter permitted within the officially approved style of socialist realism. During the Stalin era every artist was expected to give expression to ideologically defined types, not to his own actual experience. If the artist's experience did not jibe with the normative ideal of a new socialist man and society looking happily and constructively into the future; if he depicted the inherent conflicts of socialist society; if in speaking of the human condition he could not derive from socialism optimistic solutions for the problems of illness, loss, death, or even disappointment in love; then his works were branded with such labels as "bourgeois objectivism," "petty-bourgeois pessimism," and "abstract humanism." It was not until the immediate post-Stalin period, essentially, that criticism of the arts first gave sanction to the representation of passions, crises, and tragedies having nothing to do with socialism or even, at times, stemming from the abuses of Stalinism itself. Soon afterward, following the actual advent of the compromise period, an artistic avant-garde reemerged in Eastern Europe; leaving behind the conventional devices of academic socialist realism, it began to put into practice its demand for a revival of authentic and autonomous modes of expression. While these artistic aspirations received little support, they were more or less tolerated during the compromise period, especially in the more liberal Eastern European countries, and were driven into marginality only when they presented a social vision at odds with official wishes, or rejected the official view altogether. Marginalization inevitably awaited those artists who abandoned the world of historical fable and universal human drama to express in their works feelings and phenomena which had a real empirical basis in socialist society but clashed with the ideological preconceptions of the aesthetic police.

It was this empirical revisionism in the arts, ideological only in an indirect way, which first loosened the ruling elite's system of ideological controls. That in turn encouraged the technocracy to press for the introduction, in the 1960s, of social-science research, empirical study which would simply leave ideological value-judgments to one side. The narrowest professional interests of the technocracy demanded that planning be made more scientific, and that research provide an objective picture of social conditions so that the actual consequences of planning decisions could be measured with some degree of accuracy. For that reason the technocracy supported all kinds of empirical research, from econometrics and empirical sociology to structuralist literary criticism and cliometrics, looking on with approval while a positivist methodology came to pervade the social sciences; it not only tolerated their practitioners but supported them and rewarded them with high academic prestige.

It was another story when some social scientists, rigorously applying methods of research generally accepted as legitimate, began to arrive at a critique of ideology, or even made ideological goals themselves the subject of empirical study, thus implicitly giving their work an ideological significance. These empirically based critiques of ideology not only called into question the hegemony of the elite; they also offered a critique of the technocracy itself, and not just from the narrow standpoint of the intellectual class, for they articulated the interests and grievances of other social classes as well. These developments in Eastern European empirical sociology forced the elite to realize the dangers inherent in positivist social research, and so in the late 1960s it launched an ideological offensive in the course of which many empirical social scientists too were forced into marginality.

The artists and social scientists who represent empirical revisionism are, if possible, even less aware than the teleological critics of the ideological consequences of their activity. They bring hidden or even suppressed interests to light, describe concrete human grievances, relativize values, and study or depict the most diverse aspects of reality, often demanding toleration for them; thus they have an interest in a certain sort of pluralism, in the democratization of political relations, and in civil liberties permitting the expression of particular viewpoints. As a result, they are inclined to see themselves as the representatives of the overall interests of society and would be offended at being called ideologues of the intellectual class or even, more narrowly, of the technocracy. We must insist on characterizing them as such, however, for in the era of compromise nearly every important conflict in society becomes entangled in the power struggle between the technocracy and the ruling elite, and the technocracy itself is quite capable of taking from any ideology whatever notions it can use in its open or covert contest with the elite. In this second period of the history of socialism there is no social force besides the technocracy which has any real chance of breaking the hegemonic authority of the elite. Just as, on the eve of the French Revolution, the suppressed grievances of every class supplied ammunition for the bourgeoisie in its struggle for power, and even the hostile Jacobin intellectuals acted in the last analysis as bourgeois ideologues, so today the technocracy is bound to take up the cause of every injured interest, co-opting its own critics and integrating the ideology of every particular interest hostile to the ruling elite into a technocratically interpreted ethos of rational redistribution.

Paradoxically, yet understandably, the elite's ideological counteroffensive has dealt just as harshly with the teleological revisionists, who demand a reinforcement of the elite's power, as it has with the empirical revisionists, who reject the hegemony of the ruling elite even in a reformed guise. It has done so because the purpose of punishing the marginal intellectuals is to keep the technocracy in line, and it is easier to single out intellectuals whom the technocracy will not defend (even if it still views the elite's power to take reprisals with some alarm). It has done so, moreover, because while the empirical revisionists only attack the structural position of the elite, without accusing it of betraying its mission, its teleological critics go beyond disputing its empirical practice to strip it of its own ideological justification by denying its socialist character.

A common repression unites the marginal intellectuals, irrespective of their differences of opinion. They come to feel a solidarity with one another because of the similarity in the circumstances of their daily lives, including the difficulties of making a living and the periodic police harassment; and so they become more alike in their manner of living and values. They develop a special subculture of marginality, their own gallows humor, mutual tolerance, respect for one another's autonomy, a certain conspiratorial discipline even, and an antipathy to all official authority, whether embodied in the elite's political police or in the life-style of the technocracy. But the technocracy still gets more use out of the teleological critics than the ruling elite does, not only because it is more tolerant of critics of its life-style than the elite is of criticism of the police, but also and mainly because the technocracy has an interest in the creation of a more enlightened political bureaucracy, more dependable and more consistent in representing technocratic principles and strategies. Indeed, in the foreseeable third period of socialism, in which the elite's political bureaucracy will become a professional one, heralding the end of early socialism and the beginning of developed socialism, the technocracy will recall from their marginal status not only its own ideologues but its teleological critics as well. It seems certain in any case that in the third period of socialism today's marginal ideologies will not constitute any reason to force anyone to the periphery of intellectual life, because they have relevance as criticism only in the present, compromise era. Any critique of the full-blown class rule of the intelligentsia will have to be built on new varieties of critical thought.

CAN THE INTELLECTUALS ACQUIRE CRITICAL SELF-KNOWLEDGE?
SOME POSSIBILITIES AND IMPOSSIBILITIES

With the emergence of rational redistribution in Eastern Europe the intellectuals have for the first time in history acquired a class position in the social structure. Today an ever-more-united intelligentsia stands on the threshold of class power. Intellectuals have a monopoly over culture in any society, but this time the culture is that of their own class. Not only do they refuse to foster the culture of other classes; their monopoly is even stricter than that, for they appropriate and absorb the culture of other classes and strata or, failing that, disparage them. In this way they prevent the working class (for example) from becoming conscious of its own identity in its present structural position. If an able young worker wants to change his situation he has to acquire the class culture of the intelligentsia and with it the ethos of rational redistribution; there is only one legal channel of mobility for him, becoming an intellectual, perhaps even a member of the ruling elite. The ground rules of social mobility are set by the educational system, by now reduced to a selection mechanism for entry into the intellectual class; it offers only knowledge which, if it does not make everyone an intellectual, still fits every kind of consciousness into the continuous hierarchy of intellectual class culture. Under socialism culture itself has become a means of discipline, more effective for imposing the class culture of the intelligentsia than any coercive agency; those who accept this closed, manipulated, filtered culture install the police in their own minds and lose all ability to define themselves except as either full-fledged intellectuals or else underdeveloped, less-qualified "subintellectuals," relegated to the lower levels of the bureaucratic structure.

If the makers and bearers of culture are members of an intellectual class; if the culture of a society is articulated as the class culture of the intelligentsia; if the nonintellectual majority have no idea to whom to turn in order to learn what their common interests are; if it is the basic interest of the intelligentsia as a class to conceal these particular interests, then the worker can never comprehend his class situation, but neither can the intellectual; for the key ideological premise of rational redistribution, the ideal of a classless society, makes it all but an epistemological impossibility to develop any kind of class-consciousness, including the class-consciousness of the intelligentsia itself. For the first time in history the intelligentsia per se has the opportunity to acquire a class position, which also means that the social group which has always formulated the consciousness of the various classes is now becoming a distinct social class in its own right. As such it must subordinate its cognitive powers to its class interests, which demand precisely that it refrain from formulating its own class-consciousness or anyone else's, for to do so would call into question the dominant legitimating principle of rational redistribution, the notion that redistribution is governed by a collective interest above class interests; and to do that would be to jeopardize its own existence

as a class. Thus if individual intellectuals openly enunciated the
legitimating principle of the redistributive intelligentsia's class
power, their own logic would drive them (or others) on to enunciate the alternative legitimating principle of the owners of
labor-power and to a more mature and rational form of redistribution which would make possible the establishment of organs
of worker self-management at every level. It would imply, in
other words, the organization of the working class as a counter-
force within the rational-redistributive model of economic integration, which of course immediately raises the question: Would
it still be rational redistribution then?

The working class can acquire some degree of class power
only if it formulates its class-consciousness; the intelligentsia,
on the other hand, can make its class power secure only if it
refuses to formulate its class-consciousness; or, if that is impossible, if it merely assigns it a heuristic value and guards against
drawing any ideological consequences from it. For that reason
the intelligentsia is extremely diffident about its own power.
For its sake the intellectuals cling to the notion of a unitary
culture, centered upon a "constructive," hierarchical value-system derived from a universal concept of man. It is this value-
system that stands guard over the social consensus, proclaiming
a collective, anti-individual ethos, defending the integration of
roles within the personality, warding off every ironic attempt to
relativize values, and identifying culture with high culture; for
the intellectuals recognize only art and science as culture and
fence off the knowledge of other classes, which is lumped con-
descendingly into the category of "everyday life," and so defined
as nonculture. Rational-redistributive society is incapable of self-
knowledge; a unique crisis of social self-knowledge has broken
out under socialism. The intellectual class has been blinded by
the havoc wreaked upon the intelligentsia by the ruling elite,
a bloodbath so severe that it considers the mere opportunity to
reflect a luxury and would rather extend its privileges than call
them into question. Those whom the elite has driven into marginality are the only ones in a position to recognize the class
character of the intelligentsia, and they, understandably, are not
anxious to identify themselves, even as a class, with the elite.
On the other hand, the class culture of the intelligentsia is well

suited to co-opt any transcendent criticism which the marginal intelligentsia can offer, and since this class is the first one whose marginal members represent the element of transcendence within the class and its culture, rational redistribution finds it easy to appropriate any transcendent analysis for its own purposes, just as the capitalist elite can put any immanent critique to its own uses. But in so doing the intellectual class weakens its own position vis-à-vis the ruling elite, whose function it is to see that the ethos of redistribution is universally accepted as the culture for all society, thus assuring a monopoly for the class culture of the intelligentsia. If the intellectual class put an end to the hegemony of the elite its culture would become just the culture of one class, albeit the ruling class, and other alternative cultures would come to appear legitimate alongside it. And so the ruling elite installs a censor inside the intellectual's head, who prevents his recognizing himself as he really is in society. The intellectual department of the political police is the externalization of this internal censor, and it takes nothing more amiss than marginal intellectuals who talk about the intelligentsia as a class.

What first made positivist, empirical social science possible was the existence of an organic intellectual stratum which, by reason of its structural position, was able and willing to articulate other particular interests, and to develop a social science which departed not from a unitary value-hierarchy but on the contrary saw the relativization of values and interests as its task. But with the emergence of the class position and culture of the intelligentsia we can observe the agony of positivist, empirical social science, and that justifies us in asking: Was positivist social science just a historical episode, bound up with the existence of a free-market economy? And going even further: If under rational redistribution social science does nothing but articulate the class ideologies of the intellectuals, then are we perhaps living not in the twilight of ideology but rather—because of the epistemological crisis of immanent social cognition—in the era of total ideology?

To have recourse to a play on words: In our day only that which is immanent can be transcendent, but only that which transcends the existing order can be immanent. It is our conviction that in the age of the intelligentsia's coalescence into a class the first step for critical social thought is to recognize that culture is becoming the class culture of the intellectuals. We meant our essay as an immanent structural analysis; we did not intend to offer an ideological critique, or justification, of the evolution of the intelligentsia into a class by appealing to any transcendent value-system; and yet we have probably succeeded in arousing the wrath of both ideological apologists and ideological critics of the Eastern European societies. We have taken that risk because among other things we have become convinced that only immanent thinking can deal critically with societies in which the intelligentsia exercises class power; an ideological criticism must give way to the critique of ideology. Accordingly, we ourselves consider this structural analysis as only a preliminary study for a critical examination of the ethos of rational redistribution.

We further assume that only this kind of immanent critique of society and ideology can lead to the formulation of an international, East-West, New-Left strategy, by contrast with the efforts of the 1960s, which proved abortive precisely because they failed to set themselves off clearly from traditional, teleological leftism of the sort which leads only to rational redistribution. If the New Left cannot go beyond insisting that intellectuals should enunciate universal social goals and lead broad opposition movements, rather than give expression to their own particular interests, then there will be nothing in its thinking to distinguish it from traditional Bolshevism. It is not very productive to proclaim the need for the intelligentsia to intervene while at the same time condemning the interventionism of the Western technocracy in all its forms; taking this kind of dualism as a point of departure, consistent thinking can lead only to an abstractly spiritual counterculture or to apologies for rational redistribution. The criteria of left-wing thinking have to be reformulated, for what once seemed to be left-wing may now turn out to be right-wing; we must discover what elements of "left-wing" thinking are really only part of the class culture of the intelligentsia. Leftism ceases to be leftist if it only serves the ethos of redistribution.

Are there any elements of left-wing thinking which oppose

and transcend that ethos, rather than serve it? If there are, and if they are cogent, then such a thing as an immanent leftism does exist. If the Eastern European marginal intellectuals are to become the representatives of an immanent left, they must take up their position between the technocracy and the working class, becoming the organic intelligentsia of both, so that the one and the other can derive their own ideologies from the immanent critical activity of that intelligentsia. Paradoxically, no transcendent intellectual activity is thinkable in Eastern Europe so long as the intellectuals do not formulate the immanence of the intelligentsia's evolution into a class. That, however, must wait for the abolition of the ruling elite's hegemony and the consolidation of the power of the intellectual class as a whole. As to when that hypothetical third period of socialism will arrive, we can only say that when some Eastern European publisher accepts this essay for publication it will be here, and not before.

Csobánka, September 1974

GEORGE (GYÖRGY) KONRÁD, born in Hungary in 1933, studied literature at Budapest University, and worked as an editor, a librarian, and the superintendent of a child-welfare organization. Before writing his first novel, *The Case Worker,* he had published literary and sociological essays.

IVAN SZELÉNYI, a sociologist and Konrád's contemporary, also born and educated in Hungary, emigrated in 1975 and since 1976 has taught at the University of Flinders in South Australia.